6/12/17

Moral Motivation

OXFORD **PHILOSOPHICAL** CONCEPTS

Moral Motivation

A HISTORY

Edited by Iakovos Vasiliou

OXFORD
UNIVERSITY PRESS

OXFORD
UNIVERSITY PRESS

Oxford University Press is a department of the University of Oxford.
It furthers the University's objective of excellence in research, scholarship,
and education by publishing worldwide. Oxford is a registered trade mark of
Oxford University Press in the UK and certain other countries.

Published in the United States of America by Oxford University Press
198 Madison Avenue, New York, NY 10016, United States of America

© Oxford University Press 2016

Library of Congress Cataloging-in-Publication Data
Names: Vasiliou, Iakovos, 1966–editor.
Title: Moral motivation : a history / Edited by Iakovos Vasiliou.
Description: New York : Oxford University Press, 2016. | Series: Oxford
philosophical concepts | Includes bibliographical references and index.
Identifiers: LCCN 2015040583 | ISBN 9780199316571 (pbk. : alk. paper) |
ISBN 9780199316564 (hardcover : alk. paper)
Subjects: LCSH: Moral motivation.
Classification: LCC BJ324.M64 M67 2016 | DDC 170—dc23
LC record available at http://lccn.loc.gov/2015040583

1 3 5 7 9 8 6 4 2
Printed by Webcom, Inc., Canada

Contents

Contributors

JOY CONNOLLY, Professor of Classics and Dean for Humanities at New York University, is the author of *The State of Speech: Rhetoric and Political Thought in Ancient Rome* (2007), *The Life of Roman Republicanism* (2014), and essays about Roman literature and culture. Current interests include melodrama, exemplarity, and ancient literary theory.

ANNE DIEBEL received her PhD in English and Comparative Literature from Columbia University, where she now teaches in the Core Curriculum as the Robert Belknap Faculty Fellow. She has published articles on Henry James and Theodore Dreiser and is working on a book about American modernism and personality.

BRAD INWOOD is University Professor, Classics and Philosophy, at the University of Toronto and Canada Research Chair in Ancient Philosophy. He is the author of *Ethics and Human Action in Early Stoicism* (1985), *Reading Seneca: Stoic Philosophy at Rome* (2005), and *Seneca: Selected Philosophical Letters* (2007), all published by Oxford University Press.

JONATHAN JACOBS, PhD University of Pennsylvania (1983), works on moral psychology, metaethics, history of philosophy, and criminal justice. He has published over seventy articles and several books and has held fellowships and been a visiting scholar at universities in the United States and Great Britain. He is Professor and Chair of Philosophy, John Jay College, City University of New York.

CHADWICK JENKINS is an Associate Professor of Music at the City College of New York and the Graduate Center, City University of New York. He specializes in the relationships between music and philosophy, the history of music theory, Schenkerian analysis, and opera studies.

SUSAN SAUVÉ MEYER is Professor and Chair of Philosophy at the University of Pennsylvania. A scholar of Plato, Aristotle, and Stoicism, she is the author of *Aristotle on Moral Responsibility* (1993, reissued with a new introduction 2011), *Ancient Ethics* (2008) and the *Plato: Laws 1 and 2: Translation and Commentary* (Oxford, 2015).

PHILLIP MITSIS is Alexander S. Onassis Professor of Hellenic Culture and Civilization at New York University. He has published on Greek epic and tragedy, and on the history of ancient, medieval, and early modern philosophy. He is working on a larger study of Locke's use of ancient Epicurean, Stoic, and skeptic arguments, and the way that we conceptualize the origins of particular philosophical notions.

STEVEN NADLER is the William H. Hay II Professor of Philosophy at the University of Wisconsin-Madison. His books include *Spinoza: A Life* (Cambridge, 1999), and *The Best of All Possible Worlds: A Story of Philosophers, God, and Evil* (Princeton, 2011).

ANGELICA NUZZO is Professor of Philosophy at the Graduate Center and Brooklyn College, City University of New York. Among her recent publications: *History, Memory, Justice in Hegel* (Macmillan, 2012), *Hegel on Religion and Politics* (ed. 2013), *Hegel and the Analytic Tradition* (ed. 2009), *Ideal Embodiment: Kant's Theory of Sensibility* (Indiana, 2008).

STEVEN SVERDLIK is Professor of Philosophy at Southern Methodist University in Dallas, Texas, where he has taught since 1982. He writes on ethics, moral psychology, and punishment and is the author of *Motive and Rightness* (Oxford University Press, 2011). He is currently working on issues in the morality of punishment.

JACQUELINE TAYLOR is Professor of Philosophy at the University of San Francisco. She has published *Reflecting Subjects: Passion, Sympathy and Society in Hume's Philosophy* with Oxford University Press (2015). Her edited volume *Reading Hume on the Principles of Morals* is also forthcoming from Oxford University Press.

JENNIFER ULEMAN is Associate Professor of Philosophy at Purchase College, State University of New York. Her publications include *An Introduction to Kant's Moral Philosophy* (2010), "External Freedom in Kant's *Rechtslehre*: Political, Metaphysical" (2004), "On Kant, Infanticide, and Finding Oneself in a State of Nature" (2000), and various writings on art, politics, and feminism.

IAKOVOS VASILIOU is Professor of Philosophy at the Graduate Center, City University of New York. He is the author of *Aiming at Virtue in Plato* (Cambridge, 2008) and a number of articles on Plato and Aristotle.

NANCY WORMAN is Professor of Classics and Comparative Literature at Barnard College and Columbia University. She is the author of articles and books on style and the body in Greek literature and culture, including *Abusive Mouths in Classical Athens* (Cambridge, 2008) and *Landscape and the Spaces of Metaphor in Ancient Literary Theory and Criticism* (Cambridge, 2015).

Series Editor's Foreword

The Oxford Philosophical Concepts (OPC) series offers an innovative approach to philosophy's past and its relation to other disciplines. As a series, it is unique in exploring the transformations of central philosophical concepts from their ancient sources to their modern use.

The OPC series has several goals: to make it easier for historians to contextualize key concepts in the history of philosophy, to render that history accessible to a wide audience, and to enliven contemporary discussions by displaying the rich and varied sources of philosophical concepts still in use today. The means to these goals are simple enough: eminent scholars come together to rethink a central concept in philosophy's past. The point of this rethinking is not to offer a broad overview but to identify problems the concept was originally supposed to solve and investigate how approaches to them shifted over time, sometimes radically. Recent scholarship has made evident the benefits of reexamining the standard narratives about western philosophy. The editors of the OPC series look beyond the canon and explore their concepts over a wide philosophical landscape. Each volume traces a notion from its inception as a solution to specific problems through its historical transformations and to its modern use, all the while acknowledging its historical context. Each OPC volume is *a history* of its concept in that it tells a story about changing solutions to specific problems. Many editors have found it appropriate to include long-ignored writings drawn from the Islamic and Jewish traditions and the philosophical contributions of women. Volumes also explore ideas drawn from Buddhist, Chinese, Indian, and other philosophical cultures when doing so adds an especially helpful new perspective. By combining scholarly innovation with focused and astute analysis, the OPC series encourages a deeper understanding of our philosophical past and present.

One of the most innovative features of the OPC series is its recognition that philosophy bears a rich relation to art, music, literature, religion, science, and other cultural practices. The series speaks to the need for informed interdisciplinary exchanges. Its editors assume that the most difficult and profound philosophical ideas can be made comprehensible to a large audience and that materials not strictly philosophical often bear a significant relevance to philosophy. To this end, each OPC volume includes Reflections. These are short stand-alone essays written by specialists in art, music, literature, theology, science, and cultural studies that *reflect on* the volume's concept from other disciplinary perspectives. The goal of these essays is to enliven, enrich, and exemplify the volume's concept and reconsider the boundary between philosophical and extraphilosophical materials. The Reflections display the benefits of using philosophical concepts and distinctions in areas that are not strictly philosophical, and encourage philosophers to move beyond the borders of their discipline as presently conceived.

The volumes of the OPC series arrive at an auspicious moment. Many philosophers are keen to invigorate the discipline. The series aims to provoke philosophical imaginations by uncovering the brilliant twists and unforeseen turns of philosophy's past.

Christia Mercer
Gustave M. Berne Professor of Philosophy
Columbia University in the City of New York
June 2015

Acknowledgments

I thank first and foremost the contributors to the volume for their energy, expertise, and patience. Many of the chapters were first discussed at a workshop titled the History of Moral Motivation held at the Graduate Center, City University of New York, April 20, 2013. I am grateful to Columbia University, to the Academic Research Council at the Graduate Center, to the Ph.D./M.A. Program in Philosophy at the Graduate Center, and in particular to then Associate Provost Louise Lennihan at the Graduate Center for their support. Mateo Duque and Claudia Pace have my gratitude for running the workshop so smoothly, as do Joanna Smolenski and Zoey Ockenden for their meticulous help in preparing the manuscript. As always, I thank Nancy Worman for her continuous encouragement. Finally I am indebted to Christia Mercer, the series editor, for her invaluable advice and comments on all aspects of the project.

Moral Motivation

Introduction

MORAL MOTIVATION AND ITS HISTORY

Iakovos Vasiliou

The reader may be somewhat puzzled by the inclusion of a volume entitled *Moral Motivation* in a series called Oxford Philosophical Concepts. Unlike space, cause, mind, or matter, moral motivation appears to be more of a phenomenon than a concept, similar to weakness of will, political apathy, or the bystander effect. Moreover, each of its two component elements appears prima facie to be a better candidate for a concept: moral and motivation (or, at least, motive). For a time the series editor and I considered the title *Motive*, which has the distinct advantages of being more elegant and more obviously naming a concept. The problem with *Motive*, however, is that it does not isolate discretely enough the distinctive set of philosophical problems this volume treats. While a lot will be said about motives, the title *Motive* suggests a broader investigation into philosophy of psychology and philosophy of action about what moves a person (and perhaps also an animal) to act. A volume on motive as such would have its philosophical roots in Aristotle's *De Motu Animalium* and *De Anima* 3.9–11, but this volume has its roots rather in Aristotle's *Nicomachean Ethics* and the ethical dialogues of Plato. The inclusion of "moral" limits the scope to a particular class of human actions. I say at the outset, then, that while moral motivation can be thought of more neatly as a phenomenon than as a concept, it will be most apposite to consider it as naming a cluster of interrelated philosophical issues, with a complex and intricate history central to ethical theory and reflection. Thus, *moral motivation* is indeed an ideal topic for investigation in a series called "Oxford Philosophical Concepts."

As we might expect from careful scholarship in the history of philosophy, the questions and answers offered in these essays on moral motivation, which cover a range of historical figures spanning almost 2,500 years, are going to be conflicting, sometimes incompatible, and sometimes at least apparently irrelevant either to one another or to contemporary discussion. For not only do positions shift in the course of the history of philosophy, where this means that different figures offer different answers to the same question, but the questions themselves change and develop over time. Rarely do historical figures address the positions with the precise distinctions (the many "-isms") familiar in contemporary Anglo-American philosophy. While in some cases this represents a regrettable lack of clarity and precision, in others it may be a salutary reminder that one can carve up logical space in a way that may be too fine-grained for the subject in question. Of course there is no simple way to determine in advance what is going on in any particular case; we must argue it out in each instance. In line with what Christia Mercer says in the foreword to this series, one ought to be suspicious of the very notion of providing a definitive history of a philosophical concept or of the idea that there is an unchanging philosophical question that simply gets answered differently over history without the answers themselves contributing to a transformation of the question. So the aim of this volume is not to provide a definitive account of moral motivation as such, of moral motivation in this or that philosopher, or of the overall history of moral motivation but to display a broad array of positions, questions, and responses, the connections among which (as well as with contemporary work) are myriad, complex, and themselves the subject matter, we hope, for further argument.

Moral Motivation and Contemporary Philosophy

Some general remarks are in order nevertheless. First, "moral" in "moral motivation" ought to be broadly construed as including the ethical, what is right, and the virtuous. It should not be understood as referring, unless otherwise specified, to a narrow range of obligatory actions motivated solely by a concern for the moral as such; this would be, rather, a specific view of moral motivation and how it works (or ought to work). In this respect, I think the overall sense of "moral motivation" is in keeping with recent usage, where the issue of moral motivation concerns how, why, and whether moral judgments (i.e., judgments that some action is right or moral or ethical or virtuous) motivate agents to act.

Moreover, a starting point for almost all parties is that moral judgments do, at least sometimes, motivate agents to act. When I speak of "motivating an agent to act," I do not mean *overridingly motivate*, which is an extreme position that holds that whenever a moral judgment motivates, it overridingly motivates.[1] Rather, the view that moral judgments at least sometimes motivate is the view that moral judgments at least sometimes motivate *to some unspecified extent*. It may be that they sometimes provide agents with sufficient motivation to act, but this is not necessary. Internalists hold that necessarily moral judgments motivate, at least to some extent. As Christine Korsgaard says, internalists believe "moral considerations necessarily have some power to motivate us."[2] In a slightly more formal variation: "A normative reason for me to *phi* must

---

1 John L. Mackie, *Ethics: Inventing Right and Wrong* (New York: Penguin, 1977), attributes a view like this to Plato, incorrectly on my account: see chapter 1 here.

2 Christine Korsgaard, *The Sources of Normativity* (Cambridge: Cambridge University Press, 1996), 81.

be a consideration my awareness of which would motivate me to *phi* if I were thinking about it fully rationally and with full knowledge."[3] So, motivational judgment internalism (henceforth "internalism") holds that necessarily, if one sincerely judges an action right, then one is motivated to some extent to act in accordance with that judgment.[4]

Many of the figures treated in this volume are plausibly understood as taking some version of internalism to be true even if they are not explicit about this. In general, many philosophers, especially those prior to Hume and Kant, are concerned with aiding their readers to think about moral judgments with full knowledge, full rationality, and appropriate feeling, on the assumption that once one does this, one will be motivated to act morally. Furthermore, in some cases, they are concerned to argue against a moral skeptic, who might concede that moral judgments necessarily motivate to some extent but that they should not overridingly motivate.[5] So on this view one is (sometimes or often) better off acting contrary to what morality or virtue demands.

A related question concerns *how* a moral judgment motivates, via desire or belief? No one denies that a desire can motivate, but some hold that beliefs also are either themselves motivationally efficacious states or can generate them. This is often characterized as a debate about Humeanism, in so far as "the Humean," even if not Hume himself, denies that beliefs by themselves can motivate or generate motivationally

---

3 Garrett Cullity and Berys Gaut, introduction to *Ethics and Practical Reason*, edited by Garrett Cullity and Berys Gaut (Oxford: Oxford University Press, 1997), 3.

4 See Russ Shaffer-Landau, *Moral Realism: A Defense* (Oxford: Oxford University Press, 2003), 21, and Connie Rosati, "Moral Motivation," in *Stanford Encyclopedia of Philosophy* (Spring 2014 ed.), edited by Edward Zalta, http://plato.stanford.edu/entries/moral-motivation/. Such a position is going to connect quickly with issues about reasons; for what one rationally judges to be right is what one has reason to do. For a clear exposition of the many varieties of motivational internalism see Gunnar Björnsson et al., eds., *Motivational Internalism* (Oxford: Oxford University Press, 2015), 1–16.

5 An externalist, one who holds that the relationship between moral judgment and motivation is contingent, believes that an amoralist, that is, one who fully understands moral judgments yet remains *completely unmoved* by them, is possible. For two contemporary defenses of externalism about moral motivation see, e.g., David Brink, *Moral Realism and the Foundations of Ethics* (Cambridge: Cambridge University Press, 1989), and Sigrun Svavarsdottir, "Moral Cognitivism and Motivation," *Philosophical Review* 108 (1999): 161–219.

efficacious states.[6] Many contemporary philosophers, I think, would describe this problem if asked about moral motivation. One position might hold that the motivation to refrain from acting is not part of the *belief* that some action is wrong; one must already *desire* to refrain from wrongdoing. And it is this desire, rather than any belief or judgment, that motivates one to abstain from an act. If this is one's view, then one might investigate the source of this desire or how to inculcate it in someone. If one then wonders why one *ought* to have such a desire (i.e., be motivated to act morally) then we return to the challenge of the skeptic. Others maintain that beliefs themselves can motivate, without there being any desire involved. On some versions of this view, it is the *beliefs* that generate desires. More broadly, as Robert Audi puts it, moral motivation concerns "how, if at all, the behavioural will must respond to the moral intellect."[7]

In general, then, contemporary discussion of moral motivation centers on two major issues: internalism versus externalism and Humeanism versus anti-Humeanism. Stands taken on these issues often lead to further debates in metaethics concerning realism/antirealism and cognitivism/anticognitivism.[8]

MORAL MOTIVATION IN THE HISTORY OF PHILOSOPHY

While these two theoretical issues largely dominate contemporary discussion of moral motivation, the historical treatment of it does not have the narrowness of topic of much contemporary work. When thinking about moral motivation and moral motives, one prominent distinction is between the concept of what motivates one to act—what

---

6 On Hume, see chapter 7 here. The second phrase captures Thomas Nagle's "motivated desires"—that is, desires that are generated by beliefs. See Nagle, *The Possibility of Altruism* (Oxford: Oxford University Press, 1970), chap. 5.

7 Robert Audi, "Moral Judgment and Reasons for Action," in *Ethics and Practical Reason*, edited by Garrett Cullity and Berys Gaut (Oxford: Oxford University Press, 1997), 125. Audi sees the problems around moral motivation as inspired particularly by Hume.

8 See Rosati, "Moral Motivation," and further references there.

we might call in an Aristotelian manner, the "efficient-causal motive"—
and the concept of the motive of one's action, meaning the end or goal
one has in acting, what we might call "the teleological motive."⁹ In the
latter sense we say colloquially that someone has an "ulterior motive"
in acting in a certain way, meaning that the apparent end of the action,
for example generously benefiting someone, is not the real end of the
action. Over the history of the concept of moral motivation, we find a
variety of positions about what is and ought to be one's motivation, in
the efficient-causal sense and the teleological sense.

Prior to Hume, philosophers do not distinguish the cognitive from
the conative as sharply and exclusively as Hume and those who follow
him do. Both Plato and Aristotle, for example, explicitly posit a species
of desire that is itself rational—*boulēsis*, sometimes translated as "rational
wish." Aristotle's central ethical concept of decision (*prohairesis*) is described as either a "desiring understanding" (*orektikos nous*) or a "thinking
desire" (*orexis dianoētikē*) (*Nicomachean Ethics* 6.2, 1139b4–5). Moreover, as Susan Meyer discusses in chapter 2, decision functions both as an
efficient/causal motivation *and* a teleological one. Thus, perhaps, it is
not simply that Plato and Aristotle do not explicitly address the dispute
about motivational judgment internalism or about Humeanism but that
to force them to come down on one side or the other is to misunderstand
the way they are considering the matter, since they do not understand
the distinction between the cognitive and the conative as mutually exclusive, which is an assumption important for generating the philosophical problem, at least in many typical formulations of it.

Another set of issues concerns the assessment and justification of an
action *as* moral and the role that the teleological motive of that action
plays in such an assessment. We can refer to this as a puzzle about the
"deontic relevance" of motives.¹⁰ This is connected with issues about

---

9 See chapters 1 and 2 here.

10 See Steven Sverdlik, chapter 10 here, and his *Motive and Rightness* (Oxford: Oxford University
Press, 2011).

the *source* of morality: is the morality of action contained in the *action itself* or does it stem from something about the *agent*? In assessing the ethical value of a token act does one consider: (1) just the act itself; (2) just the motive of the agent; or (3) some combination of (1) and (2)? One might think that moral assessment arises most simply in the attribution of rightness and wrongness to certain action tokens and types, with the motivation of the agent irrelevant to the fact that an action of such and such a type was done. Motivation becomes important once we get into a more complicated assessment. On one hand there are questions of "apparently" wrong acts done for the "right" reason or with the "right" intention, for which an agent demands reconsideration, and perhaps, exculpation or forgiveness. On the other hand there are "apparently" virtuous or good acts that demand reassessment later given subsequent actions by or responses from the agent. For example, suppose that what initially appear to be acts of kindness turn out only to be ways of gaining a person's trust so that she can later be betrayed. After the betrayal, earlier acts of kindness seem only *apparently* kind and actually malicious.

Kant argues notoriously that the motive behind an action is determinative of what the action is. For an action to be genuinely moral it must be done because it is moral and not, as we say, for an "ulterior motive." The roots of such views about motives and moral motivation lie in Plato and Aristotle. On some interpretations Aristotle takes the reason a person does an action as at least partly constitutive of the nature of the action: for an action to be truly virtuous, it has to be (among other things) chosen "for its own sake."[11] Philosophers sometimes think of this (perhaps too hastily) as a question of the "purity" of one's motive. If a person does an action that seems, for example, kind, but we learn that the reason or motive for the action was financial profit, then we might judge that the action was not in fact kind after all. Alternatively, we might say that the person did the right thing but

---

11 *Nicomachean Ethics* 2.4, 1105a31–32; see Susan Meyer, chapter 2 here.

for the wrong reason—so the act itself is still right, there is just something wrong with the agent: she is not as she ought to be. In Aristotle's language, she has done the virtuous action but not acted *as the virtuous person would*.

Further, insofar as one holds that it is a *necessary condition* for an action's being right or moral that the agent be in a certain state when he acts, there will be a group of agents who do what the virtuous or good person would do but do not perform genuinely virtuous actions nonetheless, since they do not act from the proper motives. Alternatively, they do perform virtuous *actions* but are not (fully) virtuous *agents*. Consideration of this third set of issues has a long and illustrious history not only in philosophy but also in history, literature, and even music, as is shown in the Reflections.

A History of Moral Motivation

Philosophical reflection on moral motivation arguably begins with Socrates's call in Plato's dialogues to act virtuously above all, treating it as the supreme end of one's actions that trumps pleasure, wealth, and even survival.[12] This exhortation unsurprisingly provokes the moral skeptic's question: "why should I?" In Plato a number of interlocutors argue that they are better off doing what is in their self-interest rather than acting morally or justly. Since moral action seems in many cases to leave an agent worse off than she might otherwise be, the defender of morality must show a self-interested agent why she ought to act morally. Is the skeptic looking, at least in part, for an efficient-causal motivation to act morally? This is not always entirely clear. More typically, the skeptic's query seeks some justification or grounds for the placement of morality as the allegedly (supreme) teleological motive: as what should be the supreme end of our actions.

---

12 See chapter 1 here.

Susan Meyer considers the roles that *prohairesis* (decision) and pleasures and pains play in the moral motivation of the virtuous person according to Aristotle. She argues for a complex and subtle role for pleasures and pains in which they function not primarily as efficient-causal motivation but as a teleological motivation via their ability to reveal the reasons for our actions. Along the way, Meyer illuminates Aristotle's concept of the fine or noble (*kalon*) and contrasts the genuinely virtuous person with the one who has mere natural virtue.

As Brad Inwood and Jonathan Jacobs bring out, our pursuit of the moral is often tied in ancient and medieval thought to the notion of the good or happy life for a human being. Inwood discusses an anonymous Peripatetic author who questions the value of pursuing what is virtuous, even if, in Aristotelian fashion, being virtuous is part of a human being's perfected nature and thus (at least) part of human happiness.[13] Understanding moral motivation in the context of a type of eudaimonism also arises for Jacobs in his account of Medieval thinkers. The view of Augustine and others includes the idea that one can be motivated to act either by base desires or reason. Overall the concern of Augustine, Anselm, Maimonides, Bahya ibn Pakuda, Aquinas, and Scotus is not so much with whether it is belief or desire that motivates the agent or with whether or not moral judgment necessarily motivates, but with acting from the right efficient/causal motivations for the right ends. Inevitably in this period both the efficient causal motivation and the ends aimed at stem ultimately from God.

According to Steven Nadler, Spinoza in a way undermines the moral aspect of moral motivation. Good and evil are merely related to a model projected by us onto the world and, moreover, by us as individuals. While this means that there is no guarantee that one's own outlook is shared by others, there is nevertheless room on Spinoza's account for objectivity in the idea of a perfected specimen of humanity, which

---

13 Although there is no chapter here that is devoted exclusively to Stoic thought, Stoic views are discussed in the essays by Inwood (chapter 3), Jacobs (chapter 4), Nadler (chapter 5), and Mitsis (chapter 6).

yields maximal human activity. Spinoza's focus on the basic drive that motivates human beings, which is the same for all human beings, would seem therefore to preclude specifically moral motivation. Nevertheless, he also allows for differences in an action based on whether it stems from adequate ideas or understanding (and so from a different sort of character) rather than certain baser emotions, such as pity. In this sense, Spinoza in a way allows that efficient-causal motives may be deontically relevant.

Phillip Mitsis argues against an orthodoxy that interprets Locke's views on moral motivation as formed primarily in the context of the new philosophical frameworks of Descartes and Hobbes. Instead, Locke's position is more accurately understood as engaging with a far older tradition, namely that of the Epicureans and Stoics. It is this heritage that is responsible for what has sounded to contemporary ears to be a confused view that conflates adherence to natural law and hedonism. Some scholars reconcile this apparent conflict by seeing hedonism as what provides the psychological motivation to follow what rational understanding, itself motivationally inert, has revealed to be the natural law. Mitsis disputes this "proto-Humean" reading, presenting instead an account of Locke that may be less "distinctively modern," but that has a good claim to be more philosophically sophisticated and historically accurate.

While Jacqueline Taylor joins other scholars in debunking the attribution to Hume of a simplistic Humeanism, the focus of her essay is less well-traveled terrain concerning Hume's views about how reason, character, virtue, sentiment, and pride operate in motivating people to be moral and to act morally. Taylor begins by addressing the notorious passage of Hume's *Treatise* (2.3.3), endorsing scholarly views showing that Hume is not a crude Humean for whom reason is not at all motivationally efficacious. Rather, reason can influence the will at least "mediately" via forming beliefs about the prospects for pain or pleasure. Taylor goes on to discuss how strong but calm (as opposed to violent but momentary) passions can be shaped by habit and even directed by reason toward certain ends, so that they become deep-seated commitments. She emphasizes the crucial role of the cultivation of the virtues as part of moral motivation. Moreover, she shows that shame, and particularly pride, are important according to Hume for proper moral motivation.

Jennifer Uleman argues that Kant's account of rational autonomous willing, besides being the sole proper source for genuinely moral motivation as others have argued, is also something that should motivate us to act morally. A genuine Kantian ought to promote free, rational willing wherever it may be found as the intrinsic good it is. Uleman's account of Kant is controversial but, to my mind, exciting insofar as it makes Kant's position on moral motivation, typically characterized as extreme, both philosophically and psychologically more plausible than others have thought.

Angelica Nuzzo traces the development of the concept of motive from Kant into Fichte and Hegel. Both Fichte and Hegel reject the idea that the value of our moral action arises purely from the will as such, arguing instead that it stems from the concrete determination of the will in action. Hegel then takes this a step further. Instead of the concrete revealing the will, as on Fichte's account according to Nuzzo, Hegel reads what the will is (was) by looking at what was done. The fact that the will and intention can only be discovered after the act by interpreting it places the will into a larger social and political context. The motivation for the action is no longer just that of an individual but a matter of a social and political determination.

Finally, Steven Sverdlik focuses on the issue of the deontic relevance of motives. A motive is "deontically relevant" if it can affect whether an action is required, forbidden, or permissible. Historically, consequentialists like Bentham, Mill, Sidgwick, and Moore have generally denied deontic relevance, since what counts in the appraisal of actions are consequences rather than the motives of the agent who performs them, but Sverdlik argues that there is a way to make room for deontic relevance in a consequentialist theory.

While the value of this collection lies primarily and most obviously in the details of the individual essays, overall I would suggest that there are many more commonalities among the philosophers treating moral motivation than typical labels, such as Humean, Kantian, eudaimonist, consequentialist, and so on would suggest. When these positions are formulated in abstraction from the historical texts, as much contemporary literature does (and which I have largely tried to avoid in this introduction), the result is the formulation of more starkly opposed, but in some cases less plausible positions. By contrast, the interpretations of the figures on offer here tell a history of a complicated interrelated treatment of a constellation of issues that, while sometimes remaining less well defined, nevertheless more clearly reveal the connections and similarities among the accounts.

CHAPTER ONE

Plato and Moral Motivation

Iakovos Vasiliou

In one respect, Plato is an ideal initial figure for this volume since he addresses a wide range of issues surrounding moral motivation. He has much to tell us about why we ought to act morally, how to inculcate a motivation to be moral in people, and how and whether moral knowledge is by itself motivating.[1] In another respect, he is a problematic figure to treat for at least two reasons: first, there are puzzles about the dialogue form and developmentalism, and second, the discussions of various issues concerning moral motivation are not as sharply distinguished as we might wish, either from one another or from broader issues in ethics. The second reason makes succinct treatment of Plato's views difficult because, as I will show, in many ways treatment of moral motivation in Plato involves treatment of Plato's ethics more generally.

---

1 For the purposes of this essay, moral motivation might as well be synonymous with "ethical motivation" or "motivation to act virtuously." I do not here intend anything special by the word "moral" as opposed to "ethical" or "virtuous."

At the same time, however, this fact about Plato's arguments offers an opportunity to see how difficult the actual concept of moral motivation is and how it intersects with and affects many of our central concerns in ethics. Given these issues, and limited space, my aim in this essay is to give some overall indication of how the different aspects of moral motivation are elaborated and connected in Plato's best known ethical dialogues and then to focus a bit more narrowly on what the *Republic* tells us about how moral motivation is inculcated and on the role that knowledge, in particular knowledge of the Forms, plays in it.

A couple of brief, preliminary remarks on the dialogue form and developmentalism are in order. For the purposes of this essay I will consider the positions put forward and defended by the character "Socrates" in Plato's so-called early and middle dialogues to be Plato's.[2] Many scholars see different ethical views defended in these two periods. The guiding thought, roughly, is that Plato begins his philosophical writing with the "early" dialogues, in which he is to some more or less unknowable extent influenced by the historical Socrates, and then begins to develop his own, more mature philosophical positions in the "middle dialogues"; in dialogues of both these periods, however, a character "Socrates" remains the primary figure. I will be more concerned with similarities among dialogues of both periods than with differences.[3]

1. COMMITTING TO VIRTUE

The first and most obvious way in which moral motivation appears in Plato is in Socrates's concern with persuading people to commit to

---

2 I ignore the issue of how or whether the character "Socrates" corresponds to the historical Socrates; "Socrates" refers throughout to the character in Plato's dialogues. Early dialogues typically include (at least): the *Apology, Charmides, Crito, Euthyphro, Gorgias, Laches*, and *Protagoras*. Middle dialogues typically include (at least): *Phaedo, Phaedrus, Republic*, and *Symposium*. On the division of Plato's dialogues into developmental periods, and lists of which dialogues belong in which periods on this view, see Gregory Vlastos, *Socrates, Ironist and Moral Philosopher* (Ithaca, NY: Cornell University Press, 1991); Terence Irwin, *Plato's Ethics* (Oxford: Oxford University Press, 1995), and "The Platonic Corpus," in *The Oxford Handbook of Plato*, edited by G. Fine (Oxford: Oxford University Press, 2008), 63–87.

3 For an explicit defense of "Socratic studies," see Thomas Brickhouse and Nicholas Smith, *Socratic Moral Psychology* (Cambridge: Cambridge University Press, 2010), chap. 1.

ethical or virtuous action. In the *Apology*, Socrates tells his Athenian audience to be committed to acting virtuously above all and so to aim at being a good person above all; that is, to be someone who puts nothing ahead of virtue in acting: "Perhaps someone might say: 'Aren't you ashamed that you have pursued the sort of pursuit on account of which you are now likely to be put to death?' But I would reply to this with a just statement in saying, 'You are not right, sir, if you think that a man who is worth even some little bit ought to take under consideration the risk of living or dying and not instead look to this alone [*monon skopein*] when he acts: whether he is doing just or unjust things, the deeds of a good or a bad man'" (28b5–9).[4] Socrates urges his audience not only to act in a certain way but also to commit themselves to acting in a certain way, just as he argues that he himself has.[5]

Two questions arise at this point: (1) what is it to act virtuously (either here and now or in general)? and (2) why should I commit myself to acting in the way that Socrates insists I should?[6] The former question asks for a determination of the virtuous action: if we are committed to acting virtuously above all (and never acting contrary to virtue), then if we are to put this practical principle into action, we must be able to identify correctly the action that is required (or forbidden). The moral skeptic takes up the second question, denying that we have any (good or adequate) reason to be moral, any (good or adequate) reason to act in the way that virtue or morality requires. In Plato, the skeptic's challenge arises most starkly in Socrates's conversations with Polus and Callicles in the *Gorgias*, with Thrasymachus in *Republic* 1, and then with Glaucon's and Adeimantus's reformulated Thrasymachean challenge to the value of justice in *Republic* 2. In its most general form, the reply to the skeptic, the motivation for a person

---

4 Translations are my own unless otherwise mentioned.

5 For additional discussion, see Iakovos Vasiliou, *Aiming at Virtue in Plato* (Cambridge: Cambridge University Press, 2008), introduction and chap. 1.

6 Socrates's answer in the *Apology* is: wouldn't you be ashamed not to? Wouldn't you be ashamed, for example, to put financial profit ahead of virtue? This answer is not as bad as it may at first appear, especially to philosophers; while it will not appeal to the shameless, it will have some force for the rest of us.

to act virtuously above all is that virtuous actions affect the most important part of a person, her soul or character. Virtuous or excellent actions make one's soul excellent. Thus, the reason that it is in one's own interest to act virtuously is that acting contrary to virtue harms the most important part of oneself.[7] A short form of this argument appears even in the *Crito* (47c–48a), where Socrates is arguing with an interlocutor who is certainly no moral skeptic. The argument proceeds as follows:

1. The soul is an independent locus of harm and benefit (like the body).
2. The welfare of the soul is more important than the welfare of the body (or the condition of one's possessions).
3. A virtuous soul is generated by doing virtuous actions.
   So,
4. One ought to act virtuously above all.

This already opens up a complex issue in moral motivation. As I read Plato, appeal to the effect of virtuous actions on one's soul or character is not meant to supply a new answer to what the ultimate aim of one's actions ought to be, somehow supplanting the answer that Socrates has already given us in the *Apology*: to do the virtuous action above all. Indeed, he explicitly repeats this injunction in the *Crito* in order to secure Crito's agreement that one's ultimate aim ought *not* to be anyone's welfare or benefit but solely to do the virtuous action (48c–d, 49a–d, 54b). One's ultimate end in acting—one's motive in the teleological sense—remains doing the right/virtuous thing. It does not, as some think, change to benefiting oneself. Rather, the question focuses

---

7 This need not commit Plato to a rationalistic type of justification for the value of the virtuous life. In brief, it is not necessarily the case that what Socrates touts as the advantage to one's soul of virtuous action (in the Socratic sense) will appear as such to any agent, regardless of his or her character. Indeed, Polus, Callicles, and perhaps Thrasymachus are examples of those who remain unmoved by such an argument. The way the problem is posed precisely sets things up so that all the apparently neutral goods will not be available to be appealed to as a motivation for acting justly: money, pleasure, honor, reputation, and so on are stripped off from the putative advantages right from the start.

on why I should be thusly committed: why commit to doing the virtuous action above all? What is being supplied by this argument's
appeal to the welfare of our souls, I argue, is a motive in the efficient-
causal sense; it is not supplying a new motive in the teleological sense.[8]
What will potentially motivate me in the efficient-causal sense is the
appreciation that virtuous actions affect my soul and that my soul
(character) is the most important aspect of myself.[9]

This argument for why one should be committed to acting virtuously above all is repeated, in far greater detail, in *Republic* 4, 8, and 9.
In *Republic* 4, Socrates argues that the soul is divided into three kinds
or parts: the appetitive, spirited, and rational. The general idea of welfare of the soul from the *Crito* is now more elaborately described as the
health or harmony of this tripartite soul, with reason ruling, spirit assisting, and appetite obeying (442a–c). It is the engaging in genuinely
just actions, which is the province of the rational part of the soul's determining what ought to be done, that generates and maintains this
harmony (444b–d). In this way, Plato explains how acting justly (virtuously) is good *for* the soul. In *Republic* 8–9, the accounts of less than
virtuous characters, such as the timocratic, oligarchic, democratic, and
tyrannical characters, describe in detail the harm that comes to the soul
from acting contrary to virtue.

Although it is not usually put in these terms, a more standard reading of Plato, operating under the eudaimonist framework, understands
these descriptions as supplying new ends. If my happiness consists in

---

8 See Iakovos Vasiliou, "Aristotle, Agents, and Actions," in *Aristotle's "Nicomachean Ethics": A Critical Guide*, edited by Jon Miller, 170–190 (Cambridge: Cambridge University Press, 2011), for a defense of a distinction between motive (i.e., efficient causal motive) and end (i.e., teleological motive) in the context of a commitment to virtue in Aristotle.

9 I say "appreciation" in order to leave ambiguous whether we ought to think of this state as a belief or a desire. I think of coming to see the soul as most valuable as a cognitive/intellectual activity that is at the same time a shaping of one's motivational propensities. This makes it difficult to see Plato's po-sition as adopting either Humeanism or anti-Humeanism. John McDowell, "The Role of Eudaimonia in Aristotle's Ethics," in McDowell, *Mind, Value, and Reality* (Cambridge, MA: Harvard University Press, 1998), 3–22, and "Some Issues in Aristotle's Moral Psychology," in McDowell, *Mind, Value, and Reality,* 22–49, argues for a similar position in reading Aristotle. But there need not be agreement on this issue to agree with the general point above.

the well-being of my soul, and my happiness is my ultimate end, then what I am aiming at is my happiness, which will be brought about by or perhaps constituted by my acting virtuously. I don't have the space to raise problems with this reading of Plato here.[10] It is enough, for the purposes of elucidating moral motivation, if we can appreciate the differences in interpretation. On my view, acting virtuously is the motive in the teleological sense, while the well-being of my soul is the motive in the efficient causal sense. Another way of putting it is that Socrates consistently believes that one's supreme aim in acting ought to be to act virtuously (or not to act contrary to virtue), and the arguments in the *Crito*, *Gorgias*, and *Republic* about the effects of virtuous (and "vicious") actions on the soul are part of an argument as to why one should be so committed, not part of a new argument about what one's ultimate commitment ought to be.[11]

2. MORAL MOTIVATION AND MORAL PSYCHOLOGY

Another set of issues fitting under the heading "moral motivation," which I have already touched on briefly, stems from a broader question in philosophy of action about what *motivates* an agent to act: is it belief, desire, or some combination of both? We find this aspect of moral motivation in interpretations of Socrates's intellectualism. Socrates apparently believes that being virtuous *just is* having knowledge of virtue. So most scholars hold that Socrates maintains that knowing what virtue is is by itself sufficient for a person to be virtuous and therefore to act virtuously. Socrates's intellectualism denies the possibility of incontinence, denies the existence (or at least the motivational power) of nonrational desires when compared with the motivational power of knowledge. Plato, by contrast, moves beyond this implausible and

---

10 For some argument, see Iakovos Vasiliou, "Platonic Virtue: An Alternative Account," *Philosophy Compass* 9:9 (2014): 605–614.

11 For well-known examples of eudaimonist readings, see Julia Annas, *An Introduction to Plato's Republic* (Oxford: Oxford University Press, 1981), and Irwin, *Plato's Ethics*.

impoverished moral psychology by arguing that the soul is in fact divided into parts or kinds, only one of which is rational. He thereby allows that there can be intrapsychic conflict and so weakness of will.[12] The conflict that may ensue among the parts is vividly described in *Republic* 4, 8, and 9 and in the image of the charioteer in the *Phaedrus* (246a, 253d–256e). Thus Plato, at least in these "middle period" dialogues, acknowledges the potentially overwhelming motivational force of nonrational parts of the soul.

Each of the different parts of the soul might motivate the agent, depending on how each of them has been trained and habituated. But Plato's answer to the problem of moral motivation in its Humean form—is it belief or desire that motivates?—proves difficult to pin down. It seems that reason makes judgments about what is best for the soul as a whole but that sometimes (in characters who are unjust to varying degrees) spirited or appetitive desires overrule reason's judgment. Sometimes a person can be motivated to act by a belief (or knowledge)—when she follows her reason/rational part—while at other times, a spirited or appetitive desire would be what motivates her to act. What's more, Plato attributes to the rational part of the soul a specifically rational species of desire, which is arguably difficult to find in philosophers after Hobbes. Adding details to this account that make it both plausible in its own right and cohere with the text of *Republic* 4, 8, and 9 is quite difficult, for Plato sometimes appears to attribute beliefs and desires to each part of the soul. One then must address in more detail how to understand the parts of the soul themselves, whether all of the parts are little belief/desire homunculi, and so forth.[13] I shall not pursue these issues further here.

---

12 This account of the moral psychology often goes hand in hand with a developmental reading of the dialogues, according to which Plato has a first, "Socratic" phase, where he defends views such as the identification of virtue and knowledge (which may or may not bear a close relation to the views of the historical Socrates), but then moves into his "middle period," exemplified by such dialogues as the *Republic* and *Phaedrus*.

13 There is an extensive bibliography on this issue. See, as a sample, Christopher Bobonich, *Plato's Utopia Recast* (Oxford: Oxford University Press, 2002); Hendrick Lorenz, *The Brute Within: Appetitive*

There is another route more directly relevant to the present focus, however, that leads us back to the heart of the first set of concerns falling under moral motivation: the response to the skeptic. In *Republic* 4, when Plato tells us that justice is a harmony of the tripartite soul, he may tell us why we would be happier as just rather than unjust people, but he does not seem to give us any reason to think that a person with such a harmonious soul would be more likely to engage in actions we ordinarily consider just and to refrain from actions ordinarily considered unjust. In particular, why would someone with a well-ordered soul, a Platonically just person, show any particular concern for the well-being of others? This worry is exacerbated in book 7 when scholars ask why the Philosopher would return to the "Cave" to rule—that is, why he would agree to rule in the Kallipolis and give up what would allegedly make him happier, namely to continue to contemplate the Forms.

At this point a form of intellectualism is reintroduced, revamped to take Forms into account. Scholars concede that there is a gap between ordinary and Platonic justice but then claim that this gap will be closed by appeal to the motivational power of the philosopher's (i.e., the truly just person's)[14] knowledge of Forms.[15]

Let's look more carefully at how this is supposed to work.[16]

Desire in Plato and Aristotle (Oxford: Oxford University Press, 2006), and Jennifer Whiting, "Psychic Contingency in the *Republic*," in *Plato and the Divided Self*, edited by Rachel Barney Tad Brennan, and Charles Brittain (Cambridge: Cambridge University Press, 2012), 174–208, each of which contains further references.

14 The issue here is related to views in Irwin, *Plato's Ethics*, and Bobonich, *Plato's Utopia Recast* (more extremely), that *only* philosophers can be virtuous. And this view is (allegedly) supported by appeal to another aspect of moral motivation: only philosophers can act for the right reason (or from the right motive). For contrasting views, see Rachana Kamtekar, "What's the Good of Agreeing? Homonoia in Platonic Politics," *Oxford Studies in Ancient Philosophy* 26 (2004): 131–170; Vasiliou, *Aiming*, chap. 7, and "From the *Phaedo* to the *Republic*: Plato's Tripartite Soul and the Possibility of Non-philosophical Virtue," in Barney et al., *Plato and the Divided Self*, 9–32.

15 A feature of this strategy is that the "gap" will not be alleviated for anyone who does not know the Forms; and so not for anyone who is not a philosopher. Insofar as the *Republic* is supposed to offer an argument *to everyone* that he or she is better off being just (in the ordinary sense), this poses a problem.

16 There is some overlap in the next three sections with Iakovos Vasiliou, "Plato, Forms, and Moral Motivation," *Oxford Studies in Ancient Philosophy* 49 (2015): 37–70.

3. FORMS AS (MORAL) MOTIVATORS

I think it will be instructive to consider how the motivational power of Forms is described by the philosopher J. L. Mackie. Mackie uses Plato's Forms as vivid examples of what objective values would have to be like, describing them as follows:

> In Plato's theory the Forms, and in particular the Form of the Good, are eternal, extra-mental, realities. They are a very central structural element in the fabric of the world. But it is held also that just knowing them or "seeing" them will not merely tell men what to do but will ensure that they do it, overruling any contrary inclinations. The philosopher-kings in the *Republic* can, Plato thinks, be trusted with unchecked power because their education will have given them knowledge of the Forms. Being acquainted with the Forms of the Good and Justice and Beauty and the rest they will, by this knowledge alone, without any further motivation, be impelled to pursue and promote these ideals.[17]

> The Form of the Good is such that knowledge of it provides the knower with both a direction and an overriding motive; something's being good both tells the person who knows this to pursue it and makes him pursue it. An objective good would be sought by anyone who was acquainted with it, not because of any contingent fact that this person, or every person, is so constituted that he desires this end, but just because the end has to-be-pursuedness somehow built into it.[18]

Mackie here attributes to Plato a strong version of intellectualism and motivational internalism according to which recognition of moral facts by itself provides reason, motivation, and direction for the knower. Knowing the good "makes someone pursue it," is "an overriding

---

17 John L. Mackie, *Ethics: Inventing Right and Wrong* (New York: Penguin, 1977), 23–24.

18 Mackie, *Ethics*, 40.

motive," "overrules any contrary inclinations," and requires no further
motivation. This is in line with, at the very least, the most troubling
aspect of Socratic intellectualism: the claim that knowledge is sufficient for virtue. According to the usual interpretation of Socrates,
knowing what virtue is sufficient for being virtuous and so also for
acting virtuously; the Platonic twist on this is that knowing what
virtue is means knowing the Form of the Good and the rest of the
Forms. Views similar to Mackie's are defended in more specific ways by
Platonic scholars who claim that knowledge of the Form of Justice
itself carries with it the motivation to act justly.[19]

Contrary to orthodoxy, I deny that knowledge of the Forms by itself
motivates us to do anything other than motivate the knower to continue to contemplate Forms. We must distinguish, however, the rejection of the idea that knowledge of the Forms is by itself motivating
from the claim that *the Forms themselves* may be motivating because
they are objects of desire—at any rate at least for people with the right
natures and nurture. It seems to me that the latter claim is right, in at
least two ways: first, given that there are Forms, someone motivated to
pursue knowledge and truth is motivated to know them—whether or
not he is aware of it. And, presumably, we can be aware of this even
without knowing the Forms ourselves, as we readers of Plato are;
second, insofar as the Forms are the causes or explanations in some
sense of the various features of the sensible world, we may be motivated
to pursue beauty or goodness because of our appreciation of sensible
things participating (however imperfectly) in Beauty and the Good;

19 See John Cooper, "The Psychology of Justice in Plato," *American Philosophical Quarterly* (1977):
151–157, reprinted in Cooper, *Reason and Emotion* (Princeton, NJ: Princeton University Press, 1999),
145–148, and Cooper, "Two Theories of Justice," *Proceedings and Addresses of the American Philosophical Association* 74:2 (2000), 5–27, reprinted in Cooper, *Knowledge, Nature, and the Good* (Princeton,
NJ: Princeton University Press, 2004), 265–269. Terence Irwin, *Plato's Moral Theory* (Oxford: Oxford
University Press, 1977), and *Plato's Ethics*; Richard Kraut, "The Defense of Justice in the *Republic*," in
The Cambridge Companion to Plato, edited by Kraut (Cambridge: Cambridge University Press, 1992),
311–337, and "Return to the Cave: *Republic* 519–521," in *Plato*, vol. 2, *Ethics, Politics, Religion, and the
Soul*, edited by Gail Fine (Oxford: Oxford University Press, 1999), 235–254. Eric Brown, "Minding
the Gap in Plato's *Republic*," *Philosophical Studies* 117 (2004): 275–302, provides a good summary of
these positions.

metaphysically, Forms are prior to and responsible for (all of/lots of) the sensible world being as it is. It remains the case, however, that while the Form of the Good may motivate Socrates to pursue it and have it as his own (i.e., to know it), this does not mean that Socrates's *knowledge* of the Form of the Good, were he to have it, then motivates him to do anything further.

Let's look at some evidence that knowing the Forms leads to a kind of stasis rather than constituting a motivation to act in the sensible world.[20]

Let's begin with the *Symposium*, setting aside for the moment the famous *ascent* and just cutting to the *telos*. While the lover of beauty does many things on his ascent, once he reaches his goal—knowledge of the unchanging, intelligible, immaterial Beautiful itself—Diotima explains his position as follows:

(A) And there in life, Socrates, my friend,…there if anywhere should a person live his life, beholding that Beauty. If you once see that, it won't occur to you to measure beauty by gold or clothing or beautiful boys and youths—who, if you see them now, strike you out of your senses, and make you, you and many others, eager to be with [*sunontes*] the boys you love and look at them [*horōntes*] forever, if there were any way to do that, forgetting food and drink, everything but looking at them [*theasthai*] and being with them [*suneinai*]. But how would it be, in our view, if someone got to see the Beautiful itself, absolute, pure, unmixed, not polluted by human flesh or colors or any other great nonsense of mortality, but if he could see the divine Beauty itself in its one form? Do you think it would be a poor life for a human being to look there [*ekeise blepontos*] and to behold it [*theōmenou*] by that which he ought, and to be with it [*sunontos autō*]? (B) Or haven't you considered well, she said, that there alone, when he looks at Beauty in the only way that Beauty can

---

20 I will not try to address what contemplating the Forms might amount to.

be seen—only then will it become possible for him to give birth not
to images of virtue (because he's in touch with no images), but to
true virtue (because he is in touch with the true Beauty). The love of
the gods belongs to anyone who has given birth to true virtue and
nourished it, and if any human being could become immortal, it
would be he. (211d–212b)[21]

Let's begin with (A). When the lover finally grasps Beauty itself he
is stunned by the amazing vision of it "all it once" (210e4). The contemplation of Beauty itself is described as self-sufficient and making
life worth living. All the lover does (and all he wants) is to "contem-
plate/gaze at it" with his mind (*theaomai*; 211d2; compare 210e3,
212a2) and "to be with it" (*suneinai*; 212a2; compare 211d8).[22] In the
parallel with the love of beautiful boys, the lover's fantasy is simply
"to gaze and be with" them—forgetting food and drink and doing
nothing else. The analogy then works by suggesting that if you want
to do nothing but gaze at and be with beautiful boys, *just imagine*
how satisfying and self-sufficient simply gazing at and being with
the Form of Beauty itself would be. The upshot is that the grasping
of the Beautiful itself does not ask the contemplator to *do* anything,
nor does it *motivate* him to do anything, except contemplate it and
be with it.

Given the context of the *Symposium*, however, knowledge of the
Form must be tied in some way to immortality, since Diotima has described love as a desire for immortality (207a1–4).[23] Starting in part
(B) of the passage, Diotima explains that *only* a knower of Beauty
would be able to give birth to true virtue (and not simply to "images"
of virtue). On the ascent the lover is driven to reproduce in (the presence

---

21 *Plato "Symposium,"* translated by Alexander Nehamas and Paul Woodruff (Indianapolis: Hackett
Press, 1989); translation modified.

22 The latter is the obvious sexual image, but, as Nehamas and Woodruff translate, "to be with" retains the idea of simply being (as opposed to doing, producing, or becoming).

23 The *Symposium* does not claim that the soul itself is immortal, as is argued in other dialogues.

of) beautiful things. Since he has not yet grasped Beauty on the "way up," he is not in a position to know whether any of his productions truly participates in the Beautiful/Noble. But once he does grasp Beauty itself he will be able to give birth to instantiations of true virtue, which will be loved by the gods. And so he will be as immortal as possible.

But we need to be clear here that the *knowledge of* Beauty itself does not cause the person to "give birth." The most the passage says is that someone who knows the Beautiful is then able to give birth to true virtue rather than to images of it. His knowledge of Beauty does not move him to produce anything—*that* moves him simply to contemplate and be with the Beautiful itself. By contrast, what motivates the lover to give birth to true virtue—that is, to make things happen in the sensible world[24]—is the lover's *desire for immortality*. He will not be immortal simply by contemplating the Form of the Beautiful; he needs to do something that will last (to some degree, anyway) in the world. Thus he must perform acts in the sensible world, engendering true virtue in himself (and perhaps in his beloved) and presumably dictating practices and laws, as in the ascent (210c–d, 211c). What motivates the knower of the Form of Beauty to act in the *Symposium*, then, is his desire for immortality, not his knowledge of the Beautiful. Rather, his

24 This may well be an overreading of part (B). The interpretation I give here is in line with Irwin, *Moral Theory,* and Christopher Rowe, *Plato: "Symposium"* (Warminster, England: Aris and Phillips, 1998), among others. Frisbee Sheffield, *Plato's "Symposium": The Ethics of Desire* (Oxford: Oxford University Press, 2006), chaps. 3 and 4, argues, however, that we should not read part (B) as describing distinct ends, which implies that the philosopher does three things: (1) grasps the Form of Beauty, "by that which he ought/must" (i.e., the soul/mind); (2) engenders true virtue; (3) achieves immortality to the extent possible. Roughly, on the "traditional" view, which I follow in the text, (1) motivates (2), which is the production of external actions/products, and which, because of their lasting nature, leads to (3). In brief, Sheffield sees these three rather as different descriptions of one achievement. The philosopher's achievement of understanding (*nous*) is precisely the engendering of true, genuine virtue: the achievement of wisdom. Moreover, being wise in this way is as near to the gods and immortality as a human being can come. So the "higher mysteries" offer quite a different picture of the nature of virtue, as purely intellectual contemplation. Fortunately, I do not need to decide whether Sheffield or the "traditional" interpretation of the passage is correct, for if Sheffield is right, then the claim that knowledge of the Forms does not motivate the knower to do anything in the sensible world (other than contemplate) *is even clearer*, since according to Sheffield the true virtue the philosopher engenders *just is* contemplation.

knowledge of Beauty itself enables him to *do* something new: to knowledgably engender instances of true virtue in the world.[25]

Let us turn to the *Republic*.

Among the noncontroversial aspects of the Cave analogy in *Republic* 7 are the claims that everyday objects are analogous to the Forms (with the Sun as the Form of the Good) and that the world outside the cave is the "place" of the Forms. This is what imparts analogical force to the idea that the philosopher—the one who has "seen" the Forms (i.e., who knows them)—will want to *stay where she is* and not go back down into the Cave. We should appreciate that insofar as we understand the Cave to represent the sensible world and the outside the world of the Forms, all action, all doing of anything other than thinking of the Forms, will take place *in the Cave*. Here the analogy with the outside world breaks down:[26] there is nothing to *do* in the realm of Forms other than to be there and to contemplate them.

A well-known problem arises in book 7 concerning how to get the philosophers to play the role of rulers, which is necessary if the Kallipolis is ever to come into being. Socrates says that without active intervention, amounting as some scholars have emphasized to "force," there will never be a Kallipolis, insofar as those who have spent their whole lives being educated "will not willingly *act* (*tous de hekontes einai ou praxousin*), thinking that they have arrived at the Isles of the Blessed, while still alive" (519c4–6). I want to understand this "will not act" quite literally: they will not be interested in or care about doing anything in the ordinary world. This comment would make little sense if knowing the Forms by itself, as Mackie claims, includes having knowledge of what to do and the motivation to do it. In Plato's description here, those who know the Forms are not motivated in fact to do anything—they are done with acting. The point of the "Isles of the Blessed"

---

25 Which itself in some complicated way is a result of a desire to possess good things forever and the fact that "all of us" (206c) are pregnant in body or soul.

26 As it does in other respects, e.g., in the constant change and motion in the ordinary world.

remark is quite serious: as far as the philosophers (knowers of the Forms) are concerned, they have arrived at their final destination: knowledge. And now the only thing left to "do," in a sense, is to contemplate. Socrates is accusing these philosophers of having made a basic mistake, which is indeed *caused by* the fact that they have achieved knowledge of the Forms: they are confused about where they are; they think that they are "dead" and have gone to the afterlife, although they are in fact still embodied and alive. Far from motivating the philosophers to do anything, Plato indicates that their achievement of knowledge of the Forms puts the whole project of the *Republic* at risk because of the philosophers' complete unwillingness to act.

4. THE VARIETIES OF MOTIVATION

What are the sources of motivation according to Plato, then, given that I have denied that it stems from knowing the Forms? First, proper motivation, together with certain innate abilities, is a prerequisite for, not a result of, knowing the Forms. In the *Republic*, Plato is clear that many natural, inborn qualities need to be present in the would-be knower of Forms. At the very start of the argument concerning the just city in book 2, Socrates says: "Even as you were speaking it occurred to me that, in the first place, we aren't all born alike, but each of us differs in nature [*phusin*], one [suited for] the action in one task, another to another" (370b1–3). The natural differences among people are the starting point of the first division of the city into classes, with each person doing the type of job for which he is naturally suited. At 374e, Socrates repeats his references to peoples' differing natures before he embarks on the memorable comparison of the qualities of the young future guardians with well-bred (and, it turns out, philosophical—376b) dogs.

Nature plays no less substantial a role after we learn in book 5 that the rulers of the Kallipolis must be philosophers. A natural protophilosopher is going to be one with an insatiable, erotic love for all learning, knowledge, and truth (475b–e). This point is repeated at 485a–487a,

again with the idea of a natural erotic inclination toward wisdom and
truth, adding a list of the necessary natural qualities of the potential
philosopher, which include being a quick learner, having a good memory,
and being graceful, moderate, measured, and so forth. Throughout
these sections of the *Republic* the people Socrates describes as philosophers are philosophers in the sense of the *Phaedo* and *Symposium*: they
are *lovers* of (in the sense of yearning for, desirous of, but *lacking*)
wisdom and knowledge. They are *not* philosophers in the sense to
come in the *Republic*, where the philosophers are those who have
knowledge of the Form of the Good and the rest of the Forms, but the
people who would be able to become such philosophers.

Socrates then returns to the "nature" of the true would-be philosopher at 490a-e:

> It is the nature of the real lover of learning to struggle toward what
> is, not to remain with any of the many things that are believed to be,
> that, as he moves on, he neither loses nor lessens his erotic love until
> he grasps the being of each nature itself with the part of his soul that
> is fitted to grasp it, because of its kinship with it, and that, once get-
> ting near what really is and having intercourse with it and having
> begotten understanding and truth, he knows, truly lives, and is
> nourished, and—at that point, but not before—is relieved from the
> pains of giving birth. (490a8–b7)[27]

This passage has clear resonances with the *Symposium*.[28] For present
purposes, the important point is that all of the motivational power and
drive stemming from the potential philosopher's eros and abilities are
there *before* he has ever grasped the Forms. Once the lover of wisdom

---

27 Plato's *"Republic,"* translated by G. M. A. Grube, revised by C. D. C. Reeve (Indianapolis: Hackett
Press, 1992); translation modified.

28 Indeed, this passage supports the reading of Sheffield, *Symposium*, of the *Symposium*'s ascent.
What is "begotten" in this passage is "understanding and truth (*noun kai alētheian*)," *not* actions in the
sensible world. In the *Republic* such actions are what the philosopher performs in his role as ruler, not
philosopher, of the Kallipolis.

grasps being, he is finally *relieved* and, at that point, has knowledge, understanding, and truth. I have argued that the achievement of this knowledge is a kind of stasis, a resting point in which the philosopher will only desire to stay where he is. There is no indication that the achievement of the knowledge and understanding itself, for which he had such a passion, motivates him to do anything further.

The drive to knowledge and truth, however, is not in any ordinary sense *moral* motivation. I say "ordinary sense" because of an issue that arises with the Greek notion of virtue. An ordinary conception of virtuous action, at work throughout Plato's dialogues as I showed in the first sections of the essay, overlaps quite well with what we think of as ethical or moral action. There is something deeply right about the textbook description of *Republic* 2 as raising the question "Why be moral?" At the same time, however, *aretē* has a broader use better reflected in the translation "excellence." So an investigation into *aretē* is an investigation into varieties of excellence, which leads to questions about what is the highest or best type of excellence. For both Plato and Aristotle, the best or highest excellence is (often) taken to be understanding (*nous*) or wisdom. While the motivation and talent of the protophilosopher are among the necessary conditions for her achieving *that* highest excellence, the place of ordinary moral virtue becomes problematic in the process.[29]

Where is *moral* motivation in Plato, then, if we do not find it in the drive to wisdom and truth? The second candidate is the desire for the good. One immediate advantage of this proposal is that, unlike an "insatiable *erōs* for the truth," it is a motivation that is universal:

> Nobody is satisfied to acquire things that are merely thought to be good, but [everyone] seeks the things that really are and disdains mere opinion in this case.—That's right.

---

29 Notoriously so in the case of Aristotle's *Nicomachean Ethics*, the interpretation of which includes myriad attempts to reconcile the conception of *eudaimonia* as, essentially, moral virtue presented in books 1–9 with *eudaimonia* as *nous* in 10.7–8.

Every soul pursues [the good] and does whatever it does for its sake. (505d7–e2; compare *Gorgias* 468b–c, *Meno* 77c–78b, *Euthydemus* 278e)[30]

Now this is where eudaimonist readings of Plato blossom. The universal desire for the good holds out the prospect of a simple solution to the puzzle of moral motivation. If everyone desires (their own) good (i.e., their own *eudaimonia*), and acting virtuously/morally is essentially tied up in some way or other with *eudaimonia* (by being identical to it or a constituent of it or necessary for it, and so on) then it follows that any rational person would be motivated to act virtuously. The problem with this simple solution is why anyone would think that virtuous action (ordinarily understood) would be part of one's own happiness—given that it is often difficult, painful, frustrating and, in fact, detrimental to one's own good.[31] Nevertheless, overwhelmingly scholars believe that the ubiquitous desire for the good is the source of moral motivation and that the eudaimonist framework is where Plato finds the proper account of these issues.

Be that as it may, we should note that the motivation to pursue the good, especially in the only form that is clearly universal, which is to pursue *one's own* good, is not clearly *moral* motivation. This point is well worn, but I make it again here to contrast it with—what is at least conceptually distinct—the motivation to act morally or virtuously in the "ordinary sense" of doing what one believes to be right or virtuous. The dominant view that knowledge of the Good provides this missing moral motivation seeks to close the gap between the good and the moral in a very intimate, albeit quite metaphysical way. The philosophers' good, the philosophers' *eudaimonia*, is knowledge of the Form of the Good. If that knowledge by itself conferred the

---

30 Grube/Reeve translation, modified.

31 Of course this is to restate the challenge of *Republic* 2. And it arises again in the puzzle of why the philosophers would do their "duty" (i.e., the virtuous, moral action) and take turns ruling, given that it impedes their "possessing" their highest good (i.e., contemplating the Forms).

motivation to act virtuously (in the ordinary sense), then of course the philosophers would act virtuously, including taking their just turn at ruling.

In a sense, however, knowledge of the Form of the Good is not moral knowledge. Of course it is knowledge *about* ethics or morals, but it is not the sort of belief or knowledge that one might think of as in itself motivating, in the way that is relevant to debates about internalism versus externalism, as exemplified in the quotations from Mackie. Rather, it is in the difficult *application* of Forms to the sensible world where we actually find what we think of as moral or ethical beliefs. "Ordinary" moral beliefs—"I should jump in the river here and now to save this drowning child" or "it is wrong to take more than my fair share" or "defending one's polis is noble"—are all, to the extent that they are true and known to be true, arrived at by *application* of the knowledge of Forms to the sensible world. The knowledge of the Form of Justice, whatever it is like, is the knowledge of an essence, of what all particular justices (type or token) have in common. We get moral beliefs, in the ordinary sense, when we say that this action or this law is just or that this action or law is unjust. *These* are the sorts of beliefs that the internalist thinks of as necessarily motivating, but these are not beliefs (or knowledge) about *Forms* but are beliefs (or knowledge) about *what participates in* Forms (i.e., how the Forms apply to the sensible world). Of course such moral beliefs would be motivating, particularly to someone with the proper upbringing, but, as I shall now argue, it is that upbringing that supplies the motivation, not any knowledge of essences.[32]

---

32 This brings Plato's overall view closer to Aristotle's in the *Nicomachean Ethics* on certain readings, where upbringing is the key to acquiring the motivations and cognitive abilities of the *phronimos*. I think it is right to see Plato's view as overlapping with Aristotle's views about habituation and the role of pleasure and pain in *Nicomachean Ethics* 2.1–6. Aristotle's innovation, I would argue, lies in the "agent conditions" in 2.4, not in the idea that habituation is how one acquires character. See Iakovos Vasiliou, "Virtue and Argument in Aristotle's Ethics," in *Moral Psychology*, Poznan Studies in the Philosophy of the Sciences and Humanities, vol. 94, edited by Sergio Tenenbaum (Amsterdam: Rodopi, 2007), 35–76.

5. RULERS, PHILOSOPHERS, AND MOTIVATION

Would-be rulers of the Kallipolis must be tested, again and again, to see whether they preserve their beliefs (or even, their knowledge) in the face of pleasures and pains. After the first educational program, which consists in education only via "music" (*mousikē*), Socrates describes how they are going to select the true guardians of the city (i.e., the rulers) from among the mixed class of guardians and "auxiliaries" (412b). Those who remain completely committed to and do not discard the beliefs that have been inculcated in them about what is best for the city via their "musical" education will be the rulers (412e). While people will "voluntarily" give up their false beliefs once they realize they are false, people also "involuntarily" give up their true beliefs because of being persuaded to think something else or forgetting or being tricked or compelled by pleasure, pain, or fear. Socrates thus envisages setting up a competition to see who clings to their true beliefs in the face of pleasures, temptations, fears, and so forth (413b–414a). Assuming the musical education they have been given is correct, those receiving it will have been given true beliefs about virtue and vice, right and wrong. So the testing here is a testing of their motivation to cling to their true beliefs about what is best for the city, in the face of temptations to act otherwise. What will bring about this moral motivation is a combination of innate ability and the effect of the habituation brought about by *mousikē*, which we know in hindsight is an orderly state of soul where reason—the part that makes judgments about what is best for the soul (and city) overall—rules (compare 441e, 442c).

We receive confirmation that this is the correct way to understand this testing and what makes a person successful at it when Socrates explicitly refers back to 412a in book 4 while describing courage in the city:

> The city is courageous, then, because of a part of itself that has the power to preserve through everything its belief about what things are to be feared, namely, that they are the things and kinds of things

that the lawgiver declared to be such in the course of educating it. Or don't you call that courage?—I don't completely understand what you mean. Please, say it again.

I mean that courage is a kind of preservation.—What sort of preservation?

That preservation of the belief that has been inculcated by the law through education about what things and sorts of things are to be feared. And by preserving this belief "through everything," I mean preserving it and not abandoning it because of pains, pleasures, desires or fears.…we were doing something similar [in books 2–3] when we selected our soldiers and educated them in music and physical training. What we were contriving was nothing other than this: that because they had the proper nature and upbringing they would absorb the laws in the finest possible way, just like a dye, so that their belief about what they should fear and all the rest would become so fast that even such extremely effective detergents as pleasure, pain, fear, and desire wouldn't wash it out—and pleasure is much more potent than any powder, washing soda, or soap. This power to preserve through everything the correct and law-inculcated belief about what is to be feared and what isn't is what I call courage. (429b–430b)[33]

The topic under consideration is the testing of one's *moral motivation*, for the beliefs that have been inculcated are true beliefs about right and wrong, virtuous and "vicious" (i.e., contrary to virtue) actions. Moreover, there is no mention of what is good for the individual or of the individual's happiness; the motivation at issue concerns not an individual's desire for the good but doing what is best and what is right for the city.

---

33 Grube/Reeve translation, modified.

Once the philosophers are in the picture, after book 5, it is they who will have genuine courage (via their knowledge of the Forms), and so, one might think, the sort of habituation and testing for the "preservation" of beliefs will no longer be necessary. But Plato is explicit that the junior philosopher-kings will be similarly tested, being "pulled every which way" (*helkomenoi pantachose*; 540a1) for fifteen years. During this fifteen years the class of philosophers will be the generals, as it were, of the mature philosopher-kings, running the day-to-day operations, enacting the rules, laws, and practices that are determined by the mature philosopher-kings; all the while, however, the philosopher-kings will watch to see who does well and who does not. Although Plato does not provide details about how this vetting will proceed, we ought not to think that learning how to apply one's knowledge of the Forms to the sensible world is either an easy, automatic thing to do or something that the philosopher will *want* to do in virtue of his knowledge of Forms alone. But this exercise in application will be of paramount importance, for as I have shown, it is in the application of Forms to the sensible world that our moral beliefs arise.

Does Plato, then, actually think that one could know the Form of the Good yet still be indifferent to what is good and virtuous? That depends. If the question asks whether one could be indifferent to good things or virtuous actions in the sense of neglecting them entirely, I think the answer is yes: one might simply be motivated to contemplate the Form of the Good (and, in propitious [relatively speaking!] circumstances, one might be able to do just this). But if the objection asks whether one could be indifferent to the good when *acting in the world*, the answer is no. In this case, however, what one is doing is *using* the theoretical knowledge of the Form of the Good in order to generate manifestations of it in the sensible world; the motivation for such actions stems not from the knowledge of the Form of the Good itself but from some combination of innate ability and the proper shaping of that ability in upbringing.

Thus my reading leaves Plato an internalist about moral judgment, especially once we understand that moral judgments arise from the *application* of knowledge of the Forms to sensible tokens or types. This makes Plato's account of moral motivation persuasive in its own right and avoids the implausibility Mackie attributes to it, according to which (1) motivation stems entirely from the knowledge of the Good, and (2) the motivation is overriding. I have argued that (1) is false; moral motivation arises, as on the account of most moral philosophers, as a result of moral judgment, and moral judgment is the result of applying the knowledge of the Forms. Furthermore, again in line with most moral philosophers, the motivation is not necessarily overriding. It is a consequence of my position that the philosopher will not necessarily be more motivated to act in accordance with her ethical knowledge than an ordinary person will be motivated to act in accordance with her ethical beliefs. Anyone's steadfastness in abiding by her moral judgments will be a matter of her nature and upbringing. This is difficult to see in the case of Plato's philosophers because, of course, they are the *most* naturally talented (including athletic talent); they are the most steadfast, given their proper upbringing in *mousikē* and the trials to which they are subjected, both before and after their dialectical education; and, ultimately, and most obviously, they alone are genuinely and fully knowers. What makes philosophers qua philosophers particularly special, however, is their epistemic position, not their motivational make-up.

I have shown that Plato argues that we have a motivation to be moral (virtuous) and to commit to doing the virtuous action above all, given that our actions affect our souls/characters and our souls/characters are the most important part of ourselves (i.e., more important than our health, beauty, wealth, civic status, and so on). Moreover, contrary to many scholars, I have argued that knowledge of Forms does not by itself confer any special motivation on the philosophers who know them. Rather, Plato, like Aristotle, understands moral motivation as arising from proper education and habituation.

Acknowledgment

I thank my fellow contributors for valuable comments on an earlier draft of this essay at the workshop entitled History of Moral Motivation, held at the Graduate Center of the City University of New York, April 20, 2013.

Reflection

MORAL MOTIVATION: ACHILLES AND HOMER'S *ILIAD*

Nancy Worman

A long-standing view of ancient morality was that Homeric characters—indeed, the ancient Greeks more generally—exhibited "premoral" attitudes, having no concept of morality in a sense that we could recognize as such.[1] While this view has now been widely disputed and revised, it remains a question whether we can discern in Homeric epic characters intentionally choosing actions because they are right or assessing actions as motivated by a belief about what is right. On the surface the answer may surely appear to be yes—how would heroes defend their actions otherwise than as heroic and therefore right and in some sense moral? But in fact the most pervasive and dominant motivation for actions among Homeric warriors is *timē*, honor or valuation, as well as *kleos*, fame or good reputation. One protects and fosters one's *kleos* and *timē* by acting bravely and expecting due compensation for these actions; and if one's desire for honor and fame drives one to be braver than one might be otherwise, then that is what motivates: self-regard and public esteem.

While this kind of self-regard is not quite pride (which when overweening is deemed *hubris*), neither is it moral in any

---

1 See esp. Arthur W. H. Adkins, *Merit and Responsibility* (Oxford: Oxford University Press, 1960), and the critique of Anthony A. Long, "Morals and Values in Homer," *Journal of Hellenic Studies* 90 (1970): 121–139.

straightforward sense. It may drive one to right action, as readers of the *Iliad* have tended to think is the case with the Trojan warrior Hector, who defends his city in a manner that appears to many as altruistic, or at least noble in the sense of honorable and good. Yet the Homeric poet never frames or emphasizes any warriors' actions in this way, not even Hector's. In fact, it is difficult to find an episode in the *Iliad* or the *Odyssey* in which the poet depicts characters—male or female, warriors or servants—as doing something explicitly and intentionally because it is morally right. Rather, characters behave as they do because of their loyalties, their hostilities, and their fears, always with an eye to self-preservation or (as in the case especially of Achilles) the preservation of one's honor and reputation. Hector may appear more noble or moral because his honor and reputation center on his role as defender of the city, which includes other citizens and not just peers, unlike the warriors of the invading army.

Characters do, however, often accuse each other of acting for the wrong reasons, out of greed, say, or cravenness. In the latter case, whole groups may be deemed "women, not men," as both Achilles and the would-be rabble-rouser Thersites judge the Achaean troops early on in the *Iliad*. Certain characters tend to attract attention for their moral ambiguity, for the sense of imminent accounting that hovers around them: Agamemnon, whom the poet depicts as indecisive, craven, and excessively violent; Helen, who is the catalyst for the war and thus whose very presence in Troy demands explanation; and Odysseus, whose status as master of strategies repeatedly raises questions about the nobility of his motivations in both the *Iliad* and the *Odyssey*.

Homer positions Achilles as in some sense judge of them all. While Achilles never directly blames Helen, she is clearly the centerpiece of what he represents as a merciless and unfair calculation, in which he and others labor for another's prize.[2]

---

2 Homeric epic treats female characters, especially Helen, as ambiguous between traded object and vocal agent; for a famous formulation of this ambiguity, see Claude Lévi-Strauss, *Structural Anthropology*, translated by Claire Jacobson and Brooke Grundfest Schoepf (New York: Basic Books, 1963), 61–62.

Achilles challenges Agamemnon from the outset of the *Iliad*, which motivates this "people-eating king" (as Achilles calls him at *Iliad* 1.231) to seize Achilles's prize, Briseis (a female prisoner from another city-sacking), in compensation for losing his own (Chryseis). The emphasis in Achilles's accusations against Agamemnon is thus economic in a broad sense, focused on the chief warrior's work and his fair compensation (which the term *timē* also covers). His sense of righteousness hinges on what we might want to characterize as an ethical (i.e., socially normative), if not more strictly moral, precept: basic equality among leaders. To do wrong on this account would be to disrespect the principle of appropriate fair-sharing, although this only applies to chief warriors.

It is clear, however, that the equal distribution of prizes among leaders is not an end or value in itself; rather, it underpins the motivations that drive all actions among warriors: again, the desire for honor (*timē*) and good reputation (*kleos*). In book 9 of the *Iliad*, when a group of warriors go to Achilles to attempt to persuade him to reenter the war, he rejects the spokesman Odysseus's offer of compensation, which foregrounds the very fair-sharing he himself had emphasized in his judgment of Agamemnon.[3] Achilles now accuses Agamemnon and Odysseus of dissembling calculation—that is, of acting out of need of his services rather than for the right motives, which in this case would be an admission of having transgressed the principle of fairness and thus dishonored the best of the Achaeans. Although in book 1 Achilles had repeatedly stressed honor (using the term *timē*), now he points out that Agamemnon has not himself come to propitiate. As he puts it bitterly, "There is equal honor [*timē*] for the base man and the noble, and they die in the same way, the do-nothing and the doer of many deeds" (*Iliad* 9.319–320). He also begins his speech

---

3 On Odysseus and fair-sharing, see Nancy Worman, *The Cast of Character: Style in Greek Literature* (Austin: University of Texas Press, 2002), 69–73.

rejecting Odysseus's offer by stating that he "hates more than the gates of Hades the man who keeps one thing in his breast but says another" (*Iliad* 9.312–313); and he declares directly that Agamemnon has deceived and wronged him (9.375). Achilles's judgment, then, centers on the transgression of mutually held values; and when these values are overturned, the warrior ethos loses its undergirding, because honor and reputation are disregarded. From this bleak perspective, there is then no point in doing anything, since all are treated equally regardless of their actions.

Although Achilles now rejects his due compensation and associates Odysseus with its loss of value, Odysseus himself continues to uphold the emphasis on fair distribution and the community cohesion it fosters. In book 19, when Achilles reenters the fight to avenge the death of his beloved companion, Patroclus, Odysseus (now with Agamemnon present) attempts once again to persuade Achilles to accept his due, including the return of Briseis. But Achilles is now not only furious but also grief-stricken; set against the death of Patroclus, the value of fairness suggests to him another and far more brutal calculation. Instead of the fair-sharing of prizes among leaders, which Odysseus urges him to confirm with a meal, Achilles looks to settle his compensation elsewhere: on the field of battle, slicing up Trojans instead of sharing meat with his peers (*Iliad* 19.205–213).

Insofar as this transfer from dinner table to battlefield is motivated by the desire to avenge the death of his friend, we can see Achilles's actions as righteous, or at least in keeping with the "helping friends, harming enemies" code that was central to traditional Greek morality.[4] But Achilles is also driven from the outset by anger (*mēnis*, anger, is the first word of the *Iliad*), which

---

4 See Mary W. Blundell, *Helping Friends and Harming Enemies: A Study in Sophocles and Greek Ethics* (Cambridge: Cambridge University Press, 1989).

now in combination with his anguish makes his motivations more nebulous. Indeed, the poet's depiction of him from the moment he reenters the action in book 18 until near the very end of the epic positions him as beyond converse and contact, which has a dehumanizing effect. When he enters the field of battle in book 20, he cuts such a bloody swath through the Trojans that the river Xanthus becomes glutted with corpses; and in a surreal turn of events it rears up to fight the raging hero itself. By the end of the book the hooves of Achilles's horses and the wheels of his chariot are drenched in gore.

What kind of moral judge could such an alienated and furious warrior possibly be? And why would the Homeric poet position such a warrior as this judge? It is tempting to conclude, from the hindsight that tragedy provides, that ancient poets regarded the distance that dispute and dissension provide as fostering a clearer perspective on why and how people act in relation to right and wrong. Outcast heroes in Sophocles often achieve this new vision, once they have suffered rejection and debasement, and give voice in similarly bitter terms to a new understanding of where they and others stand in the scheme of things. And as with Achilles, we can certainly distinguish in their stringent stances an attention to motivations, but whether these are calculated in terms that we would recognize as moral remains a question.

CHAPTER TWO

Aristotle on Moral Motivation

Susan Sauvé Meyer

In the moral assessment of agents and their actions it is useful to distinguish between a person's action and her motivation for performing it. For example, you might escort an elderly man across the street (an action) from a variety of different motivations: out of concern for the elder's safety, in order to expedite the flow of traffic, from a desire to impress onlookers, and so on. Motivation here may be understood in two distinct but related senses. It might be the goal or point you have in acting, your reason[1] for acting—in Aristotle's terminology, that for the sake of which (*hou heneka*) you act. Or it might be the internal

---

1 This is "reason" in the subjective, or "internal" sense (the goal you are actually motivated to pursue). Whether such goals are also "external reasons"—what you have reason to pursue, independently of your motivation—is beyond the scope of this chapter. For the distinction between internal and external reasons, see B. Williams, "Internal and External Reasons," in Williams, *Moral Luck* (Cambridge: Cambridge University Press, 1981), 101–113. For an exceptionally clear account of the debate between internalists and externalists about reasons, see D. Brink, "Moral Motivation," *Ethics* 108:1 (1997): 5–6.

psychological state or condition (say, a desire or inclination) that is (part of) the causal apparatus that generates the action. We may call the latter the action's *efficient-causal motivation* (what *moves* one to act) and the former its *teleological motivation*. When Aristotle articulates his analysis of what it is to have, and to act from, the virtues of character, motivation in both of these senses is central to his account.

It is sometimes claimed that Aristotle takes motives to be deontically significant—that is, whether an action is right or wrong depends on the motivation with which it is performed.[2] However, when Aristotle describes the motivation characteristic of the virtuous person, he distinguishes between what just, temperate, or brave people do and the characteristic way in which they do it (1105b5–9).[3] The former are actions whose status as just, temperate, or brave is independent of the agent's motivation in performing them. In what follows I will refer to these as just, brave, or temperate actions or, in general, *virtuous actions*, and I will use *virtuous agency* (or *acting virtuously*) to refer to the characteristic way in which the just, brave, or temperate agent performs such actions.[4] Aristotle's account of the latter invokes two kinds of

---

2 On "deontic motives" see Sverdlik's essay, chapter 10 here. C. Korsgaard, "From Duty and for the Sake of the Noble," in *Aristotle, Kant and the Stoics*, edited by J. Whiting and S. Engstrom (Cambridge: Cambridge University Press, 1996), 202, 213, takes motivation to be deontically significant for Aristotle. In support of such an interpretation one might note that, for Aristotle, actions are just, temperate, brave, and so on according to whether they satisfy the doctrine of the mean (1138b18–25) and that several of his explanations of what the mean is appear to invoke the agent's motive in acting: whether one does "what one should, for the end [*hou heneka*] one should, in the manner one should" (1115b17–19; see 1106b21–24, 1109a24–30). However, not all statements of the doctrine mention the *hou heneka*: thus 1109b14–16, 1118b25–7, 1119b16–18; 1120b29–31; 1125b8–21, 30–32; 1126a13–15, 32–35, b5–6. And in two of the passages that do (1111a2–5, and 1135a30–b16) the *hou heneka* cannot be the agent's goal or motive, since this is something the agent does not know. On the latter sense of *hou heneka*, see Hendrik Lorenz, "Natural Goals of Actions in Aristotle," *Journal of the American Philosophical Association* 1:4 (Winter 2015): 583–600.

3 Unless otherwise indicated, all citations are from the *Nicomachean Ethics (EN)*; those from the *Eudemian Ethics* are indicated by *EE*. The editions cited are *Aristotelis Ethica Nicomachea*, edited by I. Bywater (Oxford: Clarendon Press, 1894), and *Aristotelis Ethica Eudemia*, edited by R. R. Walzer and J. M. Mingay (Oxford: Clarendon Press, 1991).

4 On the independence of virtuous action from virtuous agency, see J. Whiting, "*Eudaimonia*, External Results, and Choosing Virtuous Actions for Themselves," *Philosophy and Phenomenological Research* 65:2 (2002): 276, and I. Vasiliou, "Aristotle, Agents, and Actions," in *Aristotle's Nicomachean Ethics: A Critical Guide,* edited by J. Miller (Cambridge: Cambridge University Press, 2011), 170–190.

motivation: the decision (*prohairesis*) on which virtuous agents act (1105a28–33) and the feelings of pleasure and pain they feel in acting (1104b3–8). I shall first consider *prohairesis*.

1. PROHAIRESIS

In *EN* 2.4, when addressing a puzzle about his thesis that one becomes just by performing just actions, brave by performing brave actions, temperate by performing temperate actions, and so on (1105a17–21), Aristotle explains that *actions* are brave, temperate, and just as long as they themselves satisfy certain conditions (*ean auta pôs echêi*—1105a29), but that a *person* need not be brave, temperate, or just in order to perform such actions. The difference that being virtuous makes is not a matter of *what* one does but of *the way* in which one does it (*ean...pôs echôn prattêi*—1105a30–31; see 1144a18). Aristotle identifies three necessary features that distinguish virtuous activity from the mere performance of virtuous actions:

> The things that issue from the virtues [*ta de kata tas aretas ginomena*] are done justly and temperately not simply in virtue of themselves being in a certain condition, but rather in virtue of the agent who performs them being in a certain condition:
>
> (1) First of all he must act with knowledge.
> (2) Second, he must act on decision [*prohairoumenos*] and decide on them because of themselves [*prohairoumenos di' auta*].
> (3) Third, he must act from a firm and unchangeable disposition. (1105a28–33; see 1144a13–20)[5]

The second of these three conditions concerns the agent's motivation in performing the action, and will be the focus of the rest of this

---

5 Unless otherwise indicated, all translations are my own.

section. (The third condition requires that the virtuous person act from a stable disposition to have and act on such motivations.) The second condition invokes the notion of *prohairesis*. Translators often render this term as "decision," "choice," or "preferential choice." As Aristotle defines and deploys the notion, it counts as a motivation in both the teleological and efficient-causal senses distinguished above.

Prohairesis, as Aristotle defines it, is a desire (*orexis*) that is due to deliberation (1113a2–12; see 1139a23, 32–34, b4–5), and deliberation, he explains, is reasoning in the light of (*pros*) a goal (*telos*) (1112b11–34). Interpreters of Aristotle today generally agree that deliberation, as the philosopher conceives it, need not be narrowly instrumental (means-end) reasoning; rather, it can include figuring out what would *count* as realizing the goal—for example, figuring out what virtue requires in the given circumstances.[6] Nor need the reasoning be explicitly articulated by the agent before it issues in the desire.[7] The salient feature of an action done on *prohairesis* is that it issues from the agent's understanding of the action as being "for the sake of" that goal. When an action issues from your *prohairesis*, the goal for the sake of which you

---

6 A position that goes back at least to L. Greenwood, *Aristotle: Nicomachean Ethics Book VI* (1909; reprint, New York: Arno Press, 1973), 46–55, adopted in one form or another by J. Cooper, *Reason and Human Good in Aristotle* (Cambridge, MA: Harvard University Press, 1975), 19–23; D. Wiggins, "Deliberation and Practical Reason," in *Essays on Aristotle's Ethics,* edited by A. O. Rorty (Berkeley: University of California Press, 1980), 29–51; A. Kenny, *Aristotle's Theory of the Will* (London: Duckworth, 1979), 147–154; W. Hardie, *Aristotle's Ethical Theory*, 2nd ed. (Oxford: Clarendon Press, 1980), 165–169; T. Irwin, *Aristotle's First Principles* (Oxford: Clarendon Press, 1988), 335–342, 598n24; N. Sherman, *The Fabric of Character: Aristotle's Theory of Virtue* (Oxford: Clarendon Press, 1989), chap. 3; S. Broadie, *Ethics with Aristotle* (New York: Oxford University Press, 1991), 232–242; J. McDowell, "Some Issues in Aristotle's Moral Psychology," in McDowell, *Mind, Value, and Reality* (Cambridge, MA: Harvard University Press, 1998), 23–49; H. Segvic, "Deliberation and Choice in Aristotle," in *From Protagoras to Aristotle* (Princeton, NJ: Princeton University Press, 2009), 144–171; A. W. Price, *Virtue and Reason in Plato and Aristotle* (Oxford: Clarendon Press, 2011), 226–235; J. Moss, *Aristotle on the Apparent Good: Perception, Phantasia, Thought, and Desire* (Oxford: Oxford University Press, 2012), 192–198. Many of these views are inspired by a broader thesis about what "for the sake of the end" means in Aristotle, defended by J. Ackrill, "Eudaimonia in Aristotle's Ethics," in Rorty, *Essays on Aristotle's Ethics,* 15–33, reprinted from *Proceedings of the British Academy* 60 (1974): 339–359, criticized by Richard Kraut, *Aristotle on the Human Good* (Princeton, NJ: Princeton University Press, 1989), 200–203.

7 See Cooper, *Reason and Human Good in Aristotle,* 7–8, Segvic, "Deliberation and Choice in Aristotle," 147–153.

act is your *teleological* motivation, while the desire that results from deliberating *pros* that goal (and that actually moves you to act), will be your *efficient-causal motivation*. Aristotle often uses the term *prohairesis* in the *efficient-causal* sense (e.g., "*prohairesis* is the origin [*archê*] of the action, the source of the motion, not that for the sake of which," 1139a31–32). But he clearly takes the goal that figures in the relevant deliberation (the *teleological* motivation) to be an integral feature of the *prohairesis*. This is why, for example, he says that our *prohairesis* is a better indication of our characters than our actions are (1111b5–6).[8]

To return to the second requirement for virtuous agency in *EN* 2.4: In saying that the virtuous agent acts on decision (*prohairoumenos*), Aristotle is telling us something about the efficient-causal motivation characteristic of virtue: the virtuous agent is moved to act by a desire that is informed by his understanding that this action realizes or promotes a particular goal. In a more contemporary idiom, we might say that the virtuous agent acts for reasons. To continue in that idiom, we might say that Aristotle, in further specifying that the virtuous agent decides on the virtuous actions "because of themselves" (*di' auta*, 1105a32), is specifying the kind of reason for which the virtuous agent acts. In Aristotle's own idiom, he is identifying the goal or *telos* for the sake of which the agent acts—the teleological motivation of the action.

When Aristotle says, of virtuous actions, that the virtuous agent "decide[s] on them because of themselves" (*prohairoumenos di' auta*—1105a32), the antecedent of "themselves" (*auta*) is "the things that issue from the virtues" (*ta de kata tas aretas ginomena*, 1105a28–9). The "things" are actions conceived of independently of their motivations,

---

8 Thus at 1144a20–21 he uses the term *prohairesis* to refer to the *telos* of the action. On this construal (also adopted by Kenny, *Aristotle's Theory of the Will*, 103) 1144a20–21 makes the same point as 1144a6–9 and 1145a4–6 and thus does not require the ingenious but strained reading proposed by Hendrick Lorenz, "Virtue of Character in Aristotle's *Nicomachean Ethics*," *Oxford Studies in Ancient Philosophy* 37 (Winter 2009): 202–205. Oddly enough, Lorenz initially (p. 202) takes the *prohairesis* mentioned at 1144a20 to be the goal of action rather than the desire arising from deliberation in light of that goal; but on p. 204 he motivates his unorthodox reading of the passage by indicating that it is hard to construe decision as a goal of action (which seems to construe *prohairesis* as the deliberated desire rather than the goal).

that is, actions that are brave, just, or temperate, in virtue of satisfying the doctrine of the mean. But what is it to decide on such actions "because of themselves"? We are given no explanation in the immediate context, but elsewhere Aristotle uses the locution "because of X" to indicate the goal (*telos*) for the sake of which (*hou heneka, charin*). For example, in book 1, when explaining how one goal (*telos*) can be more complete (*teleioteron*) than another, he indicates that we can "choose things because of themselves" (*hairoumetha... di' auta*), or "because of something else" (*di' allo*), or for both kinds of reasons; the context makes it clear that the *dia* locution picks out the goal (*telos*) (1097a30–b6; see 1094a18–22).[9] Thus we may suppose that in the passage in *EN* 2.4, the requirement that a virtuous agent "decide [on them] because of themselves" (*prohairoumenos di' auta*, 1105a32) identifies the characteristic goal of a virtuous *prohairesis*—that is, the virtuous person's motivation in the teleological sense. Aristotle is claiming that the virtuous agent performs such actions for their own sakes. As he says in the parallel passage in *EN* 6.12, the virtuous agent acts "because of *prohairesis* and does what he does for their own sakes" (*autôn heneka tôn prattomenôn*, 1144a19–20).

Exactly what is it to decide on just, brave, or temperate actions "for their own sakes"? It is tempting, but mistaken, to suppose that the relevant contrast is with deciding on such actions because of their consequences.[10] Aristotle explicitly grants that in many cases of brave or just activity, the virtuous agent is in fact motivated by the expected consequences of her action for other people.[11] For example, the point of

---

9 The equivalence of the two locutions is even more explicit in the *Eudemian Ethics*: 1226b26–27, 1227a14, as pointed out by Moss, *Aristotle on the Apparent Good*, 181.

10 Perhaps this is what Broadie means when she says, of 1105a32, "the point is not, as some interpreters think, that the person of excellence decides on the action for its own sake" (*Ethics with Aristotle*, 300)—even though Aristotle evidently uses that locution (*autôn heneka tôn prattomenôn*, 1144a19–20) in the parallel passage in *EN* 6.12. For detailed arguments against such "deontological" readings of "deciding on them for their own sakes" see Whiting, "*Eudaimonia*, External Results, and Choosing Virtuous Actions for Themselves," 281–286, and P. Gottlieb, *The Virtue of Aristotle's Ethics* (Cambridge: Cambridge University Press, 2009), 134–150.

11 1177b1–4, 12–15; see 1169a17–30. Korsgaard, "From Duty and for the Sake of the Noble," 216, proposes a way of construing such cases as nonetheless chosen "for their own sakes."

standing one's ground in battle (a brave action) is to secure the safety of one's fellow citizens. One might alternatively suppose that deciding on just, brave, or temperate actions "because of themselves" involves thinking of them as just, brave, or temperate and deciding on them under these descriptions. However, Aristotle indicates that the agent's linguistic repertoire need not contain a term for every virtue, since some of the virtues and vices he identifies are "nameless" in Greek.[12] So this can't be precisely how Aristotle understands deciding on a virtuous action "for its own sake." There is, however, a characterization common to all virtuous actions that does figure in the virtuous person's motivation, as Aristotle describes it, in his detailed discussions of the particular virtues of character. This is the notion of the *kalon* (variously translated as "fine," "admirable," "noble")—whose opposite is the *aischron* (shameful, disgraceful).[13] In these discussions Aristotle repeatedly remarks that the virtuous person acts "for the sake of the *kalon*" or "because of the *kalon*."[14]

This attribution of motive is especially prominent in Aristotle's discussion of bravery, which provides a rich range of examples that will help us to demarcate the scope of what counts as acting "because of the fine."[15] The quintessential brave action is to stand one's ground in the face of a noble death (1115a29–35), but one can do this without having the brave person's motivation. The motivation that is characteristic of

---

12 1107b2, 1108a16–17, 1125b25, 1127a14. For example, there is no term for the virtuous disposition concerning anger (1126b19–20).

13 I do not mean to take a stand on how to understand the *kalon*. For several recent interpretations, see T. Irwin, "Aristotle's Conception of Morality," in *Proceedings of the Boston Area Colloquium in Ancient Philosophy*, vol. 1 (Leiden: Brill, 1985), 115–143, and "The Sense and Reference of *kalon* in Aristotle," *Classical Philology* 105 (2010): 381–396, J. Cooper, "Reason, Moral Virtue, and Moral Value," in *Rationality in Greek Thought*, edited by M. Frede and G. Striker (Oxford: Oxford University Press, 1996), 81–114, and G. R. Lear, "Aristotle on Moral Virtue and the Fine," in *The Blackwell Guide to Aristotle's Nicomachean Ethics* (Oxford: Blackwell, 2006), 116–136. I do however take exception to Korsgaard's proposal that an action's being *kalon* is due to its being an expression of reason ("From Duty and for the Sake of the Noble," 218) and that the *kalon* is a feature of the "action along with its purpose" (217). For Aristotle, actions can be *kalon* or *aischron* independently of their motivation.

14 "For the sake of the *kalon*" (*tou kalou heneka*): 1115b12–13, 23, 1120a24, 1122b6–7; see EE 1216a24–26; "because of the *kalon*" (*dia to kalon*): 1116b31, 1168a33; *EE* 1229a4.

15 For a discussion of these examples, see also Gottlieb, *The Virtue of Aristotle's Ethics*, 142–145.

the brave person, Aristotle says, is to perform such an action "because doing so is fine [*hoti kalon*], or because not doing so is shameful" (1116a11–12). He contrasts this with a variety of nonvirtuous motivations for performing brave actions. First, he mentions those who embrace the prospect of death as an escape from troubles: "Dying to escape from poverty, or sexual passion, or something painful, is not a feature of courage but rather of cowardice; for it is softness to run away from things because they are burdensome, and the person in this case accepts death *not because it is a fine thing to do*, but because he is running away from something bad" (1116a12–15).[16] Next, Aristotle describes a motivation that is superior to that of the coward but still deficient. This belongs to citizen-soldiers who stand their ground in battle in order to avoid legal penalties or public reproach, or in order to gain honor (1116a17–19; see 1180a8–9). Even though honor is something fine, Aristotle notes (1116a28–9), standing one's ground in order to gain it does not count as acting "because of the fine" in the way characteristic of the brave—presumably because it is the fineness of standing one's ground (in these circumstances) that is supposed to motivate the brave person. Even less worthy, Aristotle says, is the motivation of soldiers who are compelled to perform the brave action (1116a29–b3). For example, they are threatened with immediate beating (or death) if they do not stand their ground, or their commanders have stationed them in front of a ditch with no means to escape the advancing enemy. These stand their ground "because of constraint" rather than "because doing so is fine" (1116b2–3).

On the subject of generosity or liberality (*eleutheriotês*), which concerns the spending, giving, and acquisition of money, Aristotle notes that one can perform a generous act "for the sake of the fine" [*tou kalou heneka*] or one can do so "because of some other reason [*di' tin'allên aitian*]" (1120a28–29; see 1121b4–5). An example of the latter motivation

---

16 Translation by Rowe (*Aristotle: Nicomachean Ethics,* translation with introduction and commentary by Sarah Broadie and Christopher Rowe [Oxford: Oxford University Press, 2002]).

is refraining from taking what belongs to others, out of fear of repri-
sals (1121b28–30). A different ungenerous motivation (in this case,
for performing an ungenerous action) belongs to those who give too
little "in order to prevent their ever being compelled to do something
shameful" (1121b25–26).[17] On the subject of magnificence, the virtue
concerned with spending on a large scale, he classifies as vicious those
who spend lavishly "for the sake of reputation [*doxês charin*] or in
order to gain power [*di' exousian*]" (*EE* 1233b5). About the bad person
quite generally, Aristotle invokes the popular observation that such a
person "does everything for his own sake" (*heautou charin*), in contrast
with the good person who acts "because of the fine" (*dia to kalon*)
(1168a31–33).

Aristotle's view is thus that the virtuous person performs acts that
are *kalon* and decides to perform them because they are *kalon* rather
than for some other reason. It makes sense to suppose that this is what
he means in *EN* 2.4, when he speaks of "deciding on [the actions] because of themselves" (1105a32). After all, what makes a particular instance of repayment a just action—or a particular case of standing
one's ground a brave action, or a particular example of refraining from
sensual indulgence a temperate action—is that this particular action
(repayment, or withstanding, or refraining) is *kalon*. So deciding on
these actions because they are *kalon* (or for the sake of the *kalon*) will
count as deciding on them "because of themselves."

It is sometimes objected that the goal of the virtuous person's *prohairesis* is nothing as lofty as the *kalon* but is a much more determinate,
and local, objective. For example, the just person's motive is to repay
his debt, or the generous person's motive is to help his friend, and it
is under this description that she decides on the action "because of

---

17 Aristotle expresses skepticism as to whether such a self-ascription of motive is accurate (*ei phasi ge*,
1121b25); if it were, it would be analogous to the case of someone acting out of a desire for honor
(1116a28–29): a motivation aimed at something fine but not at what is fine in the action (discussed
above). In this case it would be a motivation to avoid something shameful but not attuned to what is
shameful in the action performed as a means to that end.

itself."[18] However, there is no barrier to saying this, and also saying that her reason for repaying (or helping) is that doing so is *kalon*, for Aristotle famously allows that one can pursue an end for its own sake (because of itself) and also pursue it for the sake of something else (1097a30–b5). We may suppose that the generous person, who is acting for the sake of the *kalon* when he shares with his friend, is also aiming at helping his friend. However, it is crucial to insist the he is also aiming at the *kalon*, not just at helping, because being helpful is not always *kalon*: that is why the virtue of generosity involves giving only when one ought, to whom one ought, and so on. To be helpful for the sake of the *kalon* means (at the very least) that one's aiming at being helpful on this occasion is contingent on its being *kalon* in this situation to help.[19] Where helping would be aiding and abetting a criminal act,[20] or enabling self-destructive behavior, the truly generous person will not help. Similarly, in cases where putting one's life on the line is foolish or reckless, the truly brave person will not stand her ground, and where healthy enjoyment rather than self-denial is called for, the truly temperate person will not abstain from bodily gratification.[21]

---

18 Thus Broadie, *Ethics with Aristotle*, 232–250; Williams, "Acting as the Virtuous Person Acts," in *Aristotle on Moral Realism*, edited by Robert Heinaman (San Francisco: Westview Press, 1995), 13–23, R. Hursthouse, "Reply to Bernard Williams," in *Aristotle on Moral Realism*, edited by R. Heinaman (San Francisco: Westview Press, 1995), 14–33; Korsgaard, "From Duty and for the Sake of the Noble," 216–217; Broadie and Rowe in *Aristotle: Nicomachean Ethics*, 300; Price, *Virtue and Reason in Plato and Aristotle*, 209–230.

19 For more on pursuing a subordinate goal (such as helping) for the sake of the *kalon*, see S. Meyer, "Living for the Sake of an Ultimate End," in *Aristotle's Nicomachean Ethics: A Critical Guide*, edited by J. Miller (Cambridge: Cambridge University Press, 2011), 47–65. Gottlieb, *The Virtue of Aristotle's Ethics*, 168–169, offers a different account of the way the two goals interact.

20 As in Barbara Herman's famous example of helping an art thief out of sympathy; "On the Value of Acting from the Motive of Duty," in Herman, *The Practice of Moral Judgment* (Cambridge, MA: Harvard University Press, 1993), 4–5.

21 We may accept Broadie's claim that the description under which the temperate person decides to act is "refusing excessively rich food" (Broadie, *Ethics with Aristotle*, 300). However, the standard for determining what is "excessive" must be the *kalon*; otherwise the motivation would not be temperate—as in the case of the anorexic who counts as "excessively rich" any food that contains fat. The same goes for Whiting's claim that the just person aims at "each person having his or her fair share"; "*Eudaimonia*, External Results, and Choosing Virtuous Actions for Themselves," 278.

2. NATURAL VIRTUE

This sensitivity to the *kalon* is what distinguishes a genuinely virtuous disposition (*kuria aretê*) from a similar but importantly different motivational set, which Aristotle dubs "natural virtue" (1144b3, 16). He invokes the latter in the final chapter of his discussion of the intellectual virtues, *EN* 6.13: "It seems to everyone [*pasi... dokei*] that each of these states of character can be had by nature in a way—for we are just and moderate-acting [*sôphronikoi*] and brave, and so on, right from birth. Nonetheless, the genuine good we are investigating is something different and involves having these in a different way" (1144b4–6). The "genuine good" Aristotle has in mind is genuine (*kuria*) virtue (1144b4, 16), virtue "in the strict sense" (*kuriôs*, 1144b31). Having genuine virtue is different from possessing natural virtue because the former involves having *phronêsis* (1144b16–17; *EE* 1234a29–30), the virtue of deliberating correctly about actions (1140a25–28). He is here resisting an objection articulated in the previous chapter, to the effect that the excellent disposition of the nonrational part of the soul is sufficient to guarantee right action—that one need not have *phronêsis*, an excellence of deliberative reason, in order to act correctly (1143b20–28).

Aristotle invokes the natural virtues as candidates for the sort of nonrational disposition that the objector alleges to be sufficient for virtuous action—that is, dispositions that (1) always issue in brave, temperate, or just actions but (2) are possessed by agents who lack *phronêsis*. His point, in a nutshell, is that the natural virtues fail to fit the bill because they fail to satisfy (1). He allows that people with these natural conditions will be disposed to perform with alacrity actions that most people must be habituated to perform (e.g., standing one's ground in the face of attack, exercising self-restraint, or respecting the property of others). Thus such dispositions will, on many occasions, issue in actions that are brave, temperate, just, and so on. However, he rejects the thesis that such dispositions will *always* yield such actions. Precisely because they lack *phronêsis*, Aristotle insists, the naturally virtuous are liable to make grievous errors, "like a strong body moving about without sight [who] will stumble badly [*sphallesthai ischurôs*] precisely because it lacks sight" (1144b10–12).

Interpreters of Aristotle often suppose that the error to which the naturally virtuous person is prone is a failure to implement successfully a goal that he shares with the virtuous person. For example, the naturally generous person has a Pollyannaish desire to be helpful but in certain circumstances is no good at figuring out what would actually be helpful.[22] However, this cannot be what Aristotle has in mind. As noted, not all cases of helping are generous, since not all are *kalon*. The Aristotelian virtue of generosity involves discerning which cases of helping are *kalon*, and this is the discernment for which *phronêsis is* required. Proficiency at the (admittedly difficult) task of figuring out what would be helpful will not save one from the grievous error involved in aiding and abetting, or enabling.

The latter are most likely the kinds of errors Aristotle has in mind when he says that the natural virtues are liable to grievous error. While he gives no examples in *EN* 6.13, his earlier discussion of bravery includes the remark that "the most natural" (*phusikôtatê*) kind of bravery is "due to *thumos*" (anger, or spirit—the middle part of the Platonic tripartite soul) (1117a4). *Thumos*, as he has described it a few lines earlier, is "straining to go out and meet dangers" (1116b26–27). Thus the naturally brave person is disposed to face dangers—regardless of whether doing so is *kalon*. In a similar vein, Plato in the *Statesman* (306a–308a) construes courage as a tendency toward aggression, and temperance as a tendency to "preserve the peace…in any way one can" (307e5–6); he notes that the former is prone to the error of courting ruinous conflict and the latter the error of appeasement when an

22 R. A. Gauthier and J. Y. Jolif, *L'Éthique à Nicomaque* (Louvain: Publications Universitaires, 1958–59), note on 1144b16–17; Dahl, *Practical Reason, Aristotle, and Weakness of the Will* (Minneapolis: University of Minnesota Press, 1984), 87; Natali, *The Wisdom of Aristotle* (Albany: State University of New York Press, 2001), 52–53; Moss, *Aristotle on the Apparent Good*, 195–196; see Hursthouse, "Reply to Bernard Williams," 231.

aggressive response is called for. These are not errors in executing the goals of these dispositions but failures to regulate the pursuit of these goals by an understanding of whether it is good to pursue them in particular circumstances.[23] Given this Platonic precedent, and its fit with Aristotle's sketch of natural courage in *EN* 3.8, it makes sense to suppose that these are the sort of errors that Aristotle has in mind as the grievous errors to which the natural virtues are susceptible in *EN* 6.13.

Given this way of construing the defects of the naturally virtuous, we may agree that the naturally virtuous person aims at a goal that the genuinely virtuous person shares (e.g., helping, or standing one's ground); however, it is not incompetence at realizing *this* goal that makes the naturally virtuous inferior to the genuinely virtuous. Indeed, the naturally helpful will likely be *more reliable* at helping, the naturally courageous more reliable at facing danger,[24] and the naturally temperate more reliable at exercising self-restraint than the genuinely virtuous person would be. The mark of the genuinely generous, courageous, and temperate is their success in the pursuit of a further goal, the *kalon*, and it is incompetence at realizing this goal that is the signature failure of the naturally virtuous.

3. Self-Regarding Motivation?

I now return to my original focus: the distinctive *prohairesis* of the genuinely virtuous person. I have shown that such a person is motivated to be helpful, forceful, or restrained as the occasion demands but above all is motivated to do what is *kalon*. It is sometimes supposed that the latter motivation is distinctively self-regarding (in a way that may be

---

23 Such a construal of the error fits with the accounts of natural virtue in Sherman, *The Fabric of Character*, 160; Gottlieb, *The Virtue of Aristotle's Ethics*, 109; Lawrence, "Acquiring Character: Becoming Grown-Up," in *Moral Psychology and Human Action in Aristotle*, edited by M. Pakaluk and G. Pearson (Oxford: Oxford University Press, 2011), 254–255; and Reeve, *Aristotle on Practical Wisdom* (Cambridge, MA: Harvard University Press, 2013), 256.

24 Note Aristotle's comment that the truly courageous might not make the best soldiers (1117b17–20).

objectionable to some modern moral sensibilities).[25] For instance, it is supposed that what is *kalon*, strictly construed, is not the action but the action together with its motivation.[26] So conceived, the virtuous person has a very Kantian concern with the quality of his own motivation. Or, in a more Humean mode, the virtuous person is motivated by pride.[27] But we need not construe acting for the sake of the *kalon* in such a self-regarding way.

We may conclude from Aristotle's detailed discussions of the particular virtues of character that to act "for the sake of the *kalon*" is to subordinate all one's other pursuits[28] to the pursuit of the *kalon*—that is, to be sensitive to what would be *kalon* and *aischron* in the particular circumstances. In a more contemporary idiom, the virtuous agent wants to do what is right and is reliable at guiding her conduct by this standard. Absent a compelling argument that the rightness at stake (i.e., the *kalon*) is a feature of *the way* the virtuous person acts, rather than of the action she performs, we need not conclude that Aristotle is committed to attributing such a self-regarding motivation to the virtuous.

One might suppose that he *is* committed to such an attribution by other features of his ethical theory. For example, modern readers of Aristotle sometimes worry that his *eudaimonism*—his thesis that all one's actions are ultimately for the sake of happiness—commits him to the view that the virtuous person's ultimate motivation, even in performing virtuous actions, is to promote her own happiness. Is this not an ulterior, and objectionable, motive for virtuous action? This worry is misconceived, however, insofar as it supposes that virtuous actions are instrumental to happiness, for that is not how Aristotle conceives

---

25 Thus Williams, "Acting as the Virtuous Person Acts," 13–14. For a fuller discussion of this issue, see Broadie, *Ethics with Aristotle*, 94–5, Taylor, *Aristotle: Nicomachean Ethics Books 2–4* (Oxford: Clarendon Press, 2006), 88–92, Moss, *Aristotle on the Apparent Good*, 208–219.

26 Thus Korsgaard, "From Duty and for the Sake of the Noble," 217, endorsed by Taylor, *Aristotle: Nicomachean Ethics Books 2–4*, 87n8. For criticism, see Gottlieb, *The Virtue of Aristotle's Ethics*, 145–146.

27 Thus Moss, *Aristotle on the Apparent Good*, 208.

28 On the possible exception of *theōria* (contemplation), see note 30.

the relation between virtuous activity and happiness. The famous "function argument" of *EN* 1.7 seeks to identify what happiness consists in, and its conclusion is that happiness consists in virtuous activity (1098a16–17). This is to *identify* happiness with virtuous activity, not to claim the latter is instrumental to the former. The virtuous agent who acts for the sake of the *kalon*—that is, one who decides on *kalon* actions because they are *kalon* and avoids shameful actions for the same reason—is thereby living a happy life, on Aristotle's view. We need attribute no further motive to such an agent in order to make good Aristotle's claim that such an agent is acting for the sake of happiness.[29] Acting for the sake of the *kalon* counts as acting for the sake of happiness.[30]

4. PLEASURES AND PAINS

So far we have considered virtuous motivation in the context of Aristotle's remarks on *prohairesis*, which for him is a distinctly rational kind of desire, arising as it does from deliberation, an activity of the rational part of the soul (1139a12–15).[31] The virtues of character themselves, however, are excellences of the *non*rational part of the soul (1103a2–10; *EE* 1221b28–31). This is the part of the soul that he

---

29 Defended further in S. Meyer, *Ancient Ethics* (London: Routledge, 2008), 56–59; a slightly different version of this response is worked out in detail in Whiting, "*Eudaimonia,* External Results, and Choosing Virtuous Actions for Themselves," 281–286, in response to David Charles, "Aristotle, Ontology, and Moral Reasoning," *Oxford Studies in Ancient Philosophy* 4 (1986): 119–144.

30 I set aside here the further complication that Aristotle claims that the life of *theôria* (purely intellectual activity) is a higher kind of happiness than the life of the virtues of character (*EN* 10.7–8). Commentators have worried about whether this commits Aristotle to the view that (1) virtuous practical activity is "for the sake of" *theôria*, and furthermore that (2) the former is instrumental to the latter. This question is beyond the scope of this chapter, which concerns Aristotle's own account of the motivation distinctive of the virtues of character. For alternative ways of answering yes to (1) but no to (2) see Meyer, "Living for the Sake of an Ultimate End," and G. R. Lear, *Happy Lives and the Highest Good* (Princeton, NJ: Princeton University Press, 2004); R. Kraut, *Aristotle on the Human Good* (Princeton, NJ: Princeton University Press, 1989), answers no to both.

31 This section develops the argument in S. Meyer and A. Martin, "Emotion and the Emotions," in *The Oxford Handbook of the History of Ethics,* edited by R. Crisp (Oxford: Oxford University Press, 2013), 643–646.

describes in one context as "appetitive [*epithumêtikon*] and in general desiderative [*orektikon*]" (1102b30) and in another context as the seat of *pathê*—affective or emotional states such as "appetite [*epithumia*], anger, fear, daring, envy" and the like, which he characterizes as "involving [*hois hepetai*] pleasure or pain" (1105b21–23). Thus the virtues of character "concern pleasures and pains" (1104b8–9, 1152b4–6; *EE* 1221b37–39).

More to the point, Aristotle tells us in *EN* 2.3, the pleasures and pains one experiences in acting are a sign of whether one's character is virtuous or vicious: "We should take as a sign of people's dispositions [*hexeôn*] the pleasure or pain that they take in the activities [*tên epigignomenên hedonên ê lupên tois ergois*]. For the person abstaining from bodily pleasures and taking pleasure in so doing is temperate, while the one who is vexed is intemperate. And the person enduring terrible things who enjoys it—or at any rate is not pained—is courageous, but if he is pained he is a coward" (1104b3–8). One might suppose that the pleasures and pains invoked here as signs of the agent's character are the various emotions and desires that are listed as the *pathê* of which the virtues of character are dispositions (1105b21–28). On such an interpretation, the pain that shows the abstainer to be intemperate would be the pain of frustrated appetite, and fear would be the pain that reveals the soldier standing his ground against the enemy onslaught to be a coward. This can't be right, however, for a number of reasons. First of all, the pleasures of appetite are hardly likely to be what accounts for the temperate person's pleasure in abstaining, since *ex hypothesei* he is refraining from, rather than enjoying, those pleasures. Second, fear is unlikely to be the pain that reveals cowardice, since Aristotle allows that there are some situations in which even the courageous person will feel fear, even though he must stand his ground and endure (1115b7–11). More generally, as Jessica Moss has pointed out, to the extent that the virtues are dispositions of our painful emotions (such as anger, pity, etc.), the appropriate emotion of the virtuous person will be painful, and so cannot account for the characteristic pleasure of the virtuous agent.[32] In any case, only three of the virtues of character that Aristotle discusses are defined in terms of a *pathos* or emotion; these are temperance (which concerns appetite), courage (which concerns fear and confidence), and mildness (which concerns anger). Aristotle demarcates the scope of the other virtues by invoking types of action (e.g., spending money) or objects of pursuit (e.g., wealth, honor).[33] Nonetheless, in these domains too he insists that it is characteristic of the virtuous person to act with pleasure (e.g., 1120a25–27, b29–31) or in general "to be pleased and pained as one should" (1121a3–4) or "well" (*eu*, 1105a7) or "finely" (1179b25–26) or "at what one should" (*eph'hois dei*, 1121a3–4; see 1104b12).

We can identify the objects of these pleasures and pains by paying attention to a remark Aristotle makes when he acknowledges how unpleasant the experience of facing death in battle conditions can be, even for the courageous (1117b1–13). He concludes that the courageous person's pleasure is in not in the activity itself but in achieving its *telos* (or goal) (1117b15–16). That *telos*, we may recall from our discussion of *prohairesis*, is the *kalon*. Thus it makes sense for Aristotle to indicate, in his discussion of generosity, that the generous person will be aggrieved (*achthomenos*) or pained (*lupoumenos*) if he has inadvertently spent money "contrary to what is right and fine" (1121a1–7). In general, he tells us, it is characteristic of the good person to be pleased at fine actions (*chairein tais kalais praxesin*) and to be displeased (*duscherainein*) at vicious ones (1099a13–20, 1170a8–11; see *Politics* 1340a15–18). For example, the truthful person is pained at the prospect of telling a lie (1146a21). These are the pleasures and pains that mark one's character as virtuous.[34] They indicate that the *kalon* is one's goal in acting.

---

32 Moss, *Aristotle on the Apparent Good*, 206–207. On the relation between such painful feelings and the characteristic pleasure of the virtuous, see Curzer, *Aristotle and the Virtues* (Oxford: Oxford University Press, 2012), 35–42.

33 By contrast, Curzer, *Aristotle and the Virtues*, 171–172, insists that each virtue of character has its distinctive *pathos*.

34 For more on these pleasures see Moss, *Aristotle on the Apparent Good*, 206–219, and E. Wielenberg, "Pleasure as a Sign of Moral Virtue in the *Nicomachean Ethics*," *Journal of Value Inquiry* 34 (2000): 439–448, who take issue with Broadie, *Ethics with Aristotle*, 90–95, on some points of detail.

Even the vicious person's reasons for acting are reflected in the pleasures and pains with which he acts. Thus Aristotle contrasts the deceitful person who enjoys telling lies (because this is his end in acting) with the one who tells lies in order to improve his reputation or gain wealth (1127b15–17). So, too, the stingy person, "who would choose money over acting finely" (1120a30–31), is averse to spending money and hates it, even when spending is fine. His displeasure at spending the money in such circumstances (1120a25–31) is thus a sign that he is not doing it because it is fine (i.e., he is not performing it with the teleological motivation characteristic of the virtuous person).[35] He must be performing the fine action for some other reason. Perhaps he cannot avoid making this particular expenditure without incurring some penalty or opprobrium that, in his view, would be worse than spending the money. He is taking the better of two undesirable alternatives. He is coerced or constrained to do what his virtuous counterpart does gladly and willingly, and his pain is a sign that he acts under constraint.

Such actions are ones that Aristotle classifies as "mixed" in his discussion of voluntary action (1110a4–19). The captain who throws the ship's cargo overboard (voluntarily, because he knows he must in order to save his life) may still be heartbroken at the loss of the valuable cargo—which was after all the point of the sea voyage. Thus though his action is voluntary, he acts unwillingly—hence Aristotle's verdict that such actions are mixed (1110a11–12, b3–5). The unwilling citizen who commits an act of sacrilege at the command of a tyrant who holds hostage his parents and children may similarly be pained at what he is forced to do. The pain with which such agents perform the acts they are compelled to do is therefore a sign of their unwillingness. Indeed, Aristotle insists that pain is a necessary condition of unwillingness.[36]

---

35 The pain a vicious person feels on such occasions need not be directed at the fineness of what he does; he need not be an antimoralist, who hates the very fineness of fine things and delights in shameful things as such. It is enough that he fails to delight in doing fine actions.

36 1110b11–13, b18–24; 1111a20–21, a32. On the painfulness of involuntary actions, see S. Meyer, *Aristotle on Moral Responsibility* (Oxford: Blackwell, 1993; reprint, Oxford: Oxford University Press, 2011), chap. 3, esp. 82–84.

This is how we should construe the vicious person's pains in our passage at *EN* 2.3, that is, the "pain…in the activit[y]" (1104b4–5) that shows a person to be intemperate, even though what he is does is a temperate action, and the pain that shows a soldier to be cowardly even though what he does is a brave action. The intemperate person's act of abstention and the coward's act of standing his ground are things these agents would really rather not do, and would not do except under duress or constraint. For example, a heavy drinker might turn down a drink while under the watchful eye of a spouse. Her reason for abstaining in such a case would be to avoid the censure or displeasure of the spouse rather than to do what is *kalon*. She might well be resentful of the spouse's presence because it keeps her from drinking. She would rather drink and so would prefer that her spouse not be present. But given that he is present, she would rather forgo drinking than put up with the recriminations that would follow. In such a situation, she will be pained at performing the temperate action, and that pain will be evidence of her less than virtuous motivation. Similarly, the coward who is compelled to stand his ground even though he desperately wants to flee will be aggrieved at having to stand and fight. His pain is not simply the painful emotion of fear but his distress at having to withstand the enemy assault.

This is not to say that the heavy drinker is conflicted about abstaining—for example, that she has decided to abstain but still feels a strong appetite for drink, which makes it a struggle to do what she has decided. So construed, it would be a case of *enkrateia* (continence or self-control, as contrasted with incontinence [*akrasia*] or weakness of will—1111b13–15).[37] But Aristotle states here that the pained abstainer is

---

37 The example is construed as a case of *enkrateia* by M. F. Burnyeat, "Aristotle on Learning to be Good," in *Essays on Aristotle's Ethics*, edited by A. O. Rorty (Berkeley: University of California Press, 1980), 89n10, following A. Grant, *The "Ethics" of Aristotle Illustrated with Essays and Notes*, 4th ed., vol. 2 (London: Longmans, Green, 1885; reprint, New York: Arno Press, 1973), 490, and more recently by Taylor, *Aristotle's Nicomachean Ethics Books 2–4*, 75–76, and J. Echeñique, *Aristotle's Ethics and Moral Responsibility* (Cambridge: Cambridge University Press, 2012), 182.

intemperate (*akolostos*), not that he is *enkratês*.[38] We may distinguish the two cases as follows. The intemperate abstainer is as I have described: he has decided to abstain but resents abstaining and does not think it is a *kalon* thing to do. The *enkratic* abstainer may well have decided to abstain because it is fine, but her improper appetites make it painful and difficult to act on this decision. The pains that mark her abstention as *enkratic* have their source in her unfulfilled appetites, not in her reasons for acting. The pains of the intemperate abstainer, by contrast, do reflect her reasons for acting. The same goes for the cowardly fighter of 1104b7–8. The pain that shows his disposition to be cowardly is not the fear he feels as the enemy advances; rather it is the pain that reflects the constraint under which he acts and shows that the fineness of standing his ground is not his reason for acting.

Those who perform virtuous acts unwillingly (*akontas*),[39] Aristotle tells us, are not performing these actions "because of themselves" (1144a15–16); in the idiom of our original passage from *EN* 2.4, they are not "deciding on them because of themselves" (1105a32). Thus it turns out that Aristotle's requirement in *EN* 2.3—that a virtuous person takes pleasure in performing virtuous actions—is not independent of the requirements on the virtuous agent's *prohairesis* that he articulates in *EN* 2.4. This result accords with the otherwise surprising fact that Aristotle does not mention the agent's pleasures and pains in the latter context, even though he purports to be enumerating the features that distinguish genuinely virtuous activity.

More important, the connection between the two requirements makes sense in the light of a thesis that Aristotle articulates repeatedly throughout the ethical works, when he identifies what makes one's *prohairesis* correct. *Prohairesis*, I have shown, issues from deliberation in

---

38 As noted by T. Irwin, *Aristotle: Nicomachean Ethics*, 2nd ed. (Indianapolis: Hackett, 1999), 194. Continence and incontinence: 1111b13–15; contrasted with virtue and vice: 1145a15–18; contrasted with temperance and intemperance: 1146b19–24, 1148a4–22.

39 At 1144a15 *akontas* invokes the unwillingness of constraint, rather than the involuntariness that stems from not knowing what one is doing, since the latter is captured by the next item on the list (*di' agnoian*, 1144a16).

the light of a goal. A correct *prohairesis* is one in which both the goal
and the deliberation are correct (1139a23–25). Aristotle attributes the
correctness of the deliberation to *phronêsis*, an intellectual excellence,
and attributes the correctness of the goal to virtue of character.[40] Since
the latter excellence belongs to the part of the soul that is the seat of
pleasure and pain, it follows that being pleased at performing fine actions is not simply *evidence* that the *kalon* is one's goal in acting; it is
part of what makes the *kalon* one's goal in acting.

Many commentators on Aristotle in the last century have balked at
attributing such a view to Aristotle—out of worry, for example, that it
conflicts with his general conception of virtuous character as a state in
which the nonrational part of the soul follows the rational part, or that
it saddles him with a so-called Humean theory of motivation. It is
beyond the scope of this chapter to address these worries,[41] but it is
worth noting, in conclusion, the following. The view in question is not
that blind urges or content-less drives determine the goals of our actions. The affective condition that constitutes our having the *kalon* as a
goal, on this view, is a cultivated and discerning appreciation of what is
fine and shameful in action. Nor is the view that such affective attitudes are what *make* things fine or shameful, or that we have *reason*[42] to
pursue the one and shun the other only if we are motivated to do so.
The Aristotelian thesis we are considering is simply an account of what
is involved in having something as a goal. In order to be acting for the
sake of the *kalon*, we have to love and take pleasure in the *kalon*. The
characteristic pleasures and pains of the virtuous are not their reasons
for acting, but they are necessary conditions for having reasons for
action.

---

40 *EE* 1227b22–25; *EN* 1144a7–9, 1145a4–6, 1151a15–19, 1178a16–19; see 1139a33–35. For a masterful
treatment of such passages (to which I would add 1144a20–22, discussed in note 8), see Moss, *Aristotle
on the Apparent Good,* chap. 7.

41 Moss, *Aristotle on the Apparent Good,* offers an extended response to such objections, which involves the crucial point that for Aristotle the nonrational is not the same as the noncognitive.

42 Reason in the "external" sense (see note 1).

CHAPTER THREE

A Later (and Nonstandard) Aristotelian Account of Moral Motivation

Brad Inwood

Moral motivation raises a fundamental question in ethics, though as I will show it can be a slippery issue in the context of much of the Greco-Roman philosophical tradition. I want to discuss a particular approach to the question, one that arises in an unusual context, in a little-known text from Greco-Roman antiquity. It is an Aristotelian text, but it's not by Aristotle. In fact, it's not even by one of his famous followers: not Theophrastus, not Alexander of Aphrodisias, not even Aspasius or Critolaus. In fact, we don't know the name of this particular Aristotelian, since he (presumably he) is the author of a theory that we find only in a passage from the *Anthology* by John of Stobi (fifth century AD). Stobi was a town in northern Greece, and John assembled a long (about ten inches of shelf space in very small type) collection of extracts from literature and philosophy, for the moral improvement of his son. (We have no information as to the success of this pedagogical strategy in John's day; I have my suspicions about the effectiveness of this sort of approach in our society.) Stobaeus, as he is usually called, included in book 2 of his collection three brief accounts of ethics from earlier antiquity. The one I am interested in is the third (hence often called "doxography C") and purports to be a summary version of Aristotelian ethics (just as the second, doxography B, is a version of Stoic ethics). It used to be attributed to a shadowy character named Arius Didymus, a contemporary and friend of the emperor Augustus. That is now coming to seem somewhat doubtful, especially since this Arius seems to have been a Stoic. So it is perhaps safer to refer to him simply as the author of doxography C. This author, then, probably lived and worked in the first 150 years AD, if not actually in the Augustan era, but that claim too is highly contentious, and I don't propose to burden this philosophical enquiry with any more unsolvable scholarly and historical problems.[1]

This account is entitled "The Views of Aristotle and the Other Peripatetics about Ethics"—pretty dull, but better than the label "doxography C." By implication the author is providing a version of ethical theory that Aristotle and several centuries worth of followers could support. Such is the strategy of ancient doxographical writing, but this author's account is quite different from the equally anonymous account of Stoic ethics that immediately precedes. The author of that account notes in quite a few places that different Stoics held subtly different views on several key topics. The overall effect is of a unified Stoic doctrine but not a monolithic account. This author, by contrast,

---

1 For these issues, see the collection of articles in W. W. Fortenbaugh, ed., *On Stoic and Peripatetic Ethics: The Work of Arius Didymus* (New Brunswick, NJ: Transaction Books, 1983); also T. Göransson, *Albinus, Alcinous, Arius Didymus,* Studia Graeca et Latina Gothoburgensia 61 (Göteborg: Göteborg University, 1995), with my review in *Bryn Mawr Classical Review* 7 (1996): 25–30. More general historical background can be found in H. B. Gottschalk, "Aristotelian Philosophy in the Roman Empire from the Time of Cicero to the End of the Second Century AD," in *Aufstieg und Niedergang der römischen Welt* II.36.2, edited by H. Temporini and W. Haase (Berlin: de Gruyter, 1987), 1079–1174, and P. Moraux, *Der Aristotelismus bei den Greichen,* vol. 1 (Berlin: de Gruyter, 1973), 316–434. A translation and fresh, though brief, commentary have been provided by Robert Sharples in chapter 15 of *Peripatetic Philosophy 200 BC to 200 AD* (Cambridge: Cambridge University Press, 2010). Very helpful guidance can be found in J. Annas, "The Hellenistic Version of Aristotle's Ethics," *Monist* 73 (1990): 80–96.

has only one "footnote" to Theophrastus (in section 34) and otherwise assures us by implication that the Peripatetics were of one mind on all important aspects of ethics.

That will surprise anyone who comes to this account directly from a reading of the *Nicomachean Ethics* and *Eudemian Ethics*, though of course there is a great deal of genuine Aristotelian material in this author's account. (In fact, the most authentically Aristotelian bit is probably the material from the *Politics* toward the end of his outline.) But there is also a great deal of doctrine that manifestly responds to developments in the Hellenistic period, in particular to Stoic ethical theory. It is obvious to any careful reader that the ethical theory in this account is Peripatetic, but independent-minded, showing (as has long been recognized) signs of influence from Stoic thought as well. It is not a mere summary of Aristotle's and other generic Aristotelian views—not even to the extent that the *Magna Moralia* is, a work that consists of a cribbed paraphrase of the *Eudemian Ethics* spiced with *Nicomachean* details and a significant number of its own fresh, though sometimes muddled, insights.

One of the most interesting innovations in this account concerns a difficult question about moral motivation: why should people become virtuous, or why would they strive to do so? To put the question in context, let me just revisit a couple of familiar general features of mainstream ancient ethics.[2] For the most part Greek philosophical schools

---

2 I say "mainstream" in order to allow for the persistent but minority presence of a clearly consequentialist tradition in ancient ethical thought. Glaucon and Adeimantus challenge Socrates to justify living a just life for its own sake by outlining a competing theory, that becoming just and behaving justly would be justified only for the sake of the good outcomes they can ensure, and that such good outcomes could be more reliably secured by *seeming* to be just while behaving in a self-interested manner. The *Republic* purports to show that justice on its own without any regard for consequences makes life better—that virtue really is its own reward. This becomes the mainstream, eudaimonist view. Epicurus and a handful of others embraced the frankly consequentialist justification for virtue advanced as a foil in the *Republic*. Notoriously, the hedonist Epicurus treated the cardinal virtues as choiceworthy precisely and only because they served to maximize pleasure over a lifetime. For Epicureans and the few other frank consequentialist hedonists of the ancient world, we are motivated to cultivate and acquire virtue simply because it is instrumental to the acquisition of some other goal distinct from virtue. For the other schools influenced decisively by Socrates virtue had a distinctly noninstrumental relationship to happiness.

were eudaimonistic, as we now routinely say, in that the principal organizing concept is *eudaimonia* or happiness.[3] The central insight is most crisply expressed for modern readers in the opening chapters of the *Nicomachean Ethics*. All action and endeavor aim ultimately at a single goal, and the proper name of that unified, organizing highest goal is *eudaimonia*. Striving for that goal is an expression of our nature as human beings. For Aristotle, I think it is safe to say, there are two big, top-level claims about human nature that organize his thought. "All men by nature desire to know" (the opening manifesto of the *Metaphysics*, a claim that clearly underlies a great deal of Aristotle's epistemology as well as his theory of human nature) and, at the opening of the *Nicomachean Ethics*, "every skill and every enquiry, and similarly every action and rational choice is thought to aim at some good, and so the good has been aptly described as that at which everything aims."[4]

In Aristotle's theory, as in ancient eudaimonism generally, this drive for the good is a feature of our nature. Aristotle argues that the highest, organizing good in human life is happiness, and over the course of book 1 of the *Ethics* we see him arguing that the achievement of virtue and action in accordance with the excellence of our nature constitute the happiness that is our natural goal.[5] There will, of course, be a debate about what that excellence consists in and how we come to acquire it; the rest of the *Ethics* deals at length with these issues. But given that Aristotle comes firmly to the position that character traits like justice and self-control (which we think of as important elements of "morality")

---

3 Though it is more than twenty years old, the most effective general statement of what is involved in ancient eudaimonism is to be found in Julia Annas, *The Morality of Happiness* (Oxford: Oxford University Press, 1993), and she argues that the only significant ancient school that was not eudaimonistic in this sense was the Cyrenaics. As noted, Epicureanism, with its frankly instrumentalist account of the virtues, is out of the mainstream of ancient ethics; certainly it is built on a theory of how the virtues relate to happiness that does not appear in the Socratic tradition.

4 Translation from Roger Crisp, *Aristotle: Nicomachean Ethics* (Cambridge: Cambridge University Press, 2000), 3.

5 "Constitute" rather than "lead to" or "cause." Epicurean hedonists held that happiness consists in maximization of pleasure and that virtues are instrumental to that goal. Even if the Epicureans were correct there still wouldn't be a very deep problem about moral motivation; we choose virtue, including *phronēsis*, simply to maximize pleasure, and that constitutes happiness.

are key components of that excellence, it can actually be a bit hard to see how we could even get a worry about moral motivation off the ground. If the elements of "morality" are parts of human excellence, and if excellence is just the fulfillment of our nature, how can we not be motivated to pursue it? If Aristotle is right about the relationship between "morality" and human excellence, we don't have much choice about being moral. It is almost an analytic truth that we pursue happiness, and once that is well understood in this sense we just see that what we are looking for is virtue—or perhaps, the virtues. This is a kind of template for eudaimonism. On this view, being *motivated* to become virtuous is not much of a mystery, scarcely a problem at all.[6] The key move here is the connection of the virtues to human nature, whose fulfillment in happiness is meant to be motivationally unproblematic. Most of Aristotle's real work in the *Ethics*, then, consists in unpacking the notion of virtue and the virtues and sorting out *how* rather than *why* one might go about acquiring them.

And so things remained in the Aristotelian tradition. To appreciate what is new and interesting about the account of moral motivation in doxography C, we need to review very quickly what happened in the debates of the Hellenistic period. The most relevant development is the emergence of what modern philosophers refer to as "the cradle argument."[7] Epicurus was apparently its originator. In an attempt to support his version of hedonism, he argued that we can see the status of pleasure as our natural object of desire (and so the key to our happiness) not just by observing animals in general (which is what Eudoxus

---

6 This does not stop Aristotle from asking a hard and interesting question about *phronēsis* in *EE* 5.12: what is the *use* of the virtues of thought? The challenges are complex and Aristotle's answer no less so. But his first and most decisive reply is that the virtues themselves are "choiceworthy in their own right, since each is certainly the virtue of its own part of the soul, even if neither of them accomplishes anything." The fact that wisdom, properly understood, does play a role in becoming virtuous should not distract us from the fact that Aristotle regards it as choiceworthy per se, just because it is the actualization of a distinctively human excellence. And that is equivalent to the claim I highlight in the main text, that these virtues just are constitutive of happiness, our *telos*.

7 J. Brunschwig, "The Cradle Argument in Epicureanism and Stoicism," in *The Norms of Nature*, edited by M. Schofield and G. Striker (Cambridge: Cambridge University Press, 1986), 113–144.

seems to have done) but also by concentrating on newborn animals, both human and others. Epicurus was particularly struck by the distortions imposed by artificial social norms and argued (rather like the fifth-century sophists and the Cynics) that nature was what counted and that one had to get behind social convention to understand it. The best way to do that, he thought, was to base oneself on observation of the human animal before cultural convention could distort it. Hence newborn children rather than mature adults are touted as the ideal reference point for moral theory. That newborns seek pleasure, just like all nonhuman animals, is a key support for Epicurus's hedonism, and it nicely connects his arguments to those of Eudoxus.

It is what happened next that has the greatest significance for the understanding of the Peripatetic author of doxography C and his distinctive account of moral motivation. The Stoic response to Epicurus's "cradle argument" was an elaborate theory about the foundations of moral motivation in human nature that was designed to compete with, indeed to undercut, Epicurus's argument. Though the details are probably more than are needed in the present context, the doctrine of *oikeiōsis* (natural attachment and inclination) is the Stoic response to Epicurus's cradle argument. On this theory, which we know best from combining a key passage of Diogenes Laërtius (7.85–87) with material in book 3 of Cicero's *On Goals*, what attracts newborns is not pleasure but another, equally plausible natural drive, the drive to self-preservation (*On Goals* 3.16–22). If that is right, the Stoics can rely on there being a natural motivation to preserve oneself, one's physical integrity, and more generally one's nature. How they got from there to a fundamental and overriding commitment to virtue is, as Plato would say, another, longer road, one that we need not travel at this moment.

It is now well established that by the end of the Hellenistic period the cradle argument, in particular the fundamental and probably unresolvable disagreement between Stoics and Epicureans about neonatal motivations, had become the focus of many, perhaps some of the most important, debates in ethics.[8] In book 5 of *On Goals* Cicero gives us a version of the theory that, he claims, derives ultimately from an Academic philosopher, Antiochus of Ascalon. The general consensus these days is that this theory, which is marked by Cicero as being distinctively Peripatetic, is an adaptation of the Stoic theory of *oikeiōsis*. And it is against this background that the author of doxography C works when he tackles the questions that are of greatest interest here, in particular the issue of moral motivation: what is our reason for pursuing the virtues? What *makes us* pursue them?—that is one question. But the other is harder and less clear. What makes us *want to* pursue them?

The fact that the ancient theories in question are in some sense naturalistic is what sharpens the worry. If it is in our nature to be virtuous, we may well wind up being so because we cannot help it. Take sociability, for example. Humans are naturally social animals, we might agree. It might be true that the only way I can be genuinely happy and fulfilled is to work with that feature of my nature. Only by cultivating my sociability, my sense of consideration for others and justice, can I be fulfilled and so happy. This "nature" that I find myself in possession of is not something I have chosen, any more than I chose to be a biped. Just as I would be frustrated and unfulfilled if I chose not to work with my two-footed nature and so become a healthy and vigorous walker, even a runner, so too I won't be a fulfilled and content person if I decline to cultivate my prosocial inclinations. But what if I just don't *want* to be sociable? What if I look at my sociable nature as something of an imposition, if (say) on careful reflection I conclude that most other humans are hopeless idiots and that associating with them can only be a terrible mistake? But my nature cannot be made unsociable, and so presumably I won't really be happy and my nature won't be fulfilled if I become a hermit. Yet I might conclude that that is in fact the right thing for me to do. Nature might have "plans" for me that

---

8 For this, see the recent study by Georgia Tsouni, "Antiochus and Peripatetic Ethics" (PhD diss., Cambridge University, 2010).

I cannot readily find it in my heart to embrace. I might be *caused* to be sociable, in such a case. I might even be *compelled* to be sociable, virtually blackmailed into it by my nature—otherwise I'll be unhappy. But that won't actually make me *want* to be sociable. It might well join the list of other demands and constraints imposed on me by the natural world, constraints and demands that I would avoid if I could. I'd rather not be prone to skin cancer, but by nature I am low in melanin. I'd rather not be earthbound, but terrestrial gravity is what it is, and there are limits on the strength-to-weight ratio achievable by my species. If we think of nature as a teleological force, it can have "plans" for me, but that doesn't mean I have to like them. Why, from this point of view, should I *want* to be virtuous—especially if it turns out to involve, as it does, quite a bit of hard work?

This question is particularly urgent for Stoics and those influenced by them. In another article,[9] I have tried to find in book 3 of Cicero's *On Goals*, where the Stoic spokesman Cato goes on at great length about the naturalness of virtue, some credible account of how our social nature and the attendant virtues can be linked to the neonatal drive for self-preservation and self-enhancement that Stoic theory postulates as a central element in human nature. Sadly, this search failed, and I think that all other interpreters have also failed. Stoicism assumes (and I don't claim that they are wrong to do so, but it is an assumption rather than the result of an independent argument) that there is in the course of our development a discontinuity. At some critical point in the process of maturation our nature is transformed, and we cease to be motivated solely by self-preservation and begin to be motivated by considerations that are distinctive of our rational nature. We apparently recognize the inherent structure and order in the world and that it is homologous with our own reason and *therefore* that we should shape our lives in accordance with that order—in order to achieve our *telos*. This development, outlined by Cato at *On Goals* 3.21–24, is

---

9 Brad Inwood, "The Voice of Nature," in *Cicero's De Finibus: Philosophical Approaches,* edited by J. Annas and G. Betegh (Cambridge: Cambridge University Press, 2016), 147–166.

mysterious enough, and it is not at all obvious why this realization motivates us as Cato says it does. This reorientation to virtue seems to be a
bit of magical thinking, and even more mysterious is the claim made
later in the book (3.62–63) that our rational nature entails a powerful commitment to other-regarding virtues too; we find ourselves
committed not just to self-regarding virtuous behavior (as even an
Epicurean might be able to accept) but also to other-regarding, even
self-sacrificing virtues. What is missing in all of this is an account of
why, even when we see that our nature is like this, we as rational agents
should *want* to embrace such a nature.

As I mentioned earlier, the fifth book of *On Goals* is dominated by a
Peripatetic adaptation of the Stoic theory (presented by an Academic),
an adaptation that is intended to avoid the radical discontinuity in the
development of human nature that was built into—and undermined,
one might say—the Stoic theory. But although that Peripatetic theory
avoids discontinuity—and even strengthens its claim on being a naturalistic theory because it argues not implausibly for the view that all
living things, plants included, are driven by strictly similar principles of
teleological development—nevertheless, even this account fails, I would
argue, to address the more general worry about moral motivation.
Even if my human nature develops smoothly and without implausibly
postulated transformations into a mature, other-regarding rational
nature, why should I be inclined to embrace it, develop it, and perfect
it? Arguably, the account in book 5 of *On Goals* is the best version of
Peripatetic ethics developed in the Hellenistic period; but it never
confronts the common problem of the various eudaimonisms of the
Greek tradition.

This is one of the challenges that, it seems to me, the Peripatetic
author of doxography C was prepared to take on. This is something
worth emphasizing, since his argument on the issue is normally passed
over without comment,[10] implicitly regarded as a mere bit of bungling,

---

10   It is, for example, completely neglected in Michael Trapp's book *Philosophy in the Roman Empire:
Ethics, Politics, and Society* (Aldershot, England: Ashgate, 2007).

or at best as a puzzling wrinkle in an awkward Peripatetic adaptation of a Stoic theory. It was treated rather more generously by Robert Sharples (in *Peripatetic Philosophy 200 BC to 200 AD*), who not only provided the first complete translation of the work into English but also added to it the most sensible commentary on it in decades.[11] But even this is very limited and has no room for an appreciation of the stretch of argument that interests me here. I should, therefore, say a bit more about the work as a whole.

This little treatise is indeed a curious work. It combines, into one reasonably unified whole, paraphrase and discussion of Aristotle's own ethical works with discussion of doctrines derived from unmistakably Hellenistic developments in the Peripatetic school.[12] At least, that is how it begins. By the end of the work it is a different story. The school as a whole displayed, throughout the Imperial period, a growing tendency to focus on commentary, defensive explication, and exegesis of Aristotelian texts rather than on the sort of direct dialectical exchange that, as I have argued elsewhere,[13] characterized the Aristotelianism in the Hellenistic period.[14] We may recall that the earliest commentaries on Aristotle's works, written at about the same time as this account, focused on the *Categories*, but that the first *surviving* commentary is from the pen of Aspasius, a commentary on Aristotle's *Ethics*, indeed, on the *Nicomachean Ethics*.[15] With doxography C we are clearly in the early stages of this trend toward commentary writing. It presents itself not as a commentary but as a freestanding treatise in the Aristotelian

---

11 Sharples, *Peripatetic Philosophy*, 132–133, with reference to some of the more important earlier literature.

12 On some of these developments see, for example, Annas, "The Hellenistic Version of Aristotle's Ethics."

13 See my *Ethics after Aristotle* (Cambridge, MA: Harvard University Press, 2014).

14 On the question of how Hellenistic Aristotelianism differed from that of the Imperial (post-Hellenistic) era, see most recently Andrea Falcon, *Aristotelianism in the First Century BCE: Xenarchus of Seleucia* (Cambridge: Cambridge University Press, 2012), which focuses first and foremost on a study of Xenarchus but has enlightening general remarks about the transition between these two periods. His discussion of the present text is on pp. 42–47. His account of Xenarchus on the *prōton oikeion* is on 139–157, 202–203.

15 A. Kenny, *The Aristotelian Ethics* (Oxford: Oxford University Press, 1978), 29–36.

mode, heavily dependent on paraphrase and summary of Aristotle's texts. It opens with a preface explaining the significance of the name of the discipline (ethics from *ethos*, following Aristotle very closely) and of the importance of the pair reason/passion as a foundation for ethical enquiry. The starkness of the latter pairing is familiar from the *Magna Moralia* and from developments in the Hellenistic period, though it was less apparent in Aristotle's own work.

In chapter 2 the familiar Aristotelian partitioning of the soul is set out (depending on *Nicomachean Ethics* 1.13 and other texts), but incorporating some terminology more characteristic of Stoicism (e.g., *hormē*), which had become common in the theories of the Hellenistic world. In chapter 3 the author moves with breathtaking speed from the traditional Aristotelian triad of nature (*phusis*), habit (*ethos*), and reason (*logos*) as factors in ethics to the unmistakably Hellenistic theory of *oikeiōsis* as a foundation for it.[16] The similarities to the Peripatetic account in *On Goals* 5 mentioned earlier have long been observed, though direct dependence on that work seems unlikely.[17] This fresh starting point (and it is not made particularly clear how it is meant to relate to the other prefatory material) sets the treatise on an important new track from which it only diverges when straightforward paraphrase of Aristotle's treatises returns late in the work (at chapter 28), with development of the theme of moral virtue; it then continues in this vein to the end, though the last section is based on the *Politics* rather than on the ethical treatises.[18]

---

16 It should be noted that in the past some scholars have taken the view that the theory of *oikeiōsis* had been developed originally by the early Peripatetics and that the Stoics adopted the theory from them. Von Arnim's thesis that this work relied on school documents that originated ultimately with Theophrastus has been discussed at length (see Fortenbaugh, "Arius, Theophrastus and the *Eudemian Ethics*," in Fortenbaugh, *On Stoic and Peripatetic Ethics*, 203–223) and is usually rejected or heavily qualified. F. Dirlmeier's similar view in "Die Oikeiosis-Lehre Theophrasts," *Philologus Supplementband* 30 (1937). has also been rejected. See the discussion in S. Pembroke, "Oikeiōsis," in *Problems in Stoicism*, edited by A. A. Long (London: Athlone Press, 1971), 114–149. Tsouni ("Antiochus and Peripatetic Ethics," esp. 149) emphasizes the Theophrastean features of the account in *On Goals* 5 and of doxography C.

17 Inspiration by an ultimately common source cannot be ruled out, of course.

18 This integration with the *Politics* is a feature of the *Nicomachean* rather than the *Eudemian Ethics*.

The author begins his account of human nature (at section 3) with an admission that humans "are different from other animals in both body and soul"—a significant point to make, since the distinctive traits of humans are by general agreement in the ancient world the ones pertinent to ethics—"because, since they are situated between immortals and mortals, they share a linkage with both: to the rational in virtue of what is divine in their soul and to the irrational in virtue of what is mortal in their body." This duality is clearly the key to an ethics that takes its starting point in an explicit theory of human nature. What follows from this is clear: a human being "reasonably [*kata logon*] desires [or strives for, *ephiesthai*] the perfection of both [soul and body]." But how does this fact about our nature turn into such a desire? This, in fact, is the critical move, one that starts out from Aristotle himself, who held that we, like other living things, have a fundamental desire to exist,[19] and then adopts the characteristically Hellenistic language of *oikeiōsis*. As this author puts it here:

> [a human being's] first desire [*prōton men oregesthai*] is to be, for by nature he is attached [*ōikeiōsthai*] to himself, which is why [*di' ho*] he is also suitably pleased by things that accord with nature and annoyed by things that conflict with it. He is keen to attain health, has a drive for pleasure, and strives to live because these things are in accord with nature and worth choosing for themselves and good. Contrariwise, he fights off and avoids illness, pain, and destruction because they are in conflict with nature and worth avoiding for themselves and bad. For our body is dear to us and so is our soul, and so too are their parts, their capacities, and their activities; it is our planning for the preservation of these that is the starting point for impulse, appropriate action [*kathēkon*], and virtue. *For if absolutely no error ever occurred in the pursuit and avoidance of the aforementioned things, but if we hit upon the good ones and stayed free of the bad*

---

19 Aristotle *NE* 9.9, *EE* 7.12.5–8.

ones consistently, then we would never have undertaken to seek correct and error-free selection in connection with them. But since we were in fact often misled in our pursuit and avoidance of them, sometimes passing over good things and embracing bad things as though they were good, it was necessary for us to seek out a reliable knowledge of how to distinguish them; when we also[20] found that this was harmonious with nature we labeled it "virtue" because of the splendor of its actuality and, being wonderfully impressed by this, we came to honor it more than anything else. For it has turned out that actions [*praxeis*] and what are called "appropriate actions" [*kathēkonta*] take their starting points from selecting things that accord with nature and rejecting things that conflict with it. And that is why correct actions [*katorthōseis*] and mistakes occur in connection with them [appropriate actions] and are involved with them. For pretty much the entire framework of our school has its starting point from these factors, as I will demonstrate very concisely.

This is my own translation, and I have tried to bring out the clumsiness that characterizes the Greek—it is certainly an inelegant bit of writing—and to focus on the Stoicized language of Hellenistic theory with which it is saturated. Despite the clumsiness, the basic strategy is

---

20 Sean Kelsey has suggested to me that the "also" here might show that the realization that "this" is "harmonious with nature" is meant to be a distinct, separate perception, and so that the appreciation for nature that warrants labeling it virtue and justifies honoring it (*etimēsamen* below) is just as independent of our naturalistic motivations as is the transformative moment in Cato's Stoic theory (where what we come to appreciate is *ordo et concordia*; see below). This is allegedly supported by the term *daimoniōs* applied to our reaction to the experience; I have translated this "wonderfully," but one might see here a reference to divine forces and so to nonnatural values. I am not persuaded. This interpretation doesn't fit well into the overall flow of the argument in the paragraph, which is stating that the very thing we find to be harmonious with nature is the method that enables us to reliably acquire natural goods. Furthermore, it seems quite natural to take the point of the "also" to be simply that just as natural goods like health harmonize with nature so too do effective means to get such natural goods—if you will the end, you will the means; if the desired end is impressive, so too is a uniquely reliable technique for achieving that end. There is no doubt that the phrasing in the text is designed to accentuate the impact of our valuation of these means (we are "wonderfully impressed" and hold them in honor). But there is nothing in any of the wording here to show that the importance of the rational method is based on anything other than its instrumental efficiency at achieving the natural goods under discussion.

clear. The context is established as Aristotelian right at the outset. The dual nature of human beings (body and soul, poised between beast and god) is proclaimed (without any focus on hylomorphic unity but also without any particular emphasis on Platonizing dualism). The fundamentally *natural* character of the resultant motivations (accompanied by pleasure, as one would expect of an Aristotelian) is laid out as a consequence of a basic commitment (a point made in distinctively Stoic language) to our own existence, our being what we are in our basic nature. Strikingly, in contrast to either of the accounts in Cicero's *On Goals* (which I mention and discuss briefly below), Cato's Stoic account and Piso's Peripatetic account, we do not find any sign of a cradle argument here. The radical desire to *be* what we are is not just a fact about newborns; rather, it holds throughout life.

This is a significant change from the way the Stoics, Epicureans, and earlier Peripatetics (such as Piso in Cicero's construction) chose to connect human nature to moral values. Two consequences follow. First, without a cradle argument, this account is vulnerable to charges that the values that allegedly *motivate* us may actually have been socially inculcated and so may not be reliable guides to our underlying nature. If the first motivation for developing a theory of *oikeiōsis* and the cradle argument was a desire to respond to the Epicureans, who not unreasonably demanded some reason to think that what purport to be our basic values are not just internalizations of tired old social norms, then putting forward a theory like this without addressing this demand might well be thought of as dialectically reckless. The second concern is raised by the very difficult issue of how one can make the transition from having the values of a non- or prerational animal to those of rational adult humans; but in this text, without the developmental framework of other theories of *oikeiōsis*, this issue is simply avoided.

One might well wonder why this author's approach to these standard issues of debate is so different, and any answer is bound to be speculative. But it is certainly possible that at this point in the history of the debate the idea of *oikeiōsis* was pretty much taken for granted as a relevant basic fact and no longer needed the cradle argument to prop it up; the problems that the developmental story posed for the Stoics had been pushed into the background. And in the paragraphs that follow, this author reinforces the naturalness of the network of motivations that underpin Aristotelian ethical principles in other ways (by appealing to various *endoxa* we have about love for our offspring, feelings of kinship to others in our community, and so forth).

At the end of this passage, the author declares that the *entire* framework or outline (*hupographē*) of Aristotelian ethics proceeds (*hormēsthai*) from this starting point. To my way of thinking, this seems to be a stunning bit of hyperbole. No doubt this author meant to focus on some fairly basic aspect of ethics as being the key factor in setting up a framework for a moral theory based on the natural and intrinsic value of virtue. And I think we can see how it was meant to work. He is addressing a challenge about ethical motivation. *Why* would we want to act virtuously? It is not at all obvious why we would, except for the kind of reasons that underlie Epicurean instrumentalism, and both Stoics and Peripatetics were convinced that such a strategy was inadequate. Not only was it unstable; unlike Epicurus, other ancient moral theorists were not convinced that in every case virtuous behavior of the kind they preferred could be shown to be the most efficacious means to the naturally desired end, and hedonism was perhaps even more exposed to Carneades's "lifeboat" thought experiment than the Stoics (the main target) were.[21] Worse yet, at least in Cicero's eyes, an instrumental justification for virtue was just plain *unworthy*; it conflicted with the dignity of virtue, and in fact this lack of dignity was thought to be incompatible with the concept of virtue. Instrumental virtue is not really virtue at all. So in this author's mind some argument for moral motivation was clearly needed, and having chosen not to emulate the

---

21 If there are two wise men in the water after a shipwreck and only one can be saved (by clinging to a plank, rather than a lifeboat as in the modern version), how do they decide who will sacrifice himself for the other? Why would anyone sacrifice himself for another? See Cicero *De Republica* 3.30; compare Cicero *De Officiis* 3.90 for a Stoic response.

developmental story based on the cradle argument, he turned to a basically Aristotelian insight to construct it; but it was not a bit of Aristotle that the master himself used in this way. Rather, Aristotle uses in other contexts the notion that we, like other living things, have a natural desire to *be*. The striving to exist is part of his teleological cosmology; it underlies his theology of the unmoved mover; it is also used in the *Eudemian Ethics* to address puzzling issues in the theory of friendship.[22] It is even used in connection with the delicate question of pleasure in the *Nicomachean Ethics*: "One might well think that all humans desire pleasure because all of them also strive to be alive. Life is an activity and each person is active in relation to the objects and with the faculties that he likes best.... And pleasure completes those activities, as it also completes being alive, which they desire. So it is reasonable that they strive for pleasure. For it completes being alive for each human being, and this is precisely what is worth choosing" (10.4, 1175a10–17, my translation). This point is picked up later by Alexander of Aphrodisias as well.[23] Clearly, it is a genuinely Aristotelian point to claim that for a living organism its being is to be actual, or active, and that its basic drive is to actualize its potentials and capabilities—in fact, that all living things are best explained by postulating a powerful inner drive to actualize and so to *be* in the fullest sense, rather than merely being potentially. *This* is the basic metaphysical notion that this author adapts to the needs of his argument here. He reaches into Aristotelian nonethical theory to develop a theory of deep, naturalistic motivations. And it is this that he employs as the basis for an equally naturalistic theory of moral motivation—in response, I suggest, to an unsuccessful Stoic attempt to do the same thing.

---

22 *EE* 7.11–12, noting especially the connection between activity and being, which is clearest, for Aristotle, in the case of his divinity, the unmoved mover (see *Metaphysics* 12.9).

23 See the essay in *De anima libri mantissa*, edited by I. Bruns, vol. 1, pt. 1 of *Commentaria in Aristotelem Graeca*, edited by I. Bruns (Berlin: Reimer, 1887), 150–153. A similar connection between *oikeiōsis* and the drive to live or be is developed in "Ethical Problems," in *Supplementum Aristotelicum*, edited by I. Bruns, vol. 2, pt. 1 of *Commentaria in Aristotelem Graeca*, 118.23–120.2.

To digress just slightly, we should notice too that another feature of Alexander's interpretation of Aristotle on this point is its openness to a frank and un-Stoic appreciation for the role of pleasure in the virtuous life. At the end of one essay,[24] Alexander directly connects this inborn striving for actualization with the fact that pleasure is the accompaniment of unimpeded natural activities.

> For it is not as though a man is first pleased and then as a result comes to desire that through which he was pleased. For nature is not in need of its own rational principle [*oikeios logos*] but rather, for natural entities without exception, a starting point of this kind [i.e., natural] is followed by its consequences and by an end of the same kind, providing that there is no impediment, the end not being the result of planning, as in the case of the crafts, but rather just being built that way. The end as Aristotle states it (that is, activity according to virtue) is in harmony with this kind of starting point. In book 10 of the *Nicomachean Ethics* Aristotle too says this on the topic: "One might well think that all humans desire pleasure because all of them also strive to be alive. Life is an activity and each person is active in relation to the objects and with the faculties that he likes best.[25] And pleasure completes those activities, as it also completes being alive, which they desire. So it is reasonable that they strive for pleasure. For it completes being alive for each human being, and this is precisely what is worth choosing."

This is the point that Alexander chooses as the culmination of his Peripatetic response to the Stoic theory of *oikeiōsis* with its baffling (to a developmentalist) need for a nonnaturalistic rupture in the development of our value commitments. But the integration of pleasure in

---

24 In *De anima libri mantissa*, 153.16–27, my translation.

25 Alexander here omits the examples Aristotle uses to illustrate: culture lovers are active in relation to songs with their faculty of hearing, lovers of learning are similarly active with their intellect in relation to *theōrēmata*, etc.

particular, rather than some other natural goods, suggests that the point is more than anti-Stoic; the Epicureans too come in for hard treatment at the hands of Peripatetics, and it is important to note that unlike Platonists and Stoics, Peripatetics (including this author, hapless though he sometimes seems to be) can claim to have preserved and made sense of the natural drive for pleasure that characterizes the animate world without making it a basic value.[26] This was Aristotle's achievement first, one that is often underappreciated, but later Peripatetics, including this author and Alexander, saw it for what it was and embraced it.

Let me return to doxography C. Fundamentally, its author argues, we desire and pursue virtue because we desire our own existence; that existence takes the form of our simply *being* a set of capacities that exist all the more fully when they are developed and that ultimately are fulfilled by being actualized. This is, of course, a somewhat Stoicized way of putting an Aristotelian point about desire and motivation. The teleological assumptions that do so much of the work seem not to be under debate, and specific content is given to the desire by an explication of how practical reason actually works (practical reason in the form of selection and rejection of the natural goods and evils of body and soul, both of which are dear to us by nature since we just *are* our body and soul—the point made at the outset of the account).

This account of why humans are motivated to pursue virtue is naturalistic, and not just because it sets out from a form of *oikeiōsis* and because our selections are for natural goods, such as health and freedom from pain, which no one would seriously question. The author also claims that, as we attempt to get things right, we *simply discover* that "reliable knowledge" is what we need and what we pursue in order to satisfy our basic desires. And once we learn this, inevitably by experience, we come to see that it fits smoothly into the *natural* process of

---

26 That is, the hedonistic aspects of such an Aristotelian theory avoided the instrumentalisms that were perhaps regarded as the worst aspect of Epicurean theory. Even Plato, in the *Philebus* especially, has room for pleasure as a component of the best life.

using practical reason to pursue goods; "virtue," then, turns out to be nothing more than the label we apply to this excellence of practical reason in pursuit of natural goods. The label is applied as an honorific, since we find it worthy of our respect and appreciation. This process is portrayed as being one of inevitable realization—we just *come to see* that reason is the key to getting our natural goals, and we just label its excellence "virtue." It spontaneously evokes our admiration—who wouldn't admire such a capacity so well suited to helping us get things that satisfy our basic desires? The purportedly experiential basis for this elevation of practical reason is perhaps modeled on a move made by the Stoics—we may compare Cato's account of the allegedly natural emergence of our appreciation for how well things fit together as we achieve a consistent use of reason in book 3 of *On Goals*; Cato too invoked *kathēkonta* in a way that the present passage brings to mind, and both, of course, are focused on what we learn from reflection on our use of practical rationality. (Whether the Stoic version of this is connected to what Chrysippus meant by "an experience of what happens by nature"—his *telos* formula[27]—is hard, perhaps impossible, to say.)

When we do compare these two accounts, doxography C's and Cato's, of what it is that people "just discover," we may think that the Peripatetics have the better of it. The Stoic claim, set in its developmental context, is that in the course of our intellectual and moral maturation we simply come to see the order and pattern in nature—a value they emphasized almost as emphatically as Platonists did—and that once we see that order we simply come to be more attached to that than to all the commitments we acknowledged previously.

With this established, the initial "appropriate action" (this is what I call the Greek *kathēkon*) is to preserve oneself in one's natural

---

27 See *Stoicorum Veterum Fragmenta,* III, 12–15, and my discussion in "Moral Causes: The Role of Physical Explanation in Ancient Ethics," in *Thinking about Causes: From Greek Philosophy to Modern Physics,* edited by P. Machamer and G. Wolters (Pittsburgh: University of Pittsburgh Press, 2007) 14–36.

constitution. The next is to take what is in accordance with nature and reject its opposite. Once this method of selection (and likewise rejection) has been discovered, selection then goes hand in hand with appropriate action. Then such selection becomes continuous, and, finally *stable and in agreement with nature*. At this point that which can truly be said to be good first appears and is recognized for what it is.

21. A human being's earliest concern is for what is in accordance with nature. But as soon as one has gained some understanding, or rather "conception" (what the Stoics call *ennoia*), and sees an order and as it were concordance in the things which one ought to do [*rerum agendarum ordinem et...concordiam*], one then values that concordance much more highly than those first objects of affection. Hence through learning and reason one concludes that this is the place to find the supreme human good, that good which is to be praised and sought on its own account. (*On Goals* 3.20–21)[28]

Unlike the theory offered by the author of doxography C, Cato's version of Stoic theory (and probably most other versions as well) postulates a quite striking discontinuity in our development, one that, as long as it is not properly explained and supported by observation, is nearly as disruptive as the sudden transformation of the immature human into a rational, responsible person susceptible to moral assessment and open to an appreciation of the good and virtue. Would this theory, with its apparently nonnaturalist transformation built in at the crucial stage of development, be as persuasive to anyone who was not previously committed to the Stoic school as our Peripatetic account would be to a similarly open-minded enquirer? I doubt it. Cato seems simply to help himself to the allegedly brute fact that when we are exposed to *ordo et concordia* we will be so impressed that prior value

---

28 Translation of R. Woolf in *Cicero: On Moral Ends* ed. J. Annas (Cambridge: Cambridge University Press, 2001), 71.

commitments are silenced (as some might say) or occluded.[29] Indeed, I venture to think that to most uncommitted philosophers it would look like a pure theoretical postulate and a quite implausible one at that. Moreover, the terms used here, in the Stoic theory, to attempt the linkage between natural desires and a commitment to virtue are very similar to those deployed by the author of doxography C—so much so in fact that it seems almost irresistible to hypothesize that response to the Stoic theory was one of the main reasons for developing the theory in the form he chose. Inevitably philosophers and ordinary people will disagree about what we will just "see" and experience in various predicted situations—these intuitions are no more certain than any of the other intuitions we so casually invoke in debates about moral theory and no more free from the suspicion of being tainted by a desire to support one theory over another. But even so, I do think that the Peripatetic has the better of it here and readers should consider for themselves which reaction they find more plausible.

I issue this invitation in part to support my claim that, as clumsy as this author's argument may seem, it is not reasonable to regard his work as mere eclecticism. Rather, we should see this later Aristotelian as providing at least the outline for an entire theory of the foundations of ethics and moral motivation, an outline that is meant to respond to a Stoic theory but at the same time is a highly original and updated version of Aristotelian ethics, or at least the key bits that allegedly serve to get it off the ground. And then, as the remark about *hupographē* suggests, the rest of this outline of Aristotelian ethics will try to show that everything relevant—including the nature and desirability of practical reason—follows from these natural principles.

The author's argument is heavily focused on "starting points" or principles—that is, *archai*. This indicates that in the eyes of the thinker

29 It is, I think, an open question whether Seneca's nondevelopmental account of how we come to our conception of the good and an attachment to it is any more persuasive. See Letters 120 and 121 with my commentary in *Seneca: Selected Philosophical Letters* (Oxford: Oxford University Press, 2007).

constructing this new version of Aristotelian ethics the most pressing issue to deal with was not the fine points of what makes a virtue virtuous or what role is played by pleasure, or how contemplation fits into the practical life, where friendship fits, or even the nature of the passions. Those issues had, for the time being, become routine. What *had* to be dealt with was the challenge of providing a naturalistic account of the basic *motivation* that underlies the rest. It was to be an account that linked ethics to the biological teleology that was recognized as characteristic of Aristotelian thought. It was cast in Stoic language because they were the main interlocutors. And I have suggested as well that the Stoics are also the source of the challenge to which this theory responds, a suggestion that would fit into a pattern of evolving and creative Aristotelian engagement with other schools of thought and point helpfully toward what some think is the most important contribution Aristotelian ethics can perhaps still make today: not a contribution to virtue theory in a narrow sense but rather to the search for independently plausible naturalistic foundations for ethics.

ACKNOWLEDGMENTS

I thank audiences at the University of Michigan, the University of Notre Dame, the Graduate Center at City University of New York, the University of Texas at Austin, and the University of Rochester for challenging questions and the opportunity to fill out and qualify my claims. I am particularly grateful to Babak Bakhtiarynia for helpful general discussion and to Sean Kelsey for a couple of stimulating challenges to my detailed readings of doxography C. Parts of this discussion overlap with material in chapter 4 of my *Ethics after Aristotle* (Cambridge, MA: Harvard University Press, 2014).

Reflection

CICERO ON MORAL MOTIVATION AND SEEING
(HOW) TO BE GOOD

Joy Connolly
☙

In the sixth book of Cicero's *De Republica*, in a scene that reworks Plato's myth of Er, the younger Scipio dreams that he meets his dead grandfather, the famous victor over Carthage, Scipio Africanus. Africanus informs him that a place in the heavens awaits men who devote their lives to preserving the *patria* (*De Republica* 6.13). The younger Scipio must not be motivated by desire for mortal glory, which is fleeting (6.20), but "virtue should tug you by its own charms toward true glory" (*verum decus*, my translation, 6.25). Though he expresses his wish to escape from the bondage of the body and live a "real" life in the heavens, the younger Scipio commits to living out his time on earth motivated by two ends: the ultimate reward of immortality and his immediate desire to imitate the examples of his father and grandfather.

Here, as elsewhere in his moral thought, Cicero does not explain why some men are more attracted by virtue's enticements or by the prospect of imitating virtue than others. His virtuous man seems motivated simply by the inclination of his character, which Cicero believes nature inculcates in the individual self (*De Officiis* 1.107).[1]

But Cicero has more to say in his last work, *On Moral Duties* or *De Officiis*, about the distinctive features of the human condition

---

1 See Michael Slote, *Morals from Motives* (Oxford: Oxford University Press, 2001).

that dictate why and how a man inclined to virtue may live a good, or to use his term, an "honorable" (*honesta*) life. The claims he makes in this epistle-like treatise, addressed to his son Marcus, start from two propositions that underlie his earlier work in rhetorical and political thought: first, that the impulse to live together sociably in a community is natural to human beings, and second, as he suggests in the extant opening of *De Republica*, the best human life is the life of political action.

A key point in Cicero's thinking about moral motivation (and from the perspective of his influence on early modernity, the most important one) is the fundamental role played in sustaining sociability and action by aesthetic perception, above all, sight. Scipio is motivated to live the best life by the sight of his father and grandfather, whose actions and demeanor he watches, remembers, and imitates. In turn, he will appear in public to be seen by others, who will be motivated to imitate (and compete with) him. Similarly, the strongest bonds among humans, as described in *De Officiis*, are formed by friendship between men that flourishes when two men see the honorableness in one another that each individually strives for (*cernit, videtur*, 1.55). These verbs harken back to Cicero's earlier account of the differences between human and animal, where he identifies as characteristically human the capacity to survey and see (*cernit, videt*) cause and effect, relations between things and people, and change over time (1.11). This exchange of seeing and being seen is a recurrent theme of Cicero's earlier dialogue on friendship, which transforms the relationship the Romans called *amicitia*—a word meaning friendship as well as political alliance—into a machine for motivating virtue.

Seeing and being seen also anchors the competitive practices of elite Roman life, including running for political office and leading armies on the battlefield. Embarking on these ventures is motivated by the desire for eternal life in the form of monuments in the city and around the empire that memorialize a man's achievements and enhance the glory won by his imitative descendants.

Awareness of seeing and being seen plays a determinative role in Cicero's discussion of moderation or propriety (*decorum*), the fourth of the four cardinal virtues that he reviews in *De Officiis*, translated (under the influence of the Stoic Panaetius) from Plato's *sophrosune*. His survey of propriety covers harmony with nature (100); self-control (101–106); self-knowledge, which grants understanding of the actions appropriate to one's individual capacities, and helps answer the crucial question of whom to imitate (107–125; see *De Republica* 1.16, 26); and finally, advice on action in the public arena, where men achieve divine excellence. Sight is the capacity that enables us to be aware of one another, in accordance with nature's dictate that we attend with "reverence" to the way we interact: neglect of what each man thinks of another is characteristic "not only of the arrogant man but a totally vicious one" (1.99). In the last substantive passage of book 1, Cicero identifies beauty, a sense of order, and ornament (*formositas, ordo, ornatus*) as the three elements of propriety in action. Every good man is motivated by the desire to obey, and to be seen to obey, the rules of propriety covering dress, gestures, conversation, and even interior decorating—but above all, in one's public acts.

James Porter has recently advocated for a deep realignment in our understanding of the historical development of Greek and Roman aesthetics. Against the domination of formalism and idealism in the traditional intellectual history of the ancient world, he argues that sensualism, materialism, the empirical, and the phenomenal are key terms in classical aesthetics. "To experience aesthetic pleasure in antiquity was (and still is) to be caught up within a circle of valuation, of value-production and value-consumption, a system...that ran through the entire fabric of society, and within which all social agents were implicated."[2] Porter's point underscores how Cicero's account of moral motivation—in which aesthetic perception is the guide—is socially weighted. The word Cicero chooses to denote "good" is not *bonum*, "the good" (following Plato), but *honestas*, "honorableness," a word associated with the well-off; not *malum*, "the bad," but *turpitudo*, "ugliness" or "disgrace"—a word related to *trepidus*, "fearful," or "anxious," emotions associated with the powerless. For Cicero, one's aesthetic awareness of what is "proper" emerges directly from one's social knowledge; thus one's moral motivation is inextricable from the prejudices encouraged by social hierarchies.

Implicated as it is in maintaining the conventions that underpin patterns of elite domination, the significance of Cicero's thinking cannot be limited to its role in that arena. Sight enables more than a shallow sort of imitation and responsive self-styling, or the achievement of social capital or the purely mortal glory Africanus ultimately dismisses in *De Republica* 6. Sight enables one's awareness of the other, and sight enables one to be the object of other's awareness, in a deeper sense.

Traces of sight's significance emerge even in Cicero's abstract account of virtue's appeal, with his reference to the "charms" that attract men: if one could see the "form and face" of the four virtues with physical eyes, he says, quoting Plato's *Phaedrus*, "it would arouse marvelous passions for wisdom" (*mirabiles amores, De Officiis* 1.15). The quotation from Plato's dialogue on love is significant. Cicero couches his moral and political thought in the genres of epistle and dialogue. Epistles transform the absence of a loved person into imagined presence; the dialogue represents the dynamic exchange of ideas between men in close physical proximity. In both genres, arguments unfold in the context of

---

2 James Porter, *The Origins of Aesthetic Thought in Ancient Greece: Matter, Sensation, and Experience* (Cambridge: Cambridge University Press, 2010), 13.

intense affective relationships: between writer and addressee (such as Cicero and his son in *De Officiis*), or among dear friends in the dialogues, which, following Plato, feature historical figures like the two Scipios or Cicero himself. When Cicero affectionately advises his son to reflect on moral obligations by reading Cicero's own philosophical works, he is tying together motivation to virtue with the admiring imitation of an individual for whom one feels affection. He is also offering up himself for imitation, keenly aware of being an object of the gaze of another and the responsibilities that this entails.

This literary staging foregrounds what Adriana Cavarero calls "the necessity of the other" that is characteristic of an ethics that "from beginning to end, is intertwined with other lives—with reciprocal exposures and innumerable gazes."[3] For Cicero as for Cavarero, the sight of the other and the awareness of being in another's gaze have an inescapable moral element: they motivate humans to act honorably or dishonorably, to aid human life or harm it.

These ideas have a long and so far understudied history. Cicero exerted enormous influence on the formation of moral and political thought under the conditions of radical social and political change that define early modernity. (*De Officiis* was the second book to be printed in Europe after the Bible in the 1450s.) His emphasis on aesthetic perception in general, and sight in particular, influenced Scottish and Anglo-Irish Enlightenment thinkers like Francis Hutcheson, Adam Smith, and Edmund Burke, who used the same blended aesthetico-moral lexicon and who were profoundly concerned with taste and affective relations.[4] Smith introduces his "impartial spectator" in the first section of his *Theory of Moral*

---

3 Adriana Cavarero, *Relating Narratives: Story-telling and Selfhood* (New York: Routledge, 2000), 88.
4 Terry Eagleton, *Trouble with Strangers: A Study of Ethics* (Malden, MA: Wiley-Blackwell, 2009), 29–44, 64–77.

Sentiments, titled "Of the Propriety of Action." The impact of Cicero's thinking on the eighteenth century is only now being investigated.[5] More could be said about the intriguing interconnections between his work and the recent surge of interest among poststructuralist thinkers seeking to understand what motivates us as moral agents.[6]

5 See Charles Griswold, *Adam Smith and the Virtues of Enlightenment* (Cambridge: Cambridge University Press, 1999), and Gloria Vivenza, *Adam Smith and the Classics* (Oxford: Oxford University Press, 2001).

6 Judith Butler, *Giving an Account of Oneself* (New York: Fordham University Press, 2005).

CHAPTER FOUR

Moral Motivation in Christian and Jewish Medieval Philosophy

Jonathan Jacobs

An examination of how medieval philosophers understood moral motivation has to be undertaken in the context of their philosophical anthropology. Medieval philosophers, from the period roughly, 400 CE to 1350 CE, were keenly interested in the nature of agency—especially moral agency—and in the normative aspects of human action. Claims, insights, and arguments concerning moral motivation could be examined independent of the wider context of medieval thought, but that could result in misrepresentation. By "the wider context" I mean the way medieval philosophers understood human action as occurring in a context of normatively significant relations between nature, will, and reason, and the metaphysical presuppositions that provided framing principles.

That is not to say that there is some single conception that all medieval philosophers shared, the difference between them being merely differences of detail. Medieval philosophers held quite diverse views, and there are important contrasts between numerous medieval theories of the will and action. Moreover, there were important developments in medieval thought, and there are discernible changes in the character of theorizing about agency and motivation. Nevertheless, there are some general, thematic features distinctive of medieval thought. Chief among them is that the medievals appropriated various elements of the ancient philosophical inheritance and revised them in ways informed by their conception of the world as a created order and their conception of humanity's relation to God.

In much recent and contemporary philosophy, theistic considerations are not central in the way they were central to medieval philosophy.[1] Nonetheless, familiar, difficult questions concerning determinism, the relation between reason and the will, desire and the will, weakness of the will, moral responsibility, and so forth are easily recognizable in medieval thought.[2] In addition, important debates remain about the proper framework considerations for understanding moral motivation. It is not as though *of course* medieval thought depended on mistaken or no longer relevant presuppositions and *of course* contemporary thought has got the right presuppositions. Indeed, *because* of their theistic commitments, many medieval philosophers were highly alert to issues concerning relations between naturalistic and theological considerations.[3]

---

1 In any era there are likely to be certain prevailing presuppositions or dominant philosophical methods. While it is true that theological commitments figure heavily in medieval philosophy, many of the enduringly influential medieval philosophers developed carefully articulated accounts of how their presuppositions concerning issues relevant to freedom of the will figured in their analyses, rather than using them to close off avenues of analysis. In addition, many philosophers were highly sophisticated in their analyses of the implications of their presuppositions for issues such as free will, debates concerning realism and nominalism, ethics, epistemology, and human action.

2 In my *Law, Reason, and Morality in Medieval Jewish Philosophy* (Oxford: Oxford University Press, 2010), I discuss medieval Jewish philosophical conceptions of freedom of the will, some central issues of moral psychology, and moral epistemology and explicate some respects in which those conceptions remain relevant and illuminating.

3 It might be said that for much recent philosophy, the presupposition of naturalism has played a role comparable to the presupposition of theism in medieval philosophy. One difference, though, might be that naturalism is understood in a variety of importantly different ways, whereas Abrahamic monotheism—for all the (genuinely significant) differences in faith-traditions—involved a small number of common fundamental commitments.

There is considerable analytical astuteness and rigor in a great deal of medieval philosophy, including subtle explorations of volition, the conditions for free action and for praise and blame, responsibility for one's dispositions, and so forth.

Instead of attempting comprehensive coverage of individual philosophers, this discussion focuses on a small number of especially influential thinkers and highlights a small number of significant themes. Many interesting and important medieval philosophers go unmentioned in this chapter, and there are ways of approaching action and motivation different from this approach. In addition, given limitations of space, Islamic philosophers are absent from the discussion, though they have an important place in medieval philosophy. Jewish and Christian philosophers inherited ancient philosophy largely through the mediation of Islamic thinkers, and the latter's commentaries on Aristotle were especially important. However, while Islamic thinkers had important and sophisticated views about the relations between reason and revelation and about freedom of the will, they did not address moral motivation in ways that have had pronounced, highly visible influence on western thought.

I

Most of the thinkers discussed here exhibit a broadly rationalistic cast of mind, in the respect that they take the exercise of reason to be centrally important to the well-ordered exercise of distinctively human capacities and they regard reason as having a vital role in human perfection. They are not rationalists in a Cartesian, Leibnizian, or Spinozist sense, and some of them were quite explicit about what they took to be the limits of reason. Nonetheless, they contrast with thinkers of a more mystical cast of mind and thinkers who were deeply skeptical of the powers of reason and were suspicious of its claims.

As a way of organizing the treatment of the topic the two chief themes of the discussion are these: (1) the ways that theistic commitments impacted the ancient philosophical inheritance and the understanding of human action, and (2) a transition from teleological conceptions with broadly Platonic and Aristotelian features to conceptions of will and action in which those features are much less prominent. In explicating these themes I comment on issues such as the respective roles of reason and desire in human action and the way volition and the relation between the motive of action and the end of action were understood. These themes help us to track the developments and changes in medieval theorizing about how people are moved to act, especially in regard to moral requirements.

Platonic, Aristotelian, and to some extent Stoic thought also influenced medieval philosophy profoundly. From those sources medieval philosophers inherited the notion that reason is properly authoritative with regard to human action and that reason properly asserts that authority by controlling potentially unruly passions and appetites and by guiding and ordering them even if they are not especially unruly. The Platonic notion that reason can order the soul so that a person acts in accord with a correct understanding of the good had an enduring resonance, as did Aristotle's conception of virtue as involving desire aiming at what reason understands to be good, along with virtuous activity actualizing the human *telos* pleasingly. In addition, the Stoic notion of governance of the soul belonging properly to reason is an additional current of thought ascribing normative authority to reason. The notion that knowledge of the good can shape motivation is a centrally important element of a great deal of medieval thought. According to many medieval philosophers, knowledge of the good can motivate action, and in so doing, good is actualized.

Medieval philosophers did not systematically use some particular term in the ways "motive" or "motivation" are used in modern English. Their concerns with the analysis, explanation, and evaluation of actions were somewhat different from those of modern English-language philosophers. Medieval philosophers tended to be mainly concerned with the psychology of virtuous action and with the will. Neither of those concerns is quite the same as a concern with motivation, though they have important points of contact and overlap.

That human action is intelligible through the good sought by the activity in question—whether a real or merely apparent good—figured in many medieval conceptions of human nature and action.[4] An important element of the background was the conception of human beings as created in the image of God and as being capable of imitating God, in part, by exercising the power to *realize good through agency informed by knowledge of it*. In addition, two chief reasons for defending free will were that human free will seemed necessary for the justice of divine reward and punishment, and that human beings have free will is also part of the notion that human beings are created in the image of God. That God created the world freely conflicted with some versions of a metaphysics of emanation.[5]

In general, it is fair to say that medieval philosophers understood action, volition, and motivation as *responsive*—responsive (or not) to the good, and through the good ultimately responsive to God. There is a sense in which Platonic and Aristotelian theories of action involve a central role for responsiveness to the good, through correct understanding and right desire. When a person has vices or fails to act rightly, the explanation—explicitly or implicitly—involves a failure to be properly responsive to the good. Medieval philosophers, whether Jewish, Christian, or Islamic, appropriated the ancient notion of action as

---

4 The notion that action is oriented to the good, whether real or apparent, is found throughout medieval philosophy as a basic principle of the intelligibility of rational action. Even if we abandon the objective perfectionism of many of the medievals, and if we domesticate goods to subjective conceptions, there remain reasons to interpret rational activity in terms of agents taking their actions—at least their deliberate actions—to aim at realizing or bringing about some good, some conception of that for the sake of which an action is performed.

5 In several medieval philosophers' works there is a combination of the metaphysics of emanation and Aristotelian metaphysical claims. Even in some of the views committed to the world existing by a free act of creation by God, it was held that the various levels of being emanated from the First Intelligence, created by God. Thus, in some views there was a role for emanationist procession once an act of creation brought into being something other than God. David Burrell, *Faith and Freedom: An Interfaith Perspective* (Malden: Blackwell, 2004), includes extensive discussion of emanation, creation, and the role of "Neoplatonic" thought in medieval philosophy in all three Abrahamic faith traditions.

responsiveness to good and developed and elaborated it in accord with their theological commitments. That is not an insignificant alteration. Medieval moral philosophy is not "just" Aristotle plus Christian belief, or Aristotle plus Jewish belief, and so forth. But medieval philosophical thought did, to a large extent, share with ancient thought the conception of action as properly having an orientation the rightness (or not) of which is a matter of responsiveness to that which is normatively authoritative for action.

Augustine's thought is a good example of the integration of Platonic/Aristotelian anthropology and theistic commitments. Much of Augustine's thought revolves around the ways there are obstacles and impediments to reason ruling the soul. For Augustine the soul is the locus of a contest between love of the lower (base desire) and love of the higher (through reason). There are proper and improper objects of desire; it is through reason that we have knowledge of what is good; and *libido* is the aspect of our nature through which we desire what is lower. This issue of there being (two) fundamental sources of ends and motives informs a great deal of medieval moral thought. However, it differs from ancient thought in that there is a crucially important role for the will in ways not found in Plato or Aristotle's thought. Accordingly, Augustine held that, "the mind could not become a slave of lust except through its own will. It cannot be forced to serve lust by something superior, or by an equal, because this is unjust; also, it cannot be forced by something inferior, because the inferior thing does not have the power. We conclude, therefore, that the movement which, for the sake of pleasure, turns the will from the Creator to the creature belongs to the will itself."[6] The Platonism of the view is evident in the notion of reason as properly ruling lower faculties, which, when not ruled by reason, by knowledge of the good, lead the person to pursue base(r) desires. Action flows from the way in which

---

6 Augustine, *On the Free Choice of the Will* (*On the Free Choice of the Will,* trans. Anna Benjamin [Indianapolis: Bobbs-Merrill], 1964], 87.

the person's soul is ordered with respect to different possible sources of motivation and different types of action-guiding considerations. This is a familiar feature of medieval thought concerning motivation and action; that is, one can be moved by desire or the passions on the one hand or by reason, by understanding, on the other. When action is well ordered, that is to be explained in terms of two things: the objectivity of good—and good is an object of the understanding—and our volitional capacity to act in ways that are responsive to that understanding. Thus, being motivated rightly is crucial to perfective activity, and because that is constitutive of happiness, being properly motivated is necessary to happiness.

Augustine wrote, "I cannot do any good except by my will. It is quite clear that a good God gave me the will for this purpose."[7] And: "For what lies more truly in the power of the will than the will itself? Whoever has a good will certainly has a thing to be preferred by far to all earthly realms and all pleasures of the body. Whoever does not have a good will surely lacks that very thing which is more excellent than all the goods not in our power, that thing which the will alone, in itself, may give."[8] He argued that, while it is through free will that a person can sin, free will was not given *so that* persons might sin, but so that a person can live rightly, for "if man did not have free choice of will, how could there exist the good according to which it is just to condemn evildoers and reward those who act rightly?"[9]

Free will is the basis of moral accountability. The "mind could not become a slave of lust except through its own will. It cannot be forced to serve lust by something superior, or by an equal, because this is unjust; also, it cannot be forced by something inferior, because the inferior thing does not have the power."[10] Whether the will turns to God

---

7 *On the Free Choice of the Will,* Benjamin translation, 88.
8 *On the Free Choice of the Will,* Benjamin translation, 24–25.
9 *On the Free Choice of the Will,* Benjamin translation, 36.
10 *On the Free Choice of the Will,* Benjamin translation, 87.

or pursues pleasure is due to the will itself. A good will is a "will by which we seek to live rightly and honorably and to come to the highest wisdom."[11] Later, in thinkers such as Scotus, the notion of the autonomy of the will is developed in a more radical way, one that has some important affinities with Kant's conception of the will and its role in morally worthy action.

In Anselm, seven centuries after Augustine, strong Platonist resonances remain, and we find a similar claim about the will's importance for moral accountability and its invulnerability to coercion. Anselm argued: "Since the highest good is the highest being, it follows that every good is being and every being is good. Hence nothing and nonbeing do not come from God, from whom comes only good and being."[12] This is connected with Anselm's view that "if truth and rectitude are in the essence of things because they are that which they are in the highest truth, it is certain that the truth of things is rectitude"[13]; that "these two are necessary for justice in the will, namely, to will what it ought and for the reason it ought to";[14] and "that justice is rectitude of the will that is preserved for its own sake."[15]

Anselm held that capacity to sin is not a condition of free will. God has free will and no capacity to sin. Nonetheless, when a human being sins, that is because of the wrongly ordered exercise of free will. He wrote: "The apostate angel and the first man sinned through free will, because they sinned through a judgement that is so free that it cannot be coerced to sin by anything else. That is why they are justly reprehended; when they had a free will that could not be coerced by anything else, they willingly and without necessity sinned."[16] Moreover,

---

11 *On the Free Choice of the Will*, Benjamin translation, 24.

12 Anselm, "On the Fall of the Devil," in *Anselm of Canterbury: The Major Works*, edited by Brian Davies and G. R. Evans (Oxford: Oxford University Press, 2008), 196.

13 Anselm, "On Truth," in *Anselm of Canterbury: The Major Works*, 160.

14 Anselm, "On Truth," 168.

15 Anselm, "On Truth," 170.

16 Anselm, "On Free Will," 177.

not even the strongest temptation can explain a wrong exercise of free will. "No one is deprived of this rectitude except by his own will."[17] "Who then can say that the will is not free to preserve rectitude, and free from temptation and sin, if no temptation can divert it save willingly from rectitude to sin, that is, to willing what it ought not. Therefore when it is conquered, it is not conquered by another power but by itself."[18] Anselm was primarily concerned with whether the will itself preserves the rectitude of will, "which is the task of the rational creature."[19] "What could be more obvious then than the truth of action is rectitude."[20] And: "injustice is the evil that is only a privation of the good, and makes angels and men bad and makes their will bad."[21]

In *On the Fall of the Devil* (*De casu diaboli*) Anselm extends his account of freedom and sin by discussing the first sin of the angels. In order for the angels to have the power to preserve rectitude of will for its own sake, they had to have both a will for justice and a will for happiness. If God had given them only a will for happiness, they would have been necessitated to will whatever they thought would make them happy. Their willing of happiness would have had its ultimate origin in God and not in the angels themselves. So they would not have had the power for self-initiated action, which means that they would not have had free choice. The situation is largely the same if God had given them only the will for justice. However, God gave them the will for happiness *and* the will for justice, and thus they had the power for self-initiated action.

When a person succumbs to temptation, that is attributable to the person as a volitional agent, not to compulsion that forces the will. Temptation does not force a person away from willing rightly. We might appeal to it as an irresistibly motivating cause, but Anselm denies that anything can force the will in such a way. The succumbing is an act at

---

17 Anselm, "On Free Will," 181.

18 Anselm, "On Free Will," 183.

19 Anselm, "On Truth," 151.

20 Anselm, "On Truth," 157.

21 Anselm, "On the Fall of the Devil," 206.

least in the sense that the person consents to being moved by the desire. Even when a person experiences powerful, seemingly overwhelmingly strong desire or passion, the person's act is attributable to the person as a responsible agent and this is because the will, in its nature, is something that cannot be necessitated. Anselm took that to be a conceptual truth, though not "merely" conceptual. It says something about the nature of the will. What we might call "being overcome" or "being carried away" by temptation Anselm explicated as consenting to temptation. The act simply would not be performed unless the will turned in that direction. If one is grabbed, bound, and carried off, that is a quite different kind of case; there is no role for volition in being carried away *that* way. In a literal sense an agent can be carried away, but a will cannot.

The notion that in a human being there are two fundamental sources of motivation appears in several thinkers' views, including in some that otherwise contrast with each other rather sharply. Again, Scotus is a good example. He retains the Augustinian/Anselmian notion of two sources of motivation, two fundamental affections, but his conception of the sovereignty of the will detaches it from much of the Platonist normative metaphysics of Anselm's theory.

In other thinkers an Aristotelian dimension is more pronounced. Aquinas's theory of the will and action involves elements not found in Aristotle, but there are some basically Aristotelian contours to his overall conception of human action and its end-oriented character. He argues that it is through exercise of the will that human beings engage in voluntary action and that the will desires the good in a general way, the specification of good needing to be supplied by the intellect.[22] The will is a rational appetite and it has an end, a *telos*, which is happiness, the good that is the perfection of our nature. While the intellect presents objects to the will, the will moves voluntarily, and not as a result of an external force acting on it. (Further discussion of his view follows.)

---

22 See Aquinas, *Summa Theologiae*, First Part of the Second Part, question 9, and *Disputed Question on Evil*, question 6.

Many medieval philosophers appropriated the broadly Aristotelian principle that virtuous activity is enjoyed in a distinctive manner, and also the notion that such enjoyment is a core feature of human perfection. Virtuous activity is enjoyed *as* good, *by* agents who *are* good, and that provides an additional motive for virtuous agents to sustain their virtuous activity.[23] I have noted that many medieval philosophers understood rational action as responsive to the authority of the good and that excellent activity is pleasing to the virtuous agent. In that respect, the pleasure is not a "mechanical" cause or even what the agent aims at primarily. However, finding excellent activity pleasing reinforces the disposition to engage in excellent activity. The goodness of the activity rather than the pleasure accompanying it is the primary reason for the virtuous agent to engage in it. However, the enjoyment is an important mark of the genuineness of the good that is actualized and reinforces the disposition to so act. In addition, Boethius's conception of happiness as perfective virtuous activity experienced as pleasing had considerable influence. Whether exhibiting a more Aristotelian notion of excellent activity or a more Platonic notion of harmonious order, or a combination of both, many of the most influential medieval conceptions of the soul were perfectionist in a pronounced manner. This is clearly evident in Boethius, Augustine, Alfarabi, Maimonides, and Aquinas, among others. Human beings not only have capacities for acting; they have the capacity to successfully actualize or realize their nature, and doing so is central to happiness.

2

The notion that God has supplied guidance and what we might call a "discipline of perfection" (including guidance for repentance) is

---

23 The notion that virtuous activity is naturally pleasing is developed in Aristotle's *Nicomachean Ethics* and is an important element of intellectualist *eudaimonia*. See, for example, bk. 1, chap. 8 and bk. 10, chap. 7.

centrally important to all three Abrahamic traditions.[24] This aid makes possible a perfective happiness transcending our biological nature. The concept of divine aid is relevant to this discussion, because the medievals generally held that volition and understanding are susceptible to corruption in ways that distract and alienate us from the good, whether it is a naturalistic or a transcendent good. Thus, a proper guiding concern of any person's life is whether one is seeking to realize correct ends in the correct ways, on the basis of the right motive. This is not an insoluble epistemic problem. It is not as though human beings cannot know what is required. They *can* know, at least in a broad sense. It is true that particular moral questions can involve difficult reasoning and judgment. Guidance is given to human beings through revelation, but it does not obviate the need for persons to do their own thinking and arrive at the correct specification of what is to be done. Whether and how individuals respond to divine guidance depends on their volitions and motives.

The precise role of divine activity in whether a human being attains complete happiness was understood in different ways in the different religious traditions. Despite such differences, a common implication of theistic commitments is that a virtuous individual remains capable of sinning and a vicious individual remains capable of ethical reorientation and virtue. This is a departure from Aristotle's view that a mature character typically becomes fixed and, therefore, it is not reasonable to expect a person's character, once formed, to change. Aristotle's virtuous and vicious agents are very likely to remain fixed in their respective states of character. In the religious traditions the genuineness of repentance constituted a departure from that view, and that genuineness involved a power of free will that exceeds Aristotelian voluntariness. According to the religious traditions, one should not regard one's dispositions and states of character as so fixed as to be *either* incorrigible or

---

24 The guidance provided by revelation includes guidance with regard to how repentance can enable a person to return to God. Even a very bad person is not without direction. Vices do not so obscure the path to God that a person is hopelessly abandoned to sin.

unsusceptible to sinning. The possibility of further sinning is not eliminated by repentance. But repentance, an authentic, genuine reorientation to the good, was regarded as a real prospect for human beings.

Aristotle regards the fixity of (unified) virtue as an ideal, and he is not optimistic that it will be widely attained. A great many people, on account of poor habituation, poor judgment, or incontinence are, we might say, dispositionally precluded from attaining a high degree of virtue. States of character tend to be stable and enduring, for better or worse. Fixity of character (of whatever moral quality) was part of his view. The fact that, for Aristotle, there is no revelation, no source of guidance and example other than other human beings, can also render virtue epistemically inaccessible if, for instance, the prevailing values and norms of one's community are corrupt but are not recognized as such. In that case there may be little prospect that a person will be able to reason past the impediments of the mistaken views and bad habits shaping the agent's perspective and dispositions in accord with prevailing norms.

Maimonides is an excellent example of how some important Aristotelian concepts were deployed in ways that departed from Aristotle's use of them. For instance, Maimonides agrees with Aristotle on the importance of habit with respect to the acquisition of virtues, and he agrees also on the significance of good examples. However, Maimonides argues that the will has a power of acting freely that is sufficient for making repentance possible. Even a very bad person is capable of ethical reorientation, and even an excellent person is still capable of sinning. States of character are not unrevisably fixed.

The view that a person's character is not, so to speak, naturalistically *fixed* figures in much medieval thought, in large part because of the importance of freedom of the will. While Jewish and Christian thinkers explain the good in terms that ultimately refer to God as its source and understand volition as a human likeness of a divine attribute, there is a key role for human effort in these thinkers' conceptions of the plasticity of character. The notion that a person's dispositions and volitions should be unalterable is inconsistent with the (fundamentally important) ability to be responsive—or not—to God. Maimonides is especially explicit regarding this issue, but other medievals' treatments of repentance, seeking forgiveness, forgiving, aspiring to virtue, sinning, and descending into vice also reflect the notion that one's dispositions can be revised. There is a (direct or indirect) role for God in the account of *how* they are revised but also a crucial role for the volition of the person.[25]

Maimonides insists that the Law and the commandments would be pointless without freedom of the will: "If man's actions were done under compulsion, the commandments and prohibitions of the Law would be nullified and they would all be absolutely in vain, since man would have no choice in what he does. Similarly, instruction and education, including instruction in all the productive arts, would necessarily be in vain an would all be futile."[26] He maintains that "reward and punishment would also be sheer injustice, not be be [*sic*] meted out by some of us to others nor by God to us."[27]

There is no question that humans have free will. "The truth about which there is no doubt at all is that all of man's actions are given over to him."[28] This is a robust version of "ought implies can," one in which God's wisdom and justice are at stake. The notion that a human being might lack freedom of the will is simply unsupportable, and Maimonides's argument concerning the Law has a result that comports with his critique of astrological determinism (regarding which he was derisory). With regard to the *knowledge* that might be required for

25 The Christian view of repentance and justification is complex because of the ways divine grace and human will are thought to be operative and cooperative. There is a good deal of likeness between Judaism, Christianity, and Islam regarding key elements of repentance, but Christian conceptions of the actual workings of the will and grace involve distinctive issues because of Christianity's conception of fallenness. Augustine and Aquinas are key medieval sources. See, for example, Augustine, *On Grace and Free Choice*, and Aquinas, "Treatise on Grace," in *Summa Theologiae*, First Part of the Second Part, questions 109–114.

26 Moses Maimonides, "Eight Chapters," translated by Raymond L. Weiss and Charles Butterworth, in *Ethical Writings of Maimonides*, edited by Raymond L. Weiss and Charles Butterworth (New York: Dover, 1983), 84–85.

27 "Eight Chapters," 85.

28 "Eight Chapters," 85.

repentance, to know *how* to return to the good path, the epistemic need is met by revelation and tradition, providing guidance for the effort of reorientation.

Like other Jewish philosophers, Maimonides maintained that in order to exhibit righteousness rather than mere conformity with what virtue requires, a motivating nexus of knowledge, devotion, gratitude, and humility is needed. To seek an understanding of the reasons for the commandments is itself one of the commandments, and that is a basic sense in which knowledge, an understanding of the good, is an aspect of virtuous motivation. Brittle legalism falls short of what the commandments require. Pursuing understanding of the reasons for the commandments is part of the project of more deeply and fully appreciating divine wisdom and benevolence.[29] In addition, acting rightly involves a focused commitment to do what God requires, out of devotion, and not just from fear of punishment. Perhaps, when one is not yet mature, fear of sanction plays a role in shaping the habits that establish well-ordered dispositions. But virtue in the full-fledged sense includes worshipful devotion, not simply fear of punishment. In addition, a person is to be constantly aware of the inexpressible difference, in knowledge, power, perfection, between God and oneself and to always be aware of one's dependence on God and God's graciousness. Finally, gratitude is significant, we might say, as a fundamental orientation to God.

The significance of gratitude is shared across the religious traditions. It is one of the ways theism makes a difference to philosophical anthropology and moral psychology. At the opening of *Metaphysics* Aristotle asserted: "All men by nature desire to know," which reflected his notion that intellectual activity is, or is a central element of, the *telos* of a human being.[30] The claim was not an empirical generalization about

---

29 The criticism of Judaism as emphasizing outward conduct and legalistic conformity at the cost of spiritual depth is long-standing and has appeared in every age. Kant repeated the charge in *Religion within the Limits of Reason Alone*, his version of it being a good example of the almost complete ignorance of Judaism reflected in the view.

30 Aristotle, *Metaphysics*, in *Basic Works of Aristotle*, translated by W. D. Ross (New York: Random House, 1941), bk. 1, chap. 1, 980a 21–27.

what we find every person always desiring and pursuing. It is chiefly a point about human nature and the role of intellectual activity in successfully realizing that nature. That human beings desire to know is indicated in more ways than just in the wonder that begins philosophy. It is also evidenced even by the delight we take in our senses. For thinkers in the religious traditions we might say that, to a large extent, *gratitude* replaced *wonder* as a fundamental human orientation to reality. And responsiveness to good is explicated as obedience to a divinely underwritten normative order. That responsiveness is central to moral activity and moral life. In their theism they regarded all good as ultimately coming from God, and they regarded virtuous activity as the imitation of God, activity through which good is realized and enjoyed. Gratitude as a fundamental orientation is reinforced by that enjoyment and thereby motivationally strengthens virtuous dispositions.

The aspiration to virtue, to holiness, to piety, to righteousness, to any of the things suggested as the proper end for a human being, is informed by gratitude. Jewish thinkers held that gratitude and humility are key elements of a human being's fundamental orientation to God. In human activity in general we are to be aware of God's greatness and aware of our debt to God. For instance, both Maimonides and Bahya ibn Pakuda argued that the more completely we perfect ourselves, the more we appreciate that we are to do what we do out of love of God. We find this nexus of gratitude, humility, and knowledge in Christian and Islamic thought as well. The more fully we understand God's wisdom and benevolence, the deeper our humility and the fuller our gratitude.

A vivid example in the Jewish tradition is Bahya ibn Pakuda's *Book of Direction to the Duties of the Heart*, a work that exerted considerable influence on Jewish thought and life. In that work Bahya emphasized the vital motivational importance of devotion to God, centrally including gratitude for the created order and for the commandments as a guide to perfection. The duties of the heart include a combination of gratitude, undistracted attention to God's benevolence and wisdom, and the search for enlarged understanding of the created order and of God. That combination is the core of proper motivation in all one does, not just in specific forms of worship. Like many of the medievals, Bahya held that motivation, when rightly ordered, involves attention to the good (and the source of good) and obedience as a mode of worshipful gratitude. Bahya writes of the obligation of obedience to God: "As this is a reasonable obligation of the beneficiary toward his benefactor, it is fitting to explain in the Introduction to this chapter the aspects of the various favors, and obligations of thankfulness, of men toward each other. Thence we shall ascend to our obligation of thanks and gratefulness to our Creator for His immense grace and abundant favor bestowed upon us."[31] One of the ways Judaism differs from Christianity is that Judaism does not involve the notion of fallenness in the sense so fundamental to Christianity. Jewish thinkers offered diverse interpretations of the Garden of Eden story in *Genesis,* and they typically involved the notion of human beings erring, becoming distracted from the true and the good, and setting humanity on a course involving the hardships catalogued in the story as the fallout of that distraction. This is not the place to consider the various interpretations given by important Jewish thinkers. Suffice it to say that they emphasized the ways in which pride and preoccupation with the urgency of one or another desire is corrupting, but not in quite the sense of fallenness. They emphasized the importance of profound humility but without connecting that with a notion of a fundamentally wounded, depraved nature, which can only be restored to integrity by external, supernatural salvific agency. Thus, the Garden was important to Jewish philosophers' conception of morality, even though they did not interpret the sins of Adam and Eve as the anthropological catastrophe it constitutes for Christianity. Jewish philosophers regarded the giving of Torah (the Law, the commandments constituting the Jews to be a

---

31 Bahya ibn Pakuda, *The Book of Direction to the Duties of the Heart*, translated by Menahem Mansoor (Oxford: Littman Library of Jewish Civilization, 2004), 176.

people in covenant with God) as an act of divine graciousness aiding the perfection of human beings. There is grace in Judaism, but its concern is not the Christian notion of the Fall's profound damage to human nature.

That point merits mention here because Jewish thinkers held that gratitude for the Law (and for the created order overall) combined with humility before God and obedience to the commandments are crucial to virtuously motivated activity. Appreciating the commandments as a gracious gift of divine wisdom and benevolence, as well as the humility appropriate to our finite stature and powers in contrast with God, are aspects of righteousness and of virtuous motivation. Nor is this a matter of this character of motivation being important only in some specific department of life. The commandments (and the elaboration of them, the extension of them to new sorts of circumstances, the interpretation of them, and so forth) concern all spheres and contexts of life, from worship and ritual to charity, contracts, agriculture, marriage, sexual practice, forgiveness, and so on. The Law is a discipline of perfection for all aspects of life, and there is no clean break between religious obligations and righteous living in general. A person is to strive to impart holiness to life activity overall.

In the work of some influential Jewish philosophers, such as Bahya and also Maimonides, there is emphasis on a combination of submission, the striving for knowledge, and gratitude. And "submission by way of the mind's arousal can only be purely for the sake of God, unmixed with hypocrisy, with no intention of self-adornment, for it is not based on fear or desire, but rather on knowledge and understanding of the obedience due to God from His creatures."[32] Moreover, the more a person "understands and discriminates of God's graces done to him, of His omnipotence and sovereignty, the more submissive and humble he grows before Him."[33]

---

32 Bahya, *The Book of Direction to the Duties of the Heart*, 183.
33 Bahya, *The Book of Direction to the Duties of the Heart*, 184.

Through correct understanding of the good, the grounds for gratitude are evident; the grounds are infinite (given God's inexpressible
perfection), and gratitude can figure pervasively in a human being's
conception of rightly motivated action. When we love the good on the
basis of a sound understanding of it, that understanding will involve
gratitude.

The person who pursues merely apparent goods or who leads a life
of sensual indulgence either neglects gratitude or misplaces it. It is
likely that gratitude has no place in the motivation of the vicious agent,
and in that person it may be replaced by envy or resentment. Humility
and devotion are displaced by pride. A virtuous agent's motivational
pattern exhibits a disposition of gratitude, and a vicious agent's pattern
lacks such a disposition. Selfishness, intemperate indulgence, callous
disregard of others, and all manner of other vices reflect the absence of
the kind of gratitude basic to one's relation with God. That absence is
shown in the lack of concern for the created order, including other persons. The more fully virtue is realized and the more an agent exhibits
concern for genuine good, the more fully gratitude is a feature of the
individual's overall agential disposition. In addition, it is through possession of intellect and will that we participate in the good. This Platonic notion is nearly pervasive in medieval philosophy.

Through reflection on our dependence, our finiteness, our need for
guidance, our susceptibility to error, our ignorance, corruption, and
susceptibility to distraction, we can come to the knowledge that all
that is good in us is owed to God. Thus, gratitude has an important
relation to humility. In fact, it may be that the more wisdom we have,
the better able we are to recognize that we are to be humble before
God's graciousness and power. Saadia wrote: "Humility, to go further,
is more highly rated when displayed by the great, as Scripture says:
Now the man Moses was very meek, above all men. (Num. 12:3)"[34] This

---

34 Saadia Gaon, *The Book of Beliefs and Opinions*, trans. Samuel Rosenblatt (New Haven, CT: Yale
University Press, 1976), 230.

view is quite different from the moral psychology in much ancient Greek thought, with some of the most influential of it maintaining that the more excellent the agent, the more pride is merited. The contrast with Aristotle's conception of the virtuous agent's appropriate pride is striking. Maimonides endorsed Aristotle's conception of virtue as lying in the mean, *except* with regard to anger and pride. In those cases, the extreme of minimization is urged, anger and pride being ways of being distracted from the good, corrupting judgment. Maimonides acknowledges that there are times when *feigning* anger might be appropriate, as, for example, in the moral education of children. But the virtuous agent *feels* anger as little as possible.[35]

Aristotle counseled self-awareness so that we would not be oblivious to the desires and passions by which we are moved. That awareness is helpful to us in finding the mean relative to each of us. Theistic thinkers enjoined rigorous self-examination so that we would see our stature from the correct perspective, which of course involves the contrast with God. The Jewish insistence on humility is not because Judaism regards human nature as wretched or human beings as incapable of any significant excellence. Human beings are capable of imitating God, but the more clearly the imitation is understood, including the difference between us and God, the more humble the self becomes.

The issue of "the reasons for the commandments" was centrally important to Jewish thinkers. (In this context, "commandments" refers to all of the commandments in Torah, not just the Decalogue. Tradition holds that the total number of commandments is 613; of which 248 are positive injunctions, and 365 are prohibitions.) The more rationalistically disposed thinkers held that there are reasons for all the commandments. As noted, they are not simply tests of obedience. However,

---

35 See Maimonides, "Laws Concerning Character Traits," translated by Raymond L. Weiss, in *Ethical Writings of Maimonides*, chap. 2. I discuss this issue and Maimonides's conception of the virtues in some detail in *Law, Reason, and Morality in Medieval Jewish Philosophy*, esp. chaps. 2 and 3, and in "Aristotle and Maimonides on Virtue and Natural Law," *Hebraic Political Studies* 2:1 (Spring 2007): 46–77.

human beings are not able to ascertain the reasons fully, and the reasons for many may remain uncertain, at least in detail. Still, human beings are obligated to strive to enlarge and deepen their understanding of the created order and of God, as a way of striving to understand the reasons for the commandments. The justifications of some of the commandments may be easily accessible to reason. In many other cases they are not as evident, but they can, with effort, be discerned. Many Jewish thinkers held that in no cases are the commandments arbitrary tests of obedience; they are all reflective of divine wisdom. This rationalism and the intellectualist perfectionism that sometimes accompanied it is evident in thinkers such as Bahya and Maimonides. (Saadia made a case for the rationality of many of the commandments, but he was not as explicit in regard to an intellectualist anthropology.) Many Jewish philosophers regarded knowledge as important to motivation because of how understanding can reinforce devotion and gratitude.

Some Jewish and Christian philosophers regarded gratitude to God as a rationally evident requirement. In fact, that we owe obedience and gratitude to God is the fundamental principle of Scotus's natural law theory. That can help us to understand why medieval philosophers tended not to regard moral motivation as a topic distinct from basic principles concerning the proper end for a human being and the character of the activity through which it is realized. A sort of governing conception of what is required of human beings at the most basic and most general level shaped medieval conceptions of motivation. For Saadia, it was very clear that gratitude and devotional obedience are requirements of reason. In summing up his view of those commandments whose justifications are evident to reason, Saadia wrote: "If, now, we were to combine these four classes of requirements, their sumtotal would make up all the laws prescribed for us by our Lord. For example, He made it obligatory upon us to learn to know Him, to worship Him, and to dedicate ourselves wholeheartedly to Him."[36] As

---

36 Saadia Gaon, *The Book of Beliefs and Opinions*, 139.

I have mentioned, Bahya's *Book of Direction to the Duties of the Heart* is a philosophically sophisticated, psychologically detailed study of motivation, emphasizing the combination of intellect and gratitude in obedience to the Law. Those who fulfill the requirements of the Law in the right spirit include "people who believe in the Law and take upon themselves reward and punishment both in this world and the next. These have risen from their ignorance and opened their hearts to see their obligations to God for all the favors and graces He has showered upon them. They consider neither reward nor punishment, but hasten rather to obey the Lord their God as an expression of the glory and honor He deserves, out of love and devotion to Him, for they know and understand Him."[37] Gratitude, humility, and devotion focus the will so that it is not distracted by lesser or merely apparent goods. Though the will has a *telos*, it is also free, and that is the basis for just reward and punishment for human actions.

Anselm held that "Although the free will of men differs from the free will of God and the angels, the definition of freedom expressed by the word ought to be the same"; that is, "the capacity for preserving rectitude of the will for the sake of rectitude itself."[38] Moreover, "these two are necessary for justice in the will, namely, to will what it ought and for the reason it ought to."[39] Many thinkers in each of the religious traditions held that morally sound motivation expresses human freedom but also gratitude and devotion to God as the source of good in the created order.

3

Many Christian thinkers held that there are two basic inclinations or affections in human nature: for happiness or for the self, and for

<hr>

37   Bahya ibn Pakuda, *The Book of Direction to the Duties of the Heart*, 198.
38   Anselm, "On Free Will," 176, 179.
39   Anselm, "On Truth," 168.

rectitude or for God. This is clear in Augustine, Anselm, and Scotus. In addition, because free will was thought to be a condition of moral accountability, we are accountable for whether we are moved by the former inclination or the latter.

Aquinas occupies an important place between Augustinian/Anselmian Platonism and Scotus, who, as I will show, rejects some of the Aristotelian elements of Aquinas's thought. Aquinas holds that both intellect and will are involved in choice and that the contingency of human actions and the defeasibility of practical reasoning are crucial to understanding free will. In addition, the Christian emphasis on moral accountability is no less evident in Aquinas's thought than in Augustine's or Anselm's.

In Aquinas's view we are responsible for our choices, but the will is oriented to an end, to the good, and is not a fully autonomous power of choice. We can choose well or rightly, by choosing that which we understand (correctly) to be good; or we can choose inferior or merely apparent goods. Choosing is thickly connected with practical reasoning and the intellect. The will responds to what the intellect presents to it, and choosing is a matter of appetition issuing from practical reasoning. The will is an inclination to do that for which the intellect has presented reasons for acting in a specific way. "It should be said that reason presents the good to the will as its object, and insofar as it falls under the order of reason, it pertains to the moral order and causes moral goodness in the act of the will. For reason is the principle of human and moral acts, as has been said."[40]

Intellect and will operate together in a human action. "The rectitude of reason with regard to things which are for the sake of ends consists in conformity of the desire for the obligatory end. But the very desire for the obligatory end presupposes a right grasp of the end, which is by reason."[41] And: "It should be said that the will in a certain

---

40 Thomas Aquinas, *Summa Theologiae*, q. 19, art. 1, ad. 3.
41 Aquinas, *Summa Theologiae*, q. 19, art. 3, ad. 2.

manner moves reason and reason in another manner moves the will, namely on the part of the object, as was said above."

Aquinas did not consider the general tendency toward the good as freely chosen; its orientation is grounded in our nature as humans.[42] However, he argued that it "is a heretical opinion" that the will is moved necessarily, "for it takes away the very notion of merit and demerit from human acts."[43] "It should be said that because good is the object of the will, the will can only will under the formality of the good, but because many and diverse things are contained under the formality of the good, it cannot happen that the will is necessarily moved to this or that."[44] And the good in general is that "which the will naturally tends to as any power does to its object."[45] The will is free, and volition is not necessitated by the will's general ordering to the good.

Aquinas held that "since actions are singular and are not equal to a universal power, the inclination of the will is indeterminately related to many. Just as when the artisan conceives the general form of house, under which are included different shapes of house, his will can be inclined to make a square house or a round one or one of another shape."[46] Moreover, the will is not necessarily moved by passion; it "can be moved to a particular good without the passion of sense desire. For we will and do many things by choice alone, without passion, as is evident most of all in those instances wherein reason resists passion."[47]

Scotus developed a different conception of the freedom of the will and the motivation of action. He did not eliminate or diminish the role of responsiveness in the explanation of motivation and action, but he attributed to will a power of agency independent of the intellect.

---

42 Aquinas, *Summa Theologiae*, Ia, 83, 1 ad 5.

43 Aquinas, *Summa Theologiae*, q. 6, Response.

44 Thomas Aquinas, *Disputed Questions on Evil*, q. 6, ad. 6; translated by John and Jean Oesterle (Notre Dame, IN: University of Notre Dame Press, 1995).

45 Aquinas, *Disputed Questions on Evil*, q. 10, art. 1.

46 Aquinas, *Disputed Questions on Evil*, q. 10, art. 1.

47 Aquinas, *Disputed Questions on Evil*, q. 10, art. 3, Reply to 3.

An important role for the intellect in regard to action remained. After all, the object of action had to be supplied. In this view the intellect offers information to the will but does not inform it in a broadly Aristotelian manner. In Scotus's theory the will and intellect did not have the integral complementarity found in Aquinas's view. Scotus preserved the notion of there being two fundamental affections or inclinations in human beings, the affection for happiness and the affection for justice. But he regarded the will as having independent agency, a kind of libertarianism congenial to some early modern and modern philosophers for whom natural necessity is contrasted with free will in a manner differing from the Thomistic conception.

Scotus held that the difference between the affection for happiness (or advantage) and the affection for justice (or rectitude) is that the former is an inclination of self-love and the latter is love of God. (Augustinian resonances are still detectable in this.) The Scotist view is that the will does not necessarily pursue happiness. We can be motivated in another way. "Scotus does not simply argue that a virtuous person must have a motive distinct from the desire for happiness, but also insists that virtue requires the absence of any motive that directs one's choice to oneself."[48] The right ordering of one's will is to love God. Love of self can be limited, and we are able to act out of love of God for its own sake, independent of whether so acting partly constitutes *eudaimonia*. Acting with a view to the latter is not a requirement on acting rationally. This is a sharper contrast between self-love and morality than we find in most of Scotus's predecessors. They were as concerned that a person should be rightly motivated for its own sake but they tended to see that as more directly connected with *eudaimonia*. Scotus detached acting for the sake of the just from acting for the sake of *eudaimonia*, departing from the Aristotelian view that in choosing and doing what is fine or noble for its own sake, the agent

---

48 Terence Irwin, "Scotus and the Possibility of Moral Motivation," in *Morality and Self-Interest*, edited by Paul Bloomfield (New York: Oxford University Press, 2008), 164.

enjoys *eudaimonia*. For Scotus, the affection for justice is independent of the affection for advantage.

If we could not act except with a view toward happiness, we would not be blameworthy for pursuing it even if we did so unjustly. Our ability to be motivated to do what justice requires, despite it being to the detriment of (earthly) happiness or advantage, is evidence of our being able to be motivated to will something other than our own advantage. Irwin writes of Scotus's view: "The argument depends on the claim that some choices are or are not 'directed to oneself' (ordinatum ad se). If Scotus is right, eudaemonism is incompatible with admitted facts about the virtuous person's rational choices.... The eudaemonist position is mistaken because it fails to make room for the non-self referential character of the choices required by morality."[49] It would be incorrect to conclude that Scotus eliminated teleology from his conceptions of rational action and morality. Like Aquinas, he held that in the well-ordered rational activity of a human being the agent aims at a perfective end and that the agent is perfected. The perfective object, toward which we are to move ourselves as close as possible, is God; and in so acting we perfect ourselves. He departed from Aquinas in denying that *eudaimonia* is the *telos* of well-ordered rational activity. Scotus took over an Anselmian notion of moral responsibility (one that had the putative merit of illuminating fallenness) and radicalized it, in a sense, taking it to be the basis of a notion of the sovereignty of volition. The moral worthiness of an action depends on how it is motivated, a matter determined by the will itself.

For Aquinas, intellect and will operate in an integrated manner in a person choosing and acting. In the Scotist view the will receives guidance from the intellect, but the will's act is entirely its own and is not determined by anything exterior to it.

Human beings have certain ends by nature, but the will is a capacity for unconditioned choice, with a proper, but not intrinsically determining,

---

49 Irwin, "Scotus and the Possibility of Moral Motivation," 164.

end (love of God). Freedom of the will is such that the will is not normatively governed by principles it recognizes as grounded in nature.

Contrasting Aquinas and Scotus, David Burrell writes: "What Aquinas has added to Aristotle is the immediate relation to a creator who not only inscribes the tendency [to the comprehensive good] in all rational creatures but activates it as well. That allows him to 'explain' our self-determination in a way which relies not on autonomy but on tendencies built into created natures and also identifies the initiator of willing with the free originator of all that is."[50] This passage nicely captures the notion of responsiveness, which I have highlighted as a feature of medieval thought. The Scotist conception attributes to the will independence from an inbuilt finality without denying that there is a proper end for the will. "Scotus gives manifest priority to will as an unmoved (or 'autonomous') mover."[51] That revised conception of volition, changed from rational appetite to an autonomous power of choice, went on to influence a great deal of early modern and modern moral theorizing.[52]

4

One of the chief differences between medieval philosophy concerning moral motivation and a great deal of contemporary philosophy is the contrast between the medievals' notion that human activity overall is to be understood as a response to a normatively authoritative reality. Even thinkers such as Scotus, who developed a conception of the autonomy of the will sharing important features with much later views, such as Kant's (or even Thomas Reid's, on some interpretations), held that motives and actions are to be evaluated on the basis of a conception of

---

50 David Burrell, *Freedom and Creation in Three Traditions* (Notre Dame, IN: University of Notre Dame Press, 1993), 90.

51 Burrell, *Freedom and Creation in Three Traditions*, 93.

52 On Scotus's possible influence on Thomas Reid see Alexander Broadie, "The Scotist Thomas Reid," *American Catholic Philosophical Quarterly* 74:3 (2000): 385–407.

rightness or rectitude, which is not itself "domesticated" to human volition, and not constructed by it. The medievals generally distinguished between motives exhibiting righteousness, piety, or well-ordered love and those exhibiting engagement to lesser goods or selfish distraction from true good.[53] Versions of the contrast are found in Jewish, Christian, and Islamic philosophy, and they are found in different periods of the Middle Ages.

However, there are some important affinities between medieval and contemporary thought concerning moral motivation. The notion that consent to an action-guiding consideration or that a related notion of endorsement is a key role of the will has figured prominently in recent philosophy. It is an important element of some influential compatibilist conceptions.[54] Moreover, as in Gary Watson's critique of Frankfurt, the notion of there being two fundamental sources of motivation (Watson refers to wanting and valuing, a pair not so different from the medievals' reason and desire) has shaped some important recent work on freedom of the will and moral motivation.[55] It is fair to say that while many of the presuppositions most important to the medievals are no longer widely shared by philosophers, some of the main conceptual architecture designed by the medievals continues to structure some of the most important philosophical debates. There are some contemporary nontheistic conceptions of persons as most free when acting on the basis of a correct conception of the good. However, those nontheistic views do not involve the central role for gratitude and devotion that is so pronounced in medieval thought and that makes for a significant difference in moral psychology. There is no question that medieval theorizing about moral motivation involved subtle,

---

53 Susan Wolf argues that we are most free and responsible when we are able to act on a correct conception of the true and the good. See her *Freedom within Reason* (New York: Oxford University Press), 1990.

54 An especially influential example is Harry Frankfurt, "Freedom of the Will and the Concept of a Person," *Journal of Philosophy* 68:1 (January 1971): 5–20.

55 Gary Watson, "Free Agency," *Journal of Philosophy* 72:8 (April 1975): 205–220.

sophisticated conceptions that are significant and illuminating in their own right as well as constituting a rich and important period of the history of philosophy.

Acknowledgment

A Fellowship Research Grant from the Earhart Foundation made it possible for me to spend time in London, Cambridge, and St. Andrews during the summer of 2013. I was able to meet with colleagues and have access to resources that were very helpful to the progress of this essay and several other projects. I am very grateful to the Foundation for this support and their support in the past.

CHAPTER FIVE

Act and Moral Motivation in Spinoza's *Ethics*

Steven Nadler

In his philosophical masterpiece, the *Ethics*, Spinoza has much to say about virtue, good, desire, action, and happiness, all standard topics in moral philosophy. He is also committed to a thoroughgoing egoism when it comes to motivation. All human activity—indeed, every activity of every individual in nature—derives from a striving to preserve one's being and maximize one's power of acting. While Spinoza eschews moral evaluation of action in terms of "right" and "wrong," he nonetheless believes that there are normative ways of assessing actions, according to the degree to which they do in fact contribute to an agent's egoistic striving. It would seem to follow, then, that an agent's motives do not play any role in the moral assessment of the action (although they are important for an assessment of the agent himself/herself), primarily because all agents, without exception, have one and the same basic motive—self-interest—and an action, regardless of motive, either does or does not contribute to an increase in the agent's power.

However, as is usually the case with *res Spinozana*, things are much more complicated than they may initially seem. Spinoza does, in fact, allow that one and the same action deserves a different moral evaluation depending on the motivation (which, for Spinoza, amounts to the causal factors in the mind) behind its performance. In this essay, after a general overview of some fundamental elements of Spinoza's moral philosophy, I examine just how, despite the universal egoism, there is room in Spinoza's ethics both for a normative discrimination among motives and for taking motives into account when morally assessing actions that follow from them.

1. Egoism

In Part 3 of the *Ethics*, after having explained the metaphysical and epistemological foundations of human nature, Spinoza turns his attention to what he calls, alternately, "the power of acting" (*potentia agendi*) or "force of existing" (*vis existendi*). Every individual thing in nature—every finite mode of the one eternal, necessarily existing, infinite substance—is a partial and limited expression of one and the same infinite power of God or Nature. This infinite power of Nature manifests itself as individual minds within the attribute of Thought and as individual bodies within the attribute of Extension (the only two of the infinite attributes of God or Nature of which we have knowledge). Every individual mind is a finite expression of God or Nature's infinite power through thinking; likewise, every particular body is a finite expression of God or Nature's infinite power in matter and motion. This finite quantum of power that constitutes each individual thing is what Spinoza calls *conatus*, which can be variously translated as "striving," "tendency," or "endeavor."

In any particular thing, this finite determination of power manifests itself as a striving to persevere as that individual.

IIIp6: Each thing, as far as it can by its own power, strives to persevere in its being.

Dem.: For singular things are modes by which God's attributes are expressed in a certain and determinate way (by Ip25c), i.e. (by Ip34), things that express, in a certain and determinate way, God's power, by which God is and acts. And no thing has anything in itself by which it can be destroyed, or which takes its existence away (by IIIp4). On the contrary, it is opposed to everything which can take its existence away (by IIIp5). Therefore, as far as it can, and it lies in itself, it strives to persevere in its being.[1]

There is in all things—bodies and minds—a kind of existential inertia by which they resist any attempts to destroy them or change them for the worse. It is not a temporary or accidental feature of the thing, something that the thing can be without; nor does it manifest itself only in the presence of an opposing force. Rather, it is a positive and constant striving in an individual to maintain and even increase its power, one that involves "an indefinite duration" and goes right to the heart of the thing's individuation (IIIp8). It provides a real metaphysical basis for distinguishing one thing from another, insofar as these parcels of power are distinct from each other (IIIp57d) and often strive against each other. Indeed, Spinoza insists, this *conatus* constitutes "the actual essence" of anything (IIIp7).[2] It is, he suggests elsewhere, nothing different from the thing itself.[3] It also explains a good many of the dynamic features of the world. It accounts for why stones are hard to break, why a body at rest or in motion will remain at rest or in motion unless it encounters an outside force, why the human body

---

1 References to the *Ethics* are by the standard notation of part (Roman numeral), definition (Def.), proposition (p), demonstration (dem.), scholium (s), and corollary (c). The abbreviation *G* refers to *Spinoza Opera,* 5 vols., edited by Carl Gebhardt (Heidelberg: Carl Winters Universitaetsbuchandlung, 1925); the abbreviation *C* refers to *The Collected Works of Spinoza,* vol. 1, translated by Edwin Curley (Princeton, NJ: Princeton University Press, 1984); all translations are by Curley, unless noted otherwise.

2 Within the "physical digression" of pt. 2, Spinoza had argued that the essence of any particular body consisted in a specific ratio of the communication of motion and rest among its parts (G 2:99–100/ C 1:460). Now he says that it consists in a "striving to persevere." The inconsistency here may be only apparent, since one can say that the essence of any body consists in its striving to maintain that ratio of motion and rest.

3 See "Metaphysical Thoughts," G 1:248/C 1:314.

fights disease, and why we desire many of the things we do.[4] The doctrine is much like what the ancient Stoics proclaimed, at least as this is reported by Cicero: "Immediately upon birth...a living creature feels an attachment for itself, and an impulse to preserve itself and to feel affection for its own constitution and for those things which tend to preserve that constitution; while on the other hand it conceives an antipathy to destruction and to those things which appear to threaten destruction."[5] In addition to its role in providing a foundation for force in what is otherwise a Cartesian physics, the metaphysical notion of *conatus* also lies at the heart of Spinoza's moral psychology.

Spinoza defines the affects generally as changes in *conatus*, as transitions from a greater to a lesser power of striving or vice versa. The passive affects, or passions, are those transitions in an individual's power that are caused by external things; joy (*laetitia*), for example, is a transition to a greater power of acting brought about by an external object, while sadness (*tristitia*) is an externally caused transition to a lesser power of acting. Such changes in power form the motivational basis for the things that agents do. Their pursuits and avoidances of things, their choices of action and judgments about what is good and bad, are all moved by joy and sadness, love and hate, and pleasure and pain, by the modifications in the striving to persevere in existence. We pursue the things we do because we love them, and we love them because we are conscious of the way they bring about an increase in our capacities. Similarly, we avoid the things we do because we hate them, and we hate them because we are conscious of the way they bring about a diminution in our capacities. "We strive to further the occurrence of whatever we imagine will lead to joy, and to avert or destroy what we imagine is contrary to it, or will lead to sadness" (IIIp28). (While all individuals in nature undergo affects or changes in their *conatus*, Spinoza, in his

---

4 The doctrine also amounts to a rejection by Spinoza of a central element of Cartesian physics: that a body is nothing but extension and therefore completely passive, without any dynamic powers. For Spinoza, bodies, through their conatus, appear to have an innate principle of activity.

5 *De finibus* 3.5.

discussion of the passions and their motivational role, confines himself mainly to the manifestations of *conatus* or striving in human beings. And within the human being, his focus is on mental phenomena, although each mental expression will (because of the mind-body parallelism) necessarily have its bodily correlate.)

To be more specific: in the human mind, an individual's *conatus* manifests itself as "will"—not an abstract faculty of willing but the particular mental affirmations or negations that make up much of our thinking life. When the human being is considered as a composite entity constituted by a mind and a body, its *conatus* consists in "appetite." When a person is conscious of the striving of his mind and body together, when he is aware of an appetite, it becomes "desire" (IIIp9s). In both cases, the mind and the mind-body composite, *conatus* as desire is the motivational force that lies at the root of all a person's endeavors.[6] We always and necessarily desire and strive after those things that we believe promote our well-being and the well-being of the body on which our existence depends. Motivation in a broad sense consists in the combination of belief and desire. My desire for *x*, which moves me to pursue *x*—and for Spinoza desire, as the expression of *conatus*, is the *only* motivating force—is determined and guided by my belief that *x* will bring me joy, an increase in my power. I intend to do *x* because I necessarily desire to do what is in my own best interest, and I believe that *x* is in my own best interest.[7]

---

6 In the human body, *conatus* presumably manifests itself as the body's physical resistance to any attempt to change the ratio of motion and rest among its parts to the point of dissolution.

7 I am thus attributing to Spinoza a belief/desire model of motivation; for a general discussion of this model, see Steven Sverdlik, *Motive and Rightness* (Oxford: Oxford University Press, 2011), chap. 2. In distinguishing between belief and desire here I deliberately distort Spinoza's view for the sake of simplicity of explanation (and to avoid presenting Spinoza's psychology of ideas). Strictly speaking, belief (whether an idea of reason or an idea derived from sense experience or imagination) is, as a mental event, identical with desire. In "Spinoza's Ethical Theory," in *The Cambridge Companion to Spinoza*, edited by Don Garrett (Cambridge: Cambridge University Press 1996), 296, Garrett makes this point well: "If, for example, one determines by reason that one's own advantage lies in the pursuit of knowledge…then the idea that constitutes this understanding will itself be a desire for the thing so conceived, in Spinoza's view. It will not merely direct or stimulate such a desire; it will *be* such a desire." Reason can motivate action for Spinoza, insofar as to believe that *x* is good (to have an idea that represents *x* as conducive to one's well-being) is to desire *x*.

In Spinoza's view, then, human beings are thoroughly egoistic agents. A person is moved to pursue or avoid this or that solely by the positive or negative effects that a thing is perceived to have on his condition, on his beliefs regarding the contributions that that thing makes to his project of self-preservation. The striving for perseverance is paramount. It constitutes "the very essence of man, from whose nature there necessarily follow those things that promote his preservation." Thus, he says, "man is determined to do those things [that promote his preservation]" (IIIp9s). Spinoza's egoism is similar to (and was likely influenced by) that of Thomas Hobbes, whose works Spinoza read in the 1660s while composing the *Ethics* and who claimed in his *Leviathan* that "of the voluntary acts of every man the object is some good to himself."[8]

So far, however, Spinoza offers us only a psychological egoism: every agent always and necessarily does that which he believes to be in his own best interest, which he thinks would best lead to joy or an increase in his power of acting (and correlatively, every agent always and necessarily avoids that which he believes to be counter to his own best interest, which he thinks would likely lead to a decrease in his power of acting).[9] Things get more interesting, from an ethical point of view, when we turn to Spinoza's definition of moral terms such as "good" and "virtue."

---

8 *Leviathan* 14.8. For a comparison of Spinoza and Hobbes on this question, see Edwin Curley, *Behind the Geometric Method* (Princeton, NJ: Princeton University Press, 1988), chap. 3. For Hobbes discussion of the passions generally (which is strikingly similar in important respects to Spinoza's analysis), see *Leviathan* 6.

9 It seems that, for Spinoza, a proper description of the content of my motivational beliefs should not be "doing this action or pursuing this thing will bring an increase in my power or contribute to my preservation"—especially since, empirically speaking, this just seems highly implausible. Rather, he can be read as saying that I am moved to do those things that I associate with joy and avoid those things that I associate with sadness; this is much more plausible than saying that I am moved by the desire to persevere. I am moved to be generous to my children and contribute to my friends' welfare because in my mind such things are associated with joy. Since joy just *is* the increase in my power of persevering, it can stand in as the conscious manifestation of what, at a base metaphysical level, is the urge to persevere and increase one's power. Perhaps this means, as Michael LeBuffe has argued in *From Bondage to Freedom: Spinoza on Human Excellence* (Oxford: Oxford University Press, 2010), that "hedonism" is a better term than "egoism" for Spinoza's account of motivation.

2. GOOD

Spinoza begins Part 4 of the *Ethics* with a preface in which he considers some basic ethical language: good and evil, perfect and imperfect. He insists that such terms do not refer to absolute and objective features of things, properties that they have independently of anything else (especially human agents). It follows from Spinoza's naturalism that nothing is, taken by itself and without relation to something, good or evil or perfect or imperfect, least of all when these words are understood in the normative sense. Whatever *is* just *is*, period. To put it another way, everything that exists is, if considered on its own, perfect to some degree, where "perfection" is an ontological term to be understood simply as reality, or as the power to persevere in existence. There is no evaluative element involved in saying that something has perfection in this descriptive sense. "[Things] are all equal in this regard," Spinoza says at the end of the preface; this does not imply that every thing has the *same* degree of reality/power but simply that every thing *is* simply some positive degree of reality/power.

What "good" and "evil" (and "perfect" and "imperfect") in the normative sense do refer to, if not objective, mind-independent features of the world, is an evaluative measure of the degree to which a thing corresponds to some stipulated standard or model. The most obvious case in which this is so is the evaluation of an artifact. A building, for example, is deemed more or less perfect depending on the extent to which it matches the architect's original conception, which serves as a standard to which the finished product is compared. "If someone has decided to make something, and has finished it, then he will call his thing perfect—and so will anyone who rightly knows, or thinks he knows, the mind and purpose of the author of the work." By contrast, if one has no idea of what the artificer intended to create, one will have no way of assessing how "perfect" the artifact is. Without such a model to compare the product to, the term is meaningless.

This evaluative practice gets extended to natural objects when human beings form universal ideas of kinds of things in nature. For example, from experience we conceive some ideal model of what a horse is, or a tree. We then call some particular horse or tree "perfect" or "imperfect" depending on how well it matches with that randomly created and arbitrarily adopted model. "When they see something happen in nature which does not agree with the model they have conceived of this kind of thing, they believe that Nature itself has failed or sinned, and left the thing imperfect." (What gives sustenance to this extension of normative terms from the world of artifacts to the world of nature is the human tendency to see teleology in nature, which in turn results from the traditional anthropomorphic conception of a God who acts with purposes. Things thus become "perfect" or "imperfect" to the extent that they succeed or fail in achieving the end for which God supposedly created them. But Spinoza's God, of course, does not act to achieve any ends. "Nature does nothing on account of an end," Spinoza reminds the reader in the preface to Part 4. "That eternal and infinite being we call God, or Nature, acts from the same necessity from which he exists.")

The same analysis applies to the terms "good" and "evil." These evaluative labels are, likewise, always to be understood in the context of a thing's relationship to a standard or model. Something is "good" if it is an effective means to an end. More particularly, since every individual in nature is naturally and necessarily striving to maximize its power, something is "good" if it promotes what appears to that individual (or to some observer thinking on its behalf) to be its well-being and helps move it closer to a stipulated ideal condition; and something is "evil" or "bad" if it is detrimental to what is perceived to be an individual's power and well-being. The result is that "good" and "evil," like "perfect" and "imperfect," are totally relative terms (relative, that is, to the conception of some individual's interest), and—limiting ourselves now to the case of human beings—in many cases what is good for one person may not be good for another person. "As far as good and evil are concerned, they also indicate nothing positive in things, considered in themselves, nor are they anything other than modes of thinking, or notions we form because we compare things to one another. For one and the same thing can, at the same time, be good and bad, and also indifferent. For example, music is good for one who is melancholy, bad for one who is mourning, and neither good nor bad to one who is deaf" (Part 4, preface, G 2:208/C 1:545). It may seem as if Spinoza here goes beyond an analysis of "good" and "evil" that he offered earlier in the work. In Part 3, he says that one judges that something is good because one desires it (and one desires it because it brings about an increase in one's power of acting): "We neither strive for, nor will, neither want, nor desire anything because we judge it to be good; on the contrary, we judge something to be good because we strive for it, will it, want it, and desire it" (IIIp9s). Thus, the claim that "x is good" must mean "I desire x." Such judgments would therefore seem to be not only relativized, but subjectivized.

In the preface to Part 4, however, while "good" and "evil" are still relativized, it now appears to be an objective matter of fact whether or not an individual matches up with some ideal model or whether or not some thing or action is conducive to what is taken to be some individual's interest. On the other hand the standards or models themselves that are ordinarily used for determining how perfect an individual is or whether some thing is "good" for an individual seem to remain highly subjective. One person's conception of what constitutes an ideal tree or an ideal human being will differ from another person's conception, given the differences in their experiences and thus differences in the particulars from which each abstracts his general notion, as well as in the features he focuses on in creating that notion. For this reason it is appropriate to refer to what is "perceived to be" or "appears to be" in someone's interest, and it will be the case that something will be "good" if, given what I believe about an ideal life and an individual's interests, I believe it to be good (as a means to that ideal). But there is no guarantee that my beliefs about these things are true, or even that they will be shared by others. Indeed, the framing of standards and models is strongly dependent on an individual's very particular desires, and thus so will be judgments about what is good and perfect.[10]

If this was all Spinoza had to say about "good" and "evil," then he would indeed be left with a subjectivist analysis of those important moral terms. However, he notes that while "good" and "evil" do not refer to real features of the world, nevertheless "we must retain these words," but without giving up their relativist meaning. This is because Spinoza thinks they can, while remaining context-relative, also bear a more objectivist burden. He believes that there is, in fact, a specific ideal that can serve as an objective standard according to which things can be judged as truly "good" for a human being. There is a particular kind of person and life that represents, objectively, a perfection of human nature.

Because we desire to form an idea of man, as a model of human nature which we may look to, it will be useful to us to retain these same words with the meaning I have indicated. In what follows, therefore, I shall understand by good what we know certainly is a means by which we may approach nearer and nearer to the model of human nature that we set before ourselves. By evil, what we certainly know prevents us from becoming like that model. Next, we shall say that men are more perfect or imperfect, insofar as they approach more or less near to this model. (Part 4, Preface, G 2:208/C 1:545)

This does not mean that "good" and "evil" are not relative terms. It is still the case that nothing, taken in and of itself and without comparison

---

10 See Jonathan Bennett, *A Study of Spinoza's "Ethics"* (Indianapolis: Hackett, 1984), 292: "The thesis that our value judgments are based on models is not in conflict with the earlier thesis that they are guided by our feelings and desires. Rather, the two are aspects of a single unified account, the unifying factor being the view that our feelings and desires guide our value judgments *by* guiding our selection of models."

with or utility for some standard or model, is good or evil. However, the subjectivism that was introduced with the Part 3 account of good and evil, and was carried through in the preface to Part 4, where "good" and "evil" are relativized to only haphazardly formed conceptions to serve as models for various kinds of things (including human beings), is now replaced by a more objective model. "Good" no longer means simply what one desires. Nor does it mean only "useful for making something approach what one may happen to believe to be a perfected specimen of its kind." Rather, it now means: useful for making a human being closer to what is truly a more perfected specimen of humanity.[11] What that more perfected specimen of humanity consists in is an individual of maximal power of persevering as a human being, or maximal human activity. Something is "good" if it truly contributes to an increase in an individual's *conatus*, that is, if it is the object of desire of someone who not only has beliefs about what is in his interest but true knowledge of what will actually augment his power or striving.

Spinoza thus defines "good" in Part 4 as "what we certainly know to be useful to us" (IVDef1) and "evil" as "what we certainly know prevents us from being masters of some good" (IVDef2). It is also what he has in mind when, as of IVp14, he begins speaking of "the true knowledge of good and evil," as opposed to merely "a knowledge of good and evil" (see, for example, IVp8). The latter refers to my perception of something as bringing about some increase in some partial aspect of my capacities. Some things are judged "good" because they are a source of small-scale joy and pleasure. For example, one may judge a third glass of wine to be "good" because (for a short time and with respect to only a part of one's power) it causes a pleasant state of consciousness. This judgment is grounded only in the passions, however, and thus based on inadequate knowledge of the thing and of oneself. But the

---

11 Thus, Jon Miller, "Spinoza's Axiology," *Oxford Studies in Early Modern Philosophy* 2 (2005): 149–172, rightly distinguishes between circumstantially and noncircumstantially relative value in Spinoza.

"true knowledge of good and evil" is my rational perception—derived from adequate ideas and not just random experience, based on understanding and not (in a shortsighted way) simply on the positive way something happens to affect my body and my mind—of what benefits me in a more complete and essential manner, truly bringing me as a whole individual to a more powerful condition. The difference is summed up by Spinoza in the demonstration of IVp35: "What we judge to be good or evil when we follow the dictate of reason must be good or evil."

Spinoza does not seem to be as interested in analyzing "right" and "wrong" with respect to action as he is in analyzing "good" and "evil." He does occasionally speak of the "right way of living" (III, Preface, G 2:137/C 1:491) and acts "which are called right" (III, DefAffects XXVII, G 2:197/C 1:537), but he does not explain what exactly the rightness of such acts consists in. It may be that the same conclusions he draws about "good" should apply to "right" as well. An action, then, would be "right" if it is truly conducive to the agent's well-being and brings about an increase in his power; an action is "wrong" if it brings about a decrease in his power. While it is certainly possible that one and the same action might be right for one person and wrong for another person—jumping in turbulent waters to save someone from drowning might be the right thing to do for a strong swimmer but the wrong thing to do for someone who cannot swim at all—there are some things that are right or good for all human beings. This is because we all share a certain nature as human beings, and there are some actions that naturally and objectively contribute to the preservation and striving of that nature. Such actions would be "virtuous" in a general sense and such as to be performed by the virtuous person. (Since Spinoza does not generally refer to such actions as "right," I shall in what follows speak of actions that truly contribute to an individual's power as having "moral value," as well as being "virtuous" actions or actions that are "good.")

3. VIRTUE

An agent's power or striving may be directed either by random sense experience and the imagination (or "inadequate ideas") or by knowledge ("adequate ideas"). When a person's *conatus* or desire is guided by the senses and the imagination, he pursues those things that he believes, on a deficient basis, to be good for him; when *conatus* is guided by knowledge on the other hand he will regularly and reliably do those things that really *do* increase his power of acting.

Spinoza initially defines virtue, in IVDef8, simply as power. "By virtue and power I understand the same thing, i.e. (by IIIp7), virtue, insofar as it is related to man, is the very essence, or nature, of man, insofar as he has the power of bringing about certain things, which can be understood through the laws of his nature alone." There is a lot packed into this definition, and it is important to separate the various elements that constitute living according to virtue for Spinoza. In IVp18s, Spinoza—in a statement that strongly recalls the ancient Stoic doctrine of virtue as "acting in accordance with nature"—offers a more condensed version of the definition: "virtue...is nothing but acting from the laws of one's own nature." But the nature of any thing is just its *conatus*, or striving to persevere in existence. Thus, the laws of any thing's nature prescribe that the thing strive to preserve its being. Therefore, as Spinoza concludes, "the foundation of virtue is this very striving to preserve one's own being." More precisely, the virtuous person is the person who properly follows the laws of his own nature and acts so as to preserve his own being. Virtue, in other words, is not simply the exercise of power but the *successful* striving for preservation (or, which will amount to the same thing, the cognitively informed exercise of power). "The more each one strives, and is able, to preserve his being, the more he is endowed with virtue" (IVp20dem). The opposite of virtue on the other hand—and this presumably would be vice, although Spinoza does not use this term but rather the phrase "lack of power"—is acting not according to one's own nature but according to the nature of things outside oneself. The person lacking virtue or power "allows himself to be guided by things outside him, and to be determined by them to do what the common constitution of external things demands, not what his own nature, considered in itself, demands" (IVp37s1).

Spinoza has so far provided a rather formalistic account of virtue, one that does not yet have any real content. No substantive information on what kind of person best and successfully strives for self-preservation or on *how* to act in such a way that one is following the laws of one's own nature is contained in the claim that "the more each one strives, and is able, to seek his own advantage, i.e., to preserve his own being, the more he is endowed with virtue" (IVp20). We need to be told just what the vague notions of "following the laws of one's own nature" and "striving to seek one's own advantage" imply and how a person can put them to work in his life.

This is where Spinoza's rationalism comes into play, not just as a metaphysical or epistemological principle, but as a moral one. Spinoza identifies "living according to one's own nature" with "living according to the guidance of reason." This is because a human being lives according to his own nature when the things he does have their adequate cause in that nature alone and not in the ways external things affect him; that is, he lives according to his own nature when he is active, not passive. And a human being is active—he *acts* rather than *suffers*—when what he does follows from his own adequate ideas, from his rational knowledge of things, and not from inadequate ideas or the passions.

Reason's guidance comes embodied in what Spinoza calls (in IVp18) the "dictates of reason" (*dictamina rationis*). These rational dictates are grounded in the individual's *conatus* and represent a kind of enlightened propositional expression of that natural striving. They demand "that everyone love himself, seek his own advantage, what is really useful to him, want what will really lead man to a greater perfection, and absolutely, that everyone should strive to preserve his own being as far as he can" (IVp18s). More important, reason also provides guidance on how to achieve these common human ends. It does so universally and objectively, without regard to a person's particularities. Like Kant's categorical (moral) imperatives, the dictates of reason transcend personal differences and make universal demands on human behavior, insofar as all human beings share the same basic nature. This is suggested by Spinoza's claim in IVp72, where he considers whether the person guided by reason would ever act deceptively, that "if reason should recommend that, it would recommend it to all men."

Among the first things that reason demands is that "we ought to want virtue for its own sake, and that there is not anything preferable to it, or more useful to us." But because, as Spinoza demonstrated in the metaphysical propositions of Part 1, we are necessarily always a part of Nature and unable ever to bring it about "that we require nothing outside ourselves to preserve our being, nor that we live without having dealings with things outside us," reason also prescribes that we should strive to possess the "many things outside us which are useful to us" (IVp18s). Spinoza's virtue, in other words, does not lead to an ascetic withdrawal from the world but rather a more knowledgeable and successful navigation within the world and a more efficient use of things in it. The virtuous person is able to determine what is *truly* conducive to his well-being and what is not. "Acting absolutely from virtue is nothing else in us but acting, living, and preserving our being (these three signify the same thing) by the guidance of reason, from the foundation of seeking one's own advantage" (IVp24). The virtuous person accurately discerns what is in his own best interest and actively desires and pursues that which will best serve his own power of persevering. He knows, in other words, what is truly good and strives for it.

Of course, ethics, ordinarily understood, is not just about one's own self-preservation and self-development. It must also have something to say about how one is to treat other human beings, even if it turns out that this is itself to be motivated by the pursuit of self-interest. Spinoza is aware of this and offers in Part 4 of the *Ethics* a brief discussion of the ways an individual guided by reason will necessarily act toward others.

While it is certainly possible to adopt an egoistic ethics that permits one to run roughshod over the well-being of others in the unrestricted pursuit of self-interest, Spinoza wisely argues that the egoism at the heart of his system in fact supports those benevolent and considerate ways of treating other human beings that we intuitively recognize as "ethical." While the actions are altruistic, they do not derive from an altruistic motive. It is, he insists, simply in one's own best interest to treat others in such a way that their own power and striving is increased, and this is what moves the virtuous person to so act; that is, the rational and virtuous person will act toward others so as to help them become rational and virtuous only because he sees that having other people become more like him, sharing his nature, is what is most useful to him.[12]

4. RIGHT ACTION

I can now return to the question of the relevance of motive for the moral assessment of action. What makes a right action "right" for Spinoza? It is an action that is "good" in Spinoza's sense—an action the doing of which truly benefits the agent and contributes to the preservation of his being and the augmentation of his power. Which is the same as to say that an action has moral value if and only if it is an action that is commanded by reason and in accordance with its "dictates." Put another way, an action has moral value if it follows from an agent's adequate ideas and knowledge and is therefore the virtuous thing to do. This is because such an action represents the successful striving to preserve oneself and increase one's power.

It might seem, then, that an agent's motive should have no bearing on the moral character of an action, on its goodness or badness. Helping other people in need and contributing to the flourishing and well-being of others should presumably be in one's own best interest—it should positively aid one's own power and striving by creating a

12 IVp31–p37.

condition in which one is surrounded by others who share one's nature and thus are "most useful"—regardless of what moved the agent to engage in such benevolent behavior. As Spinoza says, one and the same action can arise out of irrational passion, or it can be the effect of rational insight. "To every action to which we are determined from an affect which is a passion, we can be determined by reason, without that affect" (IVp59). One can act benevolently to others either from pity or from virtue—that is, either from a passionate motive or from a desire guided by knowledge of what is truly good for one—and it would seem not to make any difference to the moral character of the act itself.[13] It is still a good thing, the right action, insofar as it is in one's own best interest.

It is important to be clear about the connection between virtue and action on this reading. In the end, it may be that virtuous actions are performed only by virtuous people, that morally valuable actions follow only from reason and adequate ideas; perhaps the passions and inadequate ideas always lead one to mistake what is truly in one's own best interest. And it may be that adequate ideas are an infallible guide to what is in one's own best interest and that virtuous people perform only right actions. But all of this would amount to only causal claims. We can even say that a right action just *is* the action that the virtuous person, guided by reason on the basis of adequate ideas, desires (is moved) to do. It would still not establish that the moral value of the action is a function of the motivation behind it and that an action is virtuous only when it is *done as a virtuous person would do it*.[14] What makes the action virtuous and good, on this reading of Spinoza's account, is precisely that which the virtuous person knows about the action, namely, that it leads to an increase in his power.

---

13 Compare what he says about benevolence in III.Def.Affects 35 with the account of benevolence in IVp31–p36.

14 Much as Aristotle insists that true virtuous action is an action performed in the right way, as the virtuous person would do it; see, for example, *Nicomachean Ethics* 1105b. See also Kant's distinction, in the first section of the *Grounding for the Metaphysics of Morals*, between acting *in accordance with* duty versus acting *from a sense of* duty.

5. Motive and Agency

However, all is not what it seems. To read Spinoza in the way I have just described, while tempting, is to miss much of what he says about agency and to ignore especially his views on the relationship between action, virtue, adequate ideas, and power. As a matter of fact, it seems that in at least some very important cases, the motives of the agent, the beliefs and desires behind the action, are crucial for determining the moral character of the action, for assessing whether or not the action is good in Spinoza's sense of "good" (as fostering an increase in the agent's power).[15]

To see how this is so, let us return to the case of benevolence, briefly discussed earlier. First, recall what Spinoza says in IVp59: "To every action to which we are determined from an affect which is a passion, we can be determined by reason, without that affect." One and the same action can arise either out of passion or from reason and knowledge. It all depends on whether the desire to perform the action is informed by adequate ideas or inadequate ideas, by a true understanding or a deficient belief about the action's contribution to strengthening one's *conatus*. This is true of actions one might take to benefit other individuals. Spinoza explicitly says that one may act benevolently toward others either out of pity and compassion or from knowledge (adequate ideas) and a recognition that, and how, just and charitable treatment of others contributes to one's own flourishing. I have provisionally proposed that IVp59 suggests that motive is irrelevant for the moral value of the action; in fact, for Spinoza it implies just the opposite.

Spinoza defines pity at IIIp22s as "sadness that has arisen from injury to another." He explains in IIIp27 that it is grounded in what he calls "the imitation of the affects," a sympathetic reaction whereby "if we imagine a thing like us, toward which we have had no affect, to be affected with some affect, we are thereby affected with a like affect." If

---

15 My analysis here is indebted to discussion with Matt Kisner, and I am grateful for his insights.

the "thing" is another person (and thus very much like us), and if that other person is affected with sadness—that is, a decrease in his power of acting—then we will also be affected with sadness and experience a corresponding decrease in power. "This imitation of the affects, when it is related to sadness, is called pity" (IIIp27s). Pity so understood is a passive affect (or passion) because it is a decrease in my power caused by (my perception of) an external object.

This pity can then give rise to the desire to help the other person. "This will, or appetite to do good, born of our pity for the thing on which we wish to confer a benefit, is called Benevolence" (IIIp27c3s). An act of benevolence that comes about from the motive of pity still represents a decrease in one's own power of acting. It is therefore not good but bad or evil. Acting out of pity, even to benefit another, does not aid my striving but in fact works against it. It is action that is grounded in and motivated by inadequate ideas.

As I have shown, however, acts of benevolence can also arise not from passions and inadequate ideas but from knowledge and adequate ideas. In this case, a rational and virtuous person comes to the aid of another not because of a feeling of sadness but because he understands clearly that it is in his own best interest to do so. He knows that another person who is flourishing, who is rational and virtuous, has a nature that is more like his own and therefore is more useful to him; and this knowledge moves him to contribute to the virtue and rationality of that other person. In IVp50, Spinoza notes that a person who lives "according to the guidance of reason" will have no use for pity, and he knows that "the good which follows from [pity], viz. that we strive to free the man we pity from his suffering...we desire to do from the dictate of reason alone (by IVp37), and we can only do from the dictate of reason alone something that we know certainly to be good." The *rational* person's act of benevolence, unlike the pitying person's act of benevolence, is not a sadness but a joy, arising as it does from knowledge. It represents not a diminution of his power of acting but an increase; it is, therefore, a virtuous action.

This is especially so since to perform an action from adequate ideas, as the rational person does, just *is* to undergo an increase in one's power.[16] Spinoza notes that strictly speaking the mind *acts* only when it is the adequate, and not merely partial, cause of an effect; and this happens when desire is moved by adequate ideas (whereas it *suffers* or is passive when desire is moved by its inadequate ideas, by the way external things affect the body) (IIIp1). To act is to express one's power. To express one's power is virtue. Therefore, one is most virtuous when one is acting through adequate ideas. In this way, Spinoza practically defines a virtuous action as an action motivated in a certain way (i.e., by adequate ideas).

It follows, therefore, that to show benevolence toward others from the motivation of reason and adequate ideas is a virtuous action, but to show benevolence toward others from the motivation of pity is not a virtuous but an evil action. What Spinoza says in the "alternative demonstration" of IVp59 about actions in general and the affect of hate applies in particular to benevolent action and the affect of pity (which, like hate, is an "evil" affect insofar as it is a weakening of one's power): "Any action is called evil insofar as it arises from the fact that we have been affected with hate or with some evil affect.... But no action, considered in itself, is good or evil (as we have shown in the Preface of this Part); instead, one and the same action is now good, now evil. Therefore, to the same action which is now evil, or which arises from some evil affect, we can (by IVp19) be led by reason." Notice that Spinoza here identifies "an action which is evil" with "an action which arises from some evil affect." Since it is the affects that motivate actions for Spinoza, this is tantamount to saying that the moral character of an action is a function of the motive behind it. It is not just a judgment about the *agent* that is in question here—that an agent is acting virtuously only if he acts from the proper motive—or even a judgment

---

16 See Matthew Kisner, *Spinoza on Human Freedom: Reason, Autonomy and the Good Life* (Cambridge: Cambridge University, 2011), 142–145.

about the virtuous *performance* of an action, but a judgment about the action itself.

This same analysis applies to other kinds of action. Take, for example, an individual's retreat from a battle. In and of itself, the retreat from battle is neither good nor bad; it is just a certain physical activity. However, if the motive for the retreat is fear, which Spinoza calls a species of sadness (IIIp18s2), then the action (retreat) is bad, since it involves a weakening of the individual's power. On the other hand the motive for retreat in the face of danger in a person who lives by the guidance of reason is "tenacity" (*animositas*, defined at IIIp59s as "the desire by which each one strives, solely from the dictate of reason, to preserve his being," also translatable as "strength of character" or "presence of mind"). Through tenacity, a person properly estimates the danger with respect to his own capacity for overcoming it and thus engages in "timely flight" when necessary to preserve his being (IVp69). Retreat from danger out of fear is evil, but retreat from danger out of tenacity is virtuous: same activity, different motives, thus different moral status.

There is a telling passage from Spinoza's correspondence, in a letter to Willem van Blijenbergh in 1665, in which Spinoza considers the question of whether an act of killing and an act of almsgiving are, given his metaphysical conception of God (which greatly troubled Van Blijenbergh), "equally pleasing to God." He says:

> if the question is "Whether the two acts insofar as they are something real, and caused by God, are not equally perfect?" then I say that, if we consider the acts alone, and in such a way, it may well be that both are equally perfect. If you then ask "Whether the thief and the just man are not equally perfect and blessed?" then I answer "no." For by a just man I understand one who constantly desires that each should possess his own. In my *Ethics* (which I have not yet published) I show that this desire necessarily arises in the pious from a clear knowledge which they have of themselves and of God. And

since the thief has no desire of that kind, he necessarily lacks the knowledge of God and of himself, which is the principal thing that makes us men. (Letter 23, G 4:150–151/C 1:389)

Killing a person or stealing from him is, by any reasonable ethical standard, a bad thing. Giving charitably and treating others with justice is a good thing. What Spinoza is telling Blijenbergh is that the goodness and badness of these actions lies not in the actions "considered alone" and independent of the motives behind them—since from this perspective they are "equally perfect," containing the same amount of reality—but in the fact that one derives from adequate ideas and the other from ignorance, and one therefore represents an increase of the agent's power and the other represents a decrease.

There is, however, a complication for my account of Spinoza's theory that needs to be addressed. Not all cases of acting from inadequate ideas represent a decrease in one's power. There are instances where one acts on the basis of a passive affect or inadequate idea but where the operative passion is a joy. Since a joy is an *increase* in one's power, would not an action motivated by the passion of joy, while not grounded in adequate ideas, still be good? And would not an agent so motivated therefore be acting rightly?

Say, for example, that an agent acts benevolently toward another person not out of pity or sympathy (which are species of sadness) but out of love? Spinoza defines love as "nothing but joy with the accompanying idea of an external cause" (IIIp13s). One loves the thing that one believes to have brought about an increase in one's power. Therefore, does not acting benevolently toward someone because one loves him represent an instance where an action is good (represents an increase in power) *despite* the motive being a passion? And does that not suggest more generally that, for Spinoza, motive can be irrelevant in the moral evaluation of action?

The answer to this question, I believe, is no. Rather, it seems that in explaining Spinoza's account of the relationship between motive and action we need to make discriminations finer than simply between "acting from adequate idea" and "acting from inadequate idea or passion." Acting benevolently from the passion of pity (a sadness) is bad for the agent, and thus an action so motivated receives a poor moral evaluation. Acting benevolently from passionate love (a joy) is good for the agent, but only to a limited degree. Passions tend to represent only partial increases in an agent's power and only in certain and temporary respects; therefore, an act motivated by passionate love receives a higher moral evaluation than performing the same action out of pity, but it is not the best way to be moved to the action.[17] Finally, acting benevolently toward another from the dictate of reason, from true knowledge and adequate ideas, represents a real, thorough, and lasting increase in an agent's power—it is what is best for the agent—and thus an act so motivated receives the highest moral evaluation.

In other words, while acting out of passionate love is not per se an evil for the agent (as acting out of pity is), since joy as a passion is indeed an increase in a person's power, it is less good than acting on the basis of reason. And, as Spinoza insists, a lesser good is, relatively speaking, actually an evil: "A good that prevents us from enjoying a greater good is really an evil" (IVp65d). Moreover, an agent who does what he does out of passionate love is still not truly *active* in Spinoza's technical sense, since he is not the adequate cause of what he does but is only passively responding to how something else affects him.

We can conclude, then, that for Spinoza, there are many cases—and perhaps it is true of all actions subject to moral evaluation—in which the moral character of an action is indeterminate unless the motive of the agent is taken into account. Actions that consist in the benevolent treatment of others, to take only one prominent example, are not truly power-enhancing, and therefore "good," unless they are done with a

---

17 This is why Spinoza insists that certain pleasures, while increases in an agent's power, can be excessive, as can love, since they may in fact end up debilitating the agent in other ways; see IVp43–44.

certain motive, namely, the epistemic/affective condition characteristic of the virtuous and rational person. As Spinoza says, in a statement that reveals the importance of taking motive into account, "the desire to do good generated in us by our living according to the guidance of reason, I call Morality" (IVp37s).

Reflection

MORAL MOTIVATION AND MUSIC AS MORAL JUDGE

Chadwick Jenkins

꽃

Arthur Schopenhauer proclaimed music the highest of all art forms inasmuch as it alone expresses the underlying essence of the world, what he terms the Will, that endless, all-devouring striving that he identifies with the Kantian *ding an sich*. For Schopenhauer, the Will is "objectified" in the realm of Representation (the phenomenal realm). While all of the other arts engage the phenomenal realm (and thus are representations of representations), music breaks through to the underlying reality and becomes a paradoxical representation of the unrepresentable. Just as Schopenhauer claims that we experience the will through the internal understanding of our actions (we not only see our arm move, we experience our willing it to move), so music maps onto the internal workings of the will.

The idea that music embodies some aspect of striving or will has a long history that stretches back at least to eleventh-century accounts of polyphony. Music theorists claimed that the imperfect consonances (thirds and sixths) "seek their perfection," that is, that they strove to resolve to perfect consonances (namely, fifths and octaves). Theorists often assign a sense of will to dissonance. For example, Roger Kamian defines dissonance as "an unstable tone combination ... [that] *demands* an onward motion to a stable

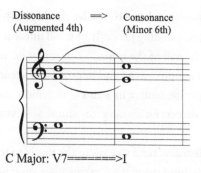

FIGURE 1. "Authentic cadence" (slurs show how the dissonance must resolve).

chord."[1] Moreover, dissonances are said to be directed not to just *any* more stable sonority but to a specific sonority. Take, for instance, a dominant seventh chord built on G. This dissonant chord indexes (points to) a specific resolution on a consonant chord built on C (this is the authentic cadence, or V7 → I; that is to say, a dominant seventh chord built on the fifth degree of the scale [here G] progresses to a chord built on the first degree of the scale [here C]) (see fig. 1).[2]

Its dissonance is not entirely satisfied by progressing to just any consonant chord. Were that not the case, we could not speak of a "deceptive" cadence, one that partially resolves the dissonance by moving to a chord, in this example, built on A (hence V7 → vi; that is to say, a dominant seventh chord built on the fifth degree of the scale [here G] progresses to a chord built on the sixth degree of the scale [here A]). A deceptive cadence does not redeem, so to speak, the promissory note of the V7 chord. The listener expects an

1 Roger Kamian, *Music, An Appreciation*, 6th brief ed. (New York: McGraw-Hill, 2008), 41. Emphasis mine.

2 The Roman numerals label chords built on scale degrees, where uppercase Roman numerals indicate major chords and lowercase indicate minor chords. Thus V7 in the key of C designates a seventh chord built on the fifth degree (that is, G). Such a chord consists of four notes: G, B, D, and F. The F creates a dissonance with the B and the G (an augmented fourth and a minor seventh, respectively).

eventual authentic cadence to resolve this higher-level dissonance. In this sense, responding properly to tonal music means attending to the implicit "will of the tones."[3] This might be usefully compared to the idea of a motive as an end or goal of an agent. Just as an agent may have a specific motive in acting—to achieve such and such an end—so too do certain dissonances aim at achieving a specific resolution.

In opera, listeners tend to look to the music to reveal the motivations behind the actions taking place on stage. The most obvious instances of the "music as guiding hand" paradigm are found in the leitmotif technique employed within the music dramas of Richard Wagner. Here Wagner famously guides the listener by using motifs that signal connections and implications within the plot, which the characters on stage may be unaware of or unwilling to express. The music "tells the truth" behind the convolutions of the plot. For example, in Wagner's *Die Wälkure*, immediately after a character declares "You cannot bring sorrow to the house where sorrow already reigns," the orchestra intones the motif variously known as the "Wälsung Motif" or "Wälsung Sorrow," depicting the despondency that haunts the Wälsung race. The motif is slow and outlines a minor and then a diminished (dissonant) harmony, and its rising sequential phrases reveal the yearning that underwrites the characters' woe (see fig. 2).

FIGURE 2. The "Wälsung Motif" from Wagner's *Die Wälkure*.

3 The phrase comes from the title of a set of pamphlets published by theorist Heinrich Schenker, *Der Tonwille: Pamphlets in Witness of the Immutable Laws of Music, Volume I: Issues 1–5 (1921–1923)*, edited by William Drabkin (New York: Oxford University Press, 2004).

Even in less extreme cases, operagoers expect the music to endorse or castigate the actions and statements of the protagonists. Hence Joseph Kerman declared: "In opera, the dramatist is the composer."[4] We might augment his dictum by adding that the composer also serves as the moral commentator.[5]

Few operas have given critics more difficulty in justifying its moral content than Claudio Monteverdi's last, *L'incoronazione di Poppea* (1643). The libretto opens with the allegorical figures of Virtue, Fortune, and Love arguing as to which is the most important. Virtue is declared "dissolute, obsolete, abhorrent." In the end, Love is triumphant and plans to demonstrate its supremacy through the story of the Roman emperor Nero and his illicit mistress Poppea. In short, Nero exiles his current wife, Ottavia, and Poppea's current husband, Ottone, in order to raise Poppea to the throne, a plan of action that the opera depicts as originating with Poppea herself. Nero first consults his advisor, the Stoic philosopher Seneca, and then not only refuses Seneca's counsel but also orders Seneca to commit suicide for his unwillingness to endorse the emperor's immoral and illegal design. (In reality, the order to die had nothing to do with Poppea and indeed occurred years after the marriage.) Ottavia and Ottone resort to attempted murder. With Seneca's death occurring roughly halfway through the opera, the plot seems to wander aimlessly in a moral vacuum. The decidedly unpalatable Nero and Poppea achieve their goals and conclude the opera with a glorious duet celebrating their love.

This opera has had critics and scholars performing acrobatic feats of interpretation to salvage the piece from becoming a mere glorification of rampant immorality. Justifications range from

---

4 Joseph Kerman, *Opera as Drama*, rev. ed. (Berkeley: University of California Press, 1988), 91.

5 One might occasionally want to describe a score as emotionally neutral, but this is clearly exceptional in an art form that traffics so heavily in the cultivation and representation of emotion.

situating the opera within the contemporaneous political struggles in Venice to grounding its salaciousness in the questionable taste of the Venetian public (as opposed to the older courtly model of opera) and to insisting that the audience would read the opera in the light of their knowledge concerning the ultimate unsavory fates of the two protagonists so that good triumphs over evil all the same, albeit outside the framework of the opera itself.

Several interpretations have taken Kerman's dictum to heart and focused on the musical language and what it can tell us about Monteverdi's (moral) interpretation of the events of the plot. Not surprisingly, many of these interpretations center on the character of Seneca.[6] After all, Seneca's writings repeatedly explore the notion of virtue. Virtue, according to Seneca, is the *only good*. Traditionally, Seneca is credited with discovering the will, owing to his emphasis on *voluntas* (willing). Indeed it is through proper willing that we become virtuous. But Seneca does not adhere to a mere list of moral rules but rather grounds his understanding of morality in contingent experiences. Finally, Seneca emphasizes the intention behind actions over the actions themselves. This would seem to offer music an ideal opportunity for revealing motivation and thus assisting in moral judgment within the realm of opera.

Interpretations of the music's understanding of Seneca, however, remain deeply divided. The libretto provides a contradictory portrait of Seneca that reflects seventeenth-century Venetian ambivalence regarding him. On the one hand he appears as the brave Stoic, ready to embrace death as the ultimate test of his convictions. On the other hand his sententious admonitions, which rely on shopworn generalities, and his reputation among the other characters as a self-serving and lascivious sophist depict him as the

---

6 This brief summary of Seneca's discussions of virtue derives, in part, from Katja Vogt, "Seneca," in *The Stanford Encyclopedia of Philosophy* (Summer 2013 ed.), edited by Edward N. Zalta, http://plato .stanford.edu/archives/sum2013/entries/seneca/.

most callous of hypocrites. Given the ambiguities of the libretto, scholars turn to the music. Susan McClary claims that "Seneca habitually reverts to silly madrigalisms [moments of text painting], which destroy the rhetorical effect of most of his statements," leaving his character "profoundly passive and impotent."[7] Iain Fenlon and Peter Miller hear irony (not silliness) in Seneca's madrigalisms, notably the melisma on "la bellezza." But Wendy Heller points out that the ludicrously long melisma actually occurs on the word "la" (meaning "the"), a word that no composer would embellish in such a manner should he want that embellishment to be taken seriously.[8] Ellen Rosand, believing Seneca to be the moral center of the opera, cites the seemingly emotion-laden chromatic music sung at the moment of Seneca's death as proof that Monteverdi viewed the philosopher as noble and heroic, while Tim Carter suggests that the texture of that music derives from the *giustiniana*, "a 'popular' genre one topos of which is three ludicrous old men singing of their supposed sexual exploits."[9] Clearly even musical experts disagree strongly about the basic moral content of the opera as a whole and the depiction of Seneca in particular.

But it was the music that was supposed to reveal the underlying motives of the opera's characters. Perhaps this points up something of a moral of its own. Earlier we said that dissonance *demands* resolution. But sounds demand nothing; people demand. We are the ones who *want* the dissonance to resolve. This wanting is not entirely subjective (it is not my whim that dissonances ought to resolve); rather it stems from my knowledge of how things go with

7 Susan McClary, *Feminine Endings: Music, Gender, and Sexuality* (Minneapolis: University of Minnesota Press, 1991), 49.

8 Iain Fenlon and Peter Miller, *The Song of the Soul: Understanding "Poppea"* (London: Royal Musical Association, 1992), 63; Wendy Heller, "Chastity, Heroism, and Allure: Women in the Opera of Seventeenth-Century Venice" (PhD diss., Brandeis University, 1995), 272–273.

9 Ellen Rosand, "Seneca and the Interpretation of *L'incoronazione di Poppea*," *Journal of the American Musicological Society* 38 (1985): 69; Tim Carter, "Re-reading *Poppea*: Some Thoughts on Music and Meaning in Monteverdi's Last Opera," *Journal of the Royal Music Association* 122:2 (1997): 194.

music and so my expectation that dissonance resolves becomes projected onto the music as *its desire*, as what it must do. Along the same lines, music doesn't make judgments but rather offers us a sense of something indeterminately meaningful; its meaning cannot simply be paraphrased. In a manner that resonates with Senecan ethics, such meaning is not merely subjective. Rather, its stake to objectivity rests on the contingency of the moment and our engagement with the musical material.

CHAPTER SIX

Locke on Pleasure, Law, and Moral Motivation

Phillip Mitsis

Locke's theory has played an influential role in subsequent philosophical thinking about moral motivation,[1] even though many believe it to be ultimately hobbled by conflicting commitments to both natural law and hedonism. More particularly, Locke initially endorsed a broadly rationalistic theory of natural law in his *Essays on the Law of Nature* (1664). In these writings, published posthumously, he argues that moral rules are rooted in universal, divine moral laws that structure and ground our moral lives. Obviously, not everyone comes to understand

---

1 Stephen Darwall, *The British Moralists and the Internal "Ought": 1640–1740* (Cambridge: Cambridge University Press, 1995), 172, credits Locke with "occupying a unique place in early modern thinking about moral obligation." Although in Darwall's view Locke is officially an externalist about moral obligation, he contributes to the idea "that the 'force of morality' and the essential practicality of 'ethics' require an intrinsic connection to motive," and he finds in Locke's theory a "surprising" contribution "to the tradition of autonomist internalism" that one would more likely find "carried out in rationalist rather than in empiricist form." On my view, giving a more historically nuanced account of "externalism" and "internalism" in Locke's intellectual context might eliminate much of this surprise in finding such "internalism" about motives in the wider framework of Locke's empiricism.

or follow them, but they are in principle discoverable by unaided natural reason. A problem that exercised his critics from the beginning is that in their view, Locke treats moral laws as a set of purely external divine commands—hence all the talk about Locke's "externalism"—and it is unclear, it is argued, that he ever explains why agents should be motivated to obey them on moral grounds, not just because of fear or the desire for rewards.

On the other hand Locke also began to take on commitments to hedonism, which makes an appearance more than a decade after the *Essays on the Law of Nature*, first in a journal entry dating from 1676 and then more fully in the second (1694) and all subsequent editions of *An Essay Concerning Human Understanding*. Accordingly, given Locke's habits of writing and revision—he typically adds rather than deletes—it is difficult to discern how, or even if, these twin commitments were meant to fit together in the span of almost thirty years of his thinking. Indeed, a majority of scholars before the mid-1980s tended to conclude that key tenets of natural law and hedonism in Locke's moral thought were at odds with one another, and some postulated a development away from his earlier endorsement of a natural law theory to a more Hobbesian account in which moral rules are justified by their instrumental effectiveness in maximizing an agent's individual pleasure. One problem with this kind of solution, however, is that Locke seems to give voice to commitments from his initial rationalistic theory of moral rules and natural law through all of his writings up until the time of his death. So one difficulty for any developmental view is that Locke never completely matured into the final view on offer to him. Moreover, the overall picture of his blossoming from a pious divine into a Hobbist seems to contradict what we know of his own richly documented slide into devoutness and his own attitudes toward Hobbes.

Two more recent interpreters, however, John Colman and Stephen Darwall, have argued that Locke's hedonism, when properly understood, is indeed compatible with his views about rational moral law, but only because his hedonism is meant as a secondary, instrumental theory about psychological motivation.[2] In their view, the hedonism of the *Essay* is meant to show how it is possible for agents to be moved practically to follow the rational precepts of natural law. In other words, hedonism is not meant to override Locke's earlier claims about what structures and grounds our moral lives—that continues to be rationally discoverable natural law—rather, hedonism is used to explain how God has made it possible for agents to come to follow their moral obligations, since rational understanding, by itself, is motivationally inert, as are God's moral commands. On this proto-Humean view, such commands, however rational and obligatory, would be incapable of motivating agents unless they were enforced by a system of eternal pleasurable rewards and painful punishments; hence the necessary role of hedonism in explaining how one can come to lead a moral life, a moral life that is grounded and justified, nonetheless, by a set of divine, natural rules. The problem with this view, however, is that it is hard to see how Locke's hedonism can be viewed as purely instrumental and as a strictly secondary psychological theory. Such a reading of Locke attempts to save consistency, perhaps, but at the cost of any plausibly straightforward reading of what he says in the *Essay* about pleasure as an end, our ultimate good, our final goal in paradise, and so on.

In examining Locke's theory of motivation, I will need to take yet another look at these two elements in his theory. But I think it will be helpful to do so from the perspective of ancient philosophy and as if Locke were looming in our future, rather than in our past, ham-handedly fumbling answers to contemporary questions about "externalism" and "internalism"—and trying to do so with a vocabulary that he does not yet have and a set of distinctions he arguably does not recognize. In my own view, Locke took himself to be writing in the long shadow of a tradition of ancient Epicurean and Stoic ethical theory, and his arguments are clearly inflected by their concerns. Many scholars of early

---

2 John Colman, *John Locke's Moral Philosophy* (Edinburgh: Edinburgh University Press, 1983).

modern philosophy,[3] especially if they follow Darwall in believing that Locke's influences on questions of motivation can be traced back perhaps only so far as Cudworth and Molyneaux,[4] are likely to find such a claim implausible. Of course, questions of philosophical influence are notoriously slippery, and in this chapter I will not be able to engage in this particular battle in sufficient textual detail.[5] I will also bracket evidence[6] that in formulating his views, Locke is consciously trying to come to terms with Epicurean and Stoic doctrines and that he ends up following lock, stock, and barrel Gassendi's attempt to bring the two ancient schools into harmony by grounding Epicurean hedonism in a Stoic-like conception of divine providential law. Nonetheless, I argue that generally viewing Locke's conceptions of law, pleasure, and moral motivation as marching in lockstep with Stoic and Epicurean arguments can not only help us to see important parallels between these ancient and early modern accounts, but also suggest how some major recent accounts of Locke's views on motivation have tended to miss the mark at key junctures.

Part of the problem is that most recent scholarship typically assumes that Locke's moral thought is shaped by two philosophical developments that might loom largest from our perspective, but not necessarily from his own: Descartes's conception of mental subjectivity and Hobbes's rejection of the sort of teleological basis for ethical theories found in ancient ethics. As a result, Locke's hedonism, for example, is

---

3 J. B. Schneewind, "Locke's Moral Philosophy," in *The Cambridge Companion to Locke,* edited by Vere Chappell (Cambridge: Cambridge University Press, 1994) 199–225.

4 Jennifer Whiting, "The Lockeanism of Aristotle," *Antiquorum Philosophia* 2 (2008): 101–136, shows how deeply Cudworth is himself indebted to Stoicism, however.

5 For detailed evidence of Locke's preoccupation with Cicero and ancient philosophers, see John Marshall, *John Locke: Resistance, Religion, and Responsibility* (Cambridge: Cambridge University Press, 1994). I set out some of the evidence for Locke's reliance on Cicero's *De Officiis* and *De Finibus* in "Locke's Offices," in *Hellenistic and Early Modern Philosophy,* edited by J. Miller and B. Inwood (Cambridge: Cambridge University Press, 2003), 45–61.

6 See Lisa T. Sarasohn, *Gassendi's Ethics: Freedom in a Mechanistic Universe* (Ithaca, NY: Cornell University Press, 1996). Fred Michael and Emily Michael, "Gassendi's Modified Epicureanism and British Moral Philosophy," *History of European Ideas* 21:6 (1995): 743–761. Edward A. Driscoll, "The Influence of Gassendi on Locke's Hedonism," *International Philosophical Quarterly* 12 (1972): 87–110.

assumed to be rooted in radically different assumptions from those of ancient hedonists like Epicurus, whose accounts of pleasure are deeply entangled in the demands and preoccupations of ancient eudaimonism. Epicurus, for his part, stipulates objective teleological criteria for individual pleasures and fails to show any particular interest in cataloguing the kinds of qualitative subjective states of consciousness or feeling that become so central in later accounts of hedonism. Indeed, for the Epicurean, such states are not even the primary goal of the hedonist's pursuit. Locke on the other hand is thought to have parted ways with ancient eudaimonism in just these respects and to have formulated the kind of readily recognizable, if problematic, hedonist theory familiar from the later British empiricist tradition. In this view, since pleasures are uniform, subjective states of consciousness of which only individuals themselves can compare and strictly be said to judge correctly,[7] our hedonic ends are inevitably so intrinsically diverse that it is senseless for a eudaimonist to try to discover or to rationally defend any sort of common *summum bonum* or objective *telos* for individuals as a whole.

The problem with this overall historical contrast is that on closer inspection Locke's hedonism often comes near enough to Epicurus's eudaimonistic version in many of its major claims that it should engender strong doubts about whether it is best understood as just being part and parcel of some putatively "new" general philosophical framework established by Descartes and Hobbes. Indeed, Locke's hedonism, I would argue, is in many respects better understood within the framework of the ancient accounts of Epicureanism that he found in Cicero's *De Finibus*, in Diogenes Laertius, and in Gassendi's exegesis of a wide variety of ancient Epicurean texts. Once we start to view Locke's account in this context it becomes difficult to categorize him either as a strict subjectivist about pleasure and happiness or as a Hobbesian

---

7 See Whiting, "Lockeanism," for discussion of the "Lockean self" and its debts to ancient Stoicism as opposed to Descartes. I would expand her argument to include Epicureanism and ancient hedonism, since, for Locke, God has attached pleasure to our states of self-awareness.

skeptic about the possibility of a commonly shared teleological good. Moreover, when viewed within the teleological and eudaimonist perspective of ancient ethical theory, Locke's defense of both hedonism and moral law appears less far-fetched than the usual improbable task he is thought to face, that of harnessing a mechanistic, Hobbesian view of pleasure and desire to a motivationally inert set of arbitrary, legalistic divine commands.

MORAL LAWS, OBLIGATION, AND MOTIVATION

Locke begins the first of his *Essays on the Law of Nature* with a discussion of the "Rule of Morals and Law of Nature." In it he begins by offering what is for all intents and purposes a laundry list of standard Stoic claims about Natural Law, which he specifically marks as being Stoic:[8]

> First then, we can equate with our law that moral good or virtue which philosophers in former times (and among them especially the Stoics) have searched for with so much zeal…and we can equate it with that single good which Seneca says man ought to be content with to which appertains so much dignity…(109). Second, there is the title of right reason, to which everyone who considers himself a human being lays claim….By reason, however, I do not think is meant here the faculty of understanding which forms trains of thought and deduces proofs, but certain definite principles of action from which spring all virtue[9] and whatever is necessary for the

---

8 While Schneewind claims Locke is following Pufendorf, and Sheridan claims he is following Aquinas (whom Locke cites once), Locke himself, throughout the *Essays*, both cites and paraphrases Aristo, Gellius, Seneca, and the Stoics generally. In addition, as Von Leyden helpfully points out, *John Locke: Essays on the Law of Nature* (Oxford: Oxford University Press, 1954), 35, Locke is often nearly paraphrasing Cicero's *De officiis* and *De legibus* for large sections of his argument even when he neglects, as was his inveterate habit, to cite Cicero by name. On Locke's indebtedness to Cicero generally and his habits of citation see note 5.

9 Von Leyden's clever but potentially misleading translation. A more literal version of Locke's attempted poetic image would be "from which the fountains of all the virtues flow." cf. note 23.)

proper moulding of morals. For that which is correctly derived from these principles is justly said to be in accordance with reason. (110)[10]

While it is certainly true that Locke argues that God is the source of the authority of moral law, it seems to me that we need to be careful about how we apply terms like "externalism" and "voluntarism" to his theory. I begin with the latter. Echoing the views of many, Schneewind draws the following strong voluntarist conclusions about Locke's theory:

> There can be nothing in nature, then, to set a moral limit to God's will. If neither law nor nature can constrain Locke's God, then Locke is taking a voluntarist position that God's will alone makes acts right. God's power makes him of course, a cause of pleasure and pain, and so he can be thought to be good or evil in a nonmoral way. But this hardly helps matters. The possession of unlimited power merely enables God to be at best a benevolent despot, at worst, a tyrant. There seems to be a good case for Burnet's claim that on Locke's view the laws that God laid down for us are "entirely arbitrary."[11]

Locke's account of our obedience to such laws, Schneewind claims, can therefore have no rational basis and can only be grounded in our fear of punishment and hope of reward. While this may be an unavoidable conclusion of some forms of voluntarism, it seems to me that Locke takes great pains to distance himself from just this kind of general conclusion, even if one thinks he ultimately must do so at the cost of theological consistency.[12] Although he readily concedes that most people need the divine carrot-and-whip approach, this in itself does not mean

---

10 Von Leyden, *John Locke*, 110.

11 Schneewind, "Locke's Moral Philosophy," 206.

12 So, for instance, at *Essay* 21.49 Locke says: "I think, we might say, That God himself cannot choose what is not good; the Freedom of the Almighty hinders not his being determined by what is best." And: "God himself is under the necessity of being happy; and the more any intelligent Being is so, the nearer is its approach to infinite perfection and happiness" (21.50).

that we feel the obligation of law only because of sanctions: "Indeed, all obligation binds conscience and lays a bond on the mind itself, so that not fear of punishment, but a rational apprehension of what is right, puts us under an obligation" (185).[13] Moreover, such obligation is not arbitrary but fitted to our natures in precisely the way that Stoics argue: "On the contrary, a manner of acting is prescribed to him that is suitable to his nature; for it does not seem to fit with the wisdom of the Creator to form an animal that is most perfect and ever active, and to endow it abundantly above all others with mind, intellect, and reason…or again to make man alone susceptible of law precisely in order that he may submit to none."

It might be, of course, that if Locke were offered a counterfactual about whether God might have constructed the world so differently that we would have obligations to violate the property of others, he might be forced to concede that his conception of God's power might allow it (though see 199 and notes 12 and 13 here). However, his own account of natural law suggests a position with a different emphasis from the one attributed to him by Schneewind. The view that emerges from these passages has an eminently Stoic pedigree and is deeply rooted in a conception of natural human *officia* and principles of reason. Moreover, as Locke puts it in his heading to *Essays* 4, human reason is capable of attaining knowledge of natural moral laws through the senses, and these moral laws indicate "what is and what is not in conformity with rational nature, and for this very reason, are commanding or prohibiting." Therefore, obedience to moral law, for Locke, essentially is "the rule of living according to nature which the Stoics so

---

13 See Patricia Sheridan, *Locke: A Guide for the Perplexed* (London: Continuum, 2010), 90, who cites the following passage in the *Essay* (1.3.6) for the claim that although most people may need rewards and punishments, "this takes nothing from the Moral and Eternal obligation, which these Rules evidently have." Locke goes on to say here in the *Essays*: "In fact, this law does not depend on an unstable and changeable will, but on the eternal order of things. For it seems to me that certain essential features of things are immutable, and that '*quaedam officia ex necessitate orta, quae aliter esse non possunt,…*' (certain proper functions have arisen from necessity that cannot be other than they are)" (199). A helpful discussion is provided by Raghuveer Singh, "John Locke and the Theory of Natural Law," *Political Studies* 9 (1961): 105–118.

often emphasize." (*Essays* 1.3) Moreover, once these moral rules come to be known, they "cannot but determine the Choice in anyone, that will but consider."[14] Thus, rather than being inert, moral laws, for Locke, have the kind of obligatory rational force that the Stoics attribute to them.[15]

For Locke, then, we are able to apprehend moral laws through our experience and by means of our reason; as such, rational apprehension ultimately determines our actions because rational moral requirements themselves compel us, independently of sanctions or reward and punishment, to live according to their dictates. In defense of this claim Locke approvingly endorses the view that man's *officium* (or proper function) is acting in conformity to reason, so much so that man must of necessity perform what reason prescribes (113). This seems to be in strict keeping with the Stoic claim that reason alone is sufficient to motivate and that divine law obligates through its rational fit with man's nature. In following reason, one has no alternative but to follow the mandates of natural law and one's own nature. In making this argument, Locke cites Aristotle in support of this particular view of acting in accord with right reason, but it is fully Stoic as well both in thought and terminology. So too the prominent Ciceronian claim that there is a harmony (*congruentia*) between man's rational nature and natural law:

---

14 See *Essay* 21.70. Sheridan makes a distinction between the content of natural law—which is an outgrowth of human nature—and its obligatory force, which is solely derived from its divine authorship. "Pirates, Kings and Reasons to Act: Moral Motivation and the Role of Sanctions in Locke's Moral Theory," *Canadian Journal of Philosophy* 37:1 (2007): 38. For a detailed defense of this distinction in the context of the early modern reception of medieval natural law theories, see the brilliant account of Francis Oakley, "Locke, Natural Law, and God; Note" (1966), Natural Law Forum, paper 119, http://scholarship.law.nd.edu/nd_naturallaw_forum/119. However, in passages such as these, Locke claims that characteristic features of our rationality and what Sheridan is calling the content of natural law are themselves what determine choice and oblige rational agents to act morally; see "Tertio homines obligat, omnia enim quae ad obligationem requiruntur in se continent" (Thirdly it [natural law] binds men, for it contains in itself all that is requisite to create an obligation.) Von Leyden, *John Locke*, 112.

15 See Sheridan, "Pirates, Kings, and Reasons to Act," 42, for a discussion of Locke's appeal to conscience in *Essays* 4. She makes a compelling case that, in Locke's view, acting in accordance with one's conscience depends not on motives of fear or other sanctions but on a rational apprehension of the obligations of moral law.

"For it seems to me that certain essential features of things are immutable, and that certain proper functions [officia] arise out of necessity and cannot be other than they are. And this is not because nature or God (as I should say more correctly) might not have created man differently. Rather, the cause is that, since man has been made such as he is, equipped with reason and his other faculties and destined for this mode of life, there necessarily result from his inborn constitution [nativa constitutione] certain definite proper functions [officia], which cannot be other than they are" (199).[16]

It is perhaps worth noticing at this point how questions about "externalism" would arise in such an intellectual context for Locke and his contemporaries since many in the period take on board the Stoic notion that our rational essence mirrors the rationality of divine law. For the Stoics, questions about "internalism" and "externalism" would sound odd because we are all rational sparks that are parts of a providential divine nature, and in following moral laws we are fulfilling both the demands of our own particular natures and those of nature writ large. Locke, of course, has a Christian God in mind who is not part of his creation or immanent in his creatures. God is clearly an external moral authority in that sense, and Locke certainly makes no bones about our pitiful distance from an all-powerful creator. At the same time, however, Locke's own description of our relation to God's commands mimics the Stoic account in ways that can blur distinctions between "external" and "internal" because of the harmony between natural law and the structure of human rationality; moreover, he treats divine *doctrina*—Seneca's term for moral principles—in a recognizably Stoic manner by claiming that they are practical rational principles of action

---

16 In contrasting Locke with Culverwell and ascribing a purely juridical notion of obligation to Locke, it seems to me that Darwall completely overlooks passages such as these that show Locke's familiarity and reliance on Stoic claims about the congruency of man's rational essence and divine law; he consequently overstates the differences between Locke and Culverwell (Darwall, *British Moralists*, 33. Von Leyden, *John Locke*, 4, rightly in my view, suggests the *Discourse of the Light of Nature* as a possible source of "silent borrowings" on Locke's part.

that structure our virtuous choices and actions. Locke argues as well that the moral law from which these principles are derived is "insitam" (placed, implanted, etc.) in our hearts by God (legem…pectoribus nostris insitam) (III). Now, given that he later denies both that our knowledge of these principles is innate and that he stops short of claiming that our natural instincts lead us to a knowledge of natural law, Locke nonetheless seems to be holding on to an assumption, however weak, that there is some inner natural propensity that propels us in the direction of our proper duties. Locke had planned in the *Essays* to write on the question of whether man can come to know the law of nature through natural inclination, but seemingly balked at formulating a clear and open rejection of this central tenet of Stoic *oikeiosis*.[17] The fact that he never completed such an argument, however, is suggestive and perhaps points to a gap that pleasure and pleasurable self-awareness would come to fill in his mature thought.[18]

In any case, it should be clear on the one hand why for Locke, moral laws are not merely an inert set of juridical commands enforceable only by nonmoral sanctions and on the other why it is unlikely that he would think that motives for obedience can be entirely furnished by nonmoral psychological drives aiming solely at reward and punishment. Rather, Locke, like the Stoics, claims that moral laws have obligatory force because of the nature of our rationality and that we cannot help but be motivated by them as reasoning agents. Rational agents who come to understand these laws do not need sanctions to follow them; this is because "they cannot but determine the Choice in anyone, but that will consider."

As I now turn to Locke's hedonism, it is worth keeping in mind that however one construes these doctrines in the *Essays,* Locke thereafter gives us mostly occasional glimpses of his views about moral laws. Accordingly, it would be foolhardy to suggest that anything like a detailed

---

17 Von Leyden, *John Locke,* 158.

18 Whiting, "Lockeanism," shows how central the Stoic notion of *oikeiosis* comes to be for Locke's conceptions of self-consciousness and personal identity.

and fully defended account of these matters appears in the *Essay*. Nonetheless, if these Stoicizing features of Locke's theory are taken seriously and are understood to continue resonating in his later thought,[19] it forces us to reappraise the nature of his mature thinking on the role of pleasure in motivation and the nature of moral motivation generally.

PLEASURE, OBLIGATION, AND MOTIVATION

I would like to begin with a passage where Locke is typically taken to reject the *eudaimonism* of ancient philosophers and to be justifying an irreducible diversity in individual motivation (21.55): "Hence it was, I think, that the Philosophers of old did in vain enquire, whether *Summum bonum* consisted in Riches, or bodily Delights, or Virtue, or Contemplation: And they might have reasonably disputed, whether the best Relish were to be found in Apples, Plumbs, or Nut: and have divided themselves into Sects upon it." Of course, the subjectivity of individual pleasures is insufficient to establish the claim that Locke views pleasure as merely a secondary psychological theory. Those who claim that pleasures provide only motive force in the form of sanctions take the further step of linking Locke's view of desire to Hobbes's and to his claim that human desire lacks any teleological structure.[20] Thus, for comparison's sake, Locke says at 21.46: "We are seldom at ease, and free enough from the solicitation of our natural or adopted desires, but a constant succession of uneasinesses out of that stock which natural wants or acquired habits have heaped up, take the will in turns; and no sooner is one action dispatched, which by a determination of the will are set upon, but another uneasiness is ready to set us to work." It is tempting to read such passages as echoing Hobbes's rejection of a natural human *telos* and of breaking down motivation into a mere succession

---

19 See notes 11 and 12 here, with Sheridan's discussion.

20 See John Yolton's careful and convincing criticism, "Locke on the Laws of Nature," *Philosophical Review* 67:4 (1958): 490, of Leo Strauss's attempt to identify Locke's views on natural law and politics with those of Hobbes.

of movements, or in Lockean terms, a succession of "uneasinesses." The much-quoted passage at *Leviathan* 6.58, for instance, might seem to provide the appropriate Hobbesian parallel:

> *Continual success* in obtaining those things which a man from time to time desireth, that is to say continual prospering, is that men call FELICITY; I mean the felicity of this life. For there is no such thing as perpetual tranquility of mind while we live here; because life itself is but motion, and can never be without desire, nor without fear, no more without sense. What kind of felicity God has ordained to them that devoutly honor Him, a man shall no sooner know than enjoy, being joys that are now as incomprehensible as the word of school-men *beatifical vision* is unintelligible.

In addition to his claim that desires are merely types of motion, presumably strictly material ones, Hobbes contrasts his overall view "with accounts of felicity given by traditional defenders of *eudaimonism*, in this case Aquinas, who made the standard of felicity supernatural happiness, or blessedness, attained through the beatifical vision of God."[21] Hobbes insists, of course, that we are able to reason only about the natural condition of human beings in this life, but he also takes aim at Epicureans and Stoics who associate happiness in this life with *ataraxia*. He dismisses the possibility of attaining in life a psychological state of "tranquility"—a life without continual wants and fears, especially the fear of death.

Hobbes's skepticism about an objective final good, as evidenced by his claim that happiness is merely the continual success in obtaining things that our desires move us toward, is also often attributed to Locke on the basis of this similarly much-quoted passage from the *Essay*: "And therefore it was the right answer of the physician to his

---

21 Donald Rutherford, "In Pursuit of Happiness: Hobbes's New Science of Ethics," *Philosophical Topics* 31 (2003): 360–393. As Rutherford points out, even Hobbes at times appeals to wider teleological criteria in setting out his accounts of desire and motivation.

patient that had sore eyes:—If you have more pleasure in the taste of wine than in the use of your sight, wine is good for you; but if the pleasure of seeing be greater to you than that of drinking, wine is naught" (21.55). But it is important to understand such passages in the larger context of Locke's argument. He is describing what our condition would be if "Men in this Life only have hope; if in this Life they can only enjoy" (21.55). Locke thinks it was useless for *pagan* philosophers to dispute about a *summum bonum* because they had inadequate conceptions of the possibility of eternal felicity. In direct opposition to Hobbes, however, Locke claims that agents fail in their pursuit of happiness precisely by disregarding the "absent good" of eternal felicity in favor of a diversity of present subjective pursuits that appear to them to suit their individual palates. Locke goes on to claim that without the secure anchor of eternal felicity, all of our pursuits might just as well be random and subjective:

> For if there be no Prospect beyond the Grave, the inference is certainly right, *Let us eat and drink,* let us enjoy what we delight in, *for tomorrow we shall die.* This, I think, may serve to shew us the Reason, why, though all Men's desires tend to Happiness, yet they are not moved by the same Object. Men may chuse different things, and yet all chuse right, supposing them only like a Company of poor Insects, whereof some are Bees, delighted with Flowers, and their sweetness; others Beetles, delighted by other kinds of Viands; which having enjoyed for a season, they should cease to be, and exist no more for ever. (21.55)

Of course, no ancient eudaimonist would think that there is nothing to be said about a choice between the pleasures of sight and the pains of blindness, even if death means our annihilation. But Locke claims that without the prospect of eternal life, such choices are meaningless. He certainly does not think, however, that such subjectivity about the good still infects our choices and pleasures in view of God's gift of eternal life and the possibility of eternal felicity. Locke continually laments throughout the *Essay* that we place our happiness in the wrong things. But he does not conclude, like Hobbes, that there is nothing to be said about the goodness or badness of these pursuits objectively. Indeed, he merely reproduces a familiar ancient reply to a familiar ancient objection. By delineating the diversity of pursuits and the fact that some engage in pursuits destructive of true happiness, Locke tries to show the foolishness of those who fail to pursue the common *telos* of eternal felicity (21.46). He therefore feels impelled to explain "*How Men come to prefer the worse to the better*" (21.56–57), especially when the better joys of our future state are so manifestly superior. In some sense, he feels his task is more difficult than that of ancient philosophers, since those pursuing the present goods of earthly pleasure require less strength of mind than those Lockean agents who must correctly judge from a great distance the absent pleasures of eternity—pleasures with which they are entirely unacquainted. (21.65).

Locke claims that if there were not infinite degrees of happiness that are not yet in our possession—that is, eternal life—our happiness might indeed consist of a life of moderate pleasure with all uneasiness being removed—that is, something close to *ataraxia*. (see 21.45–46) And this is perhaps Locke's most important divergence from ancient *eudaimonists*. He thinks that any account of the final good must also include mention of an eternal life and the prospects of eternal pleasure or pain. In so doing, however, he dismisses common subjectivist challenges to those eternal pleasures of the following sort. What if it turns out that I do not like the pleasures of eternity or what if I grow tired of them? Or what if I find them "insipid and nauseous" in comparison to earthly delights? Am I not the only judge of what gives me pleasure and might I not trade intense present pleasures for potentially long-term desiccated ones? Locke insists that such objections reflect a false way of judging since they must assume that "God cannot make those happy he designs to be so. For that being intended for a State of Happiness, it must certainly be agreeable to everyone's wish and desire:

Could we suppose their relishes there as different as they are here, yet the manna in heaven will suit every one's plate" (21.65).

What characterizes intellectual beings, for Locke, is "their constant endeavor after and a steady prosecution of true felicity," which he describes both as an obligation and as a motive to pursue as their good. Indeed, higher beings are more steadily determined in their choice of happiness (21.49); even "God Almighty himself is under the necessity of being happy" (21.50). Locke thus claims that the pursuit of happiness itself is a duty that obligates agents and provides them with motives to try to approach infinite perfection and happiness. "For the inclination, and tendency of their happiness is an obligation, and motive to them, to take care not to mistake or miss it; and so necessarily puts them upon caution, deliberation, and wariness, in the direction of their particular actions, which are the means to obtain it. Whatever necessity determines to the pursuit of real Bliss, the same necessity, with the same force establishes *suspence, deliberation,* and scrutiny of each successive desire, whether the satisfaction of it, does not interfere with our true happiness and mislead us from it" (21.52). In the same way that Locke characterizes the mandates of natural law as being obligatory and as providing motives that cannot but determine the actions of rational agents, he takes our eternal happiness as being similarly obligatory and motivating. He claims, moreover, that it is likewise incumbent on us to coolly reflect on each of our desires and, like a good Epicurean or Stoic, to "suspend" the course of particular desires and to hold up to fair examination the good or evil in them, since this is "the great privilege of finite intellectual Beings." "This we are able to do; and when we have done it, we have done our duty,[22] and all that is in our power; and indeed all that needs" (21.52).

It still remains to be seen, of course, what this package of claims about our various obligations and motives amounts to, but Locke

---

22   In his Latin writings, Locke uses the terminology of *officia*. It may be that he is still using "duty" in a more neutral sense of *officium* or "proper function," but the way he couples duty with obligation in these passages suggests a stronger deontic sense.

seems to offer two principles for regulating our action—pleasure and moral law—that are both obligatory and that provide us with motives for acting. He also thinks that it is our duty to coolly step back and reflect on our desires in the light of these rational principles, a claim to which I can now turn.

RATIONALITY, MOTIVES, AND AUTONOMOUS ACTIONS

At times, Locke says things that make it appear that he is following Hobbes on questions of desire and action and that he holds a similarly naturalistic view of human volitions. Take, for instance, the following claim about the nature of voluntary actions: "But we being in this world beset with sundry uneasinesses, distracted with different desires, the next inquiry naturally will be,—Which of them has the precedency in determining the will to the next action? and to that the answer is,—That ordinarily which is the most pressing of those that are judged capable of being then removed.... But these set apart, the most important and urgent uneasiness we at that time feel, is that which ordinarily determines the will, successively, in that train of voluntary actions which makes up our lives" (*Essay* 2.21.41). In the kind of stimulus-response model that Locke describes in this passage, human action would appear to be the natural causal outcome or consequence of prior "uneasinesses," that is, the desires, pains, pleasures, and so on that serve as the causes that determine the operations of the will. Our individual experiences of various feelings of "uneasiness" move the will and determine its choices according to their motive strength. Thus, from passages such as these, one can easily conclude, as many commentators have, that Locke endorses a model of human volition in which stimuli causally determine our volitions, which in turn cause the actions that flow from them. Locke, moreover, sometimes seems to characterize a free action as one that is in accordance with the preference or direction of an agent's mind or will, and thus, accordingly, "as that particular power of rational agents that enables them to act or not to act." This might suggest that Locke, like Hobbes, straightforwardly identifies free actions with voluntary ones and, like Hobbes, thinks that agents are acting freely just insofar as they are willing what they are doing. This kind of naturalistic project of explaining action can be schematized as follows:

(1) Human actions are part of a causal chain and have sufficient prior causes.

(2) Motives, which are psychological states, are sufficient prior causes of actions.

Thus, for any agent (F) with a set of motives (M), if (F) performs action (G) at time (T), then there is some member of set (M) that is F's strongest motive and that causes F to perform (G) at time (T).

So, for instance, at 2.21.29, Locke writes: "The motive, for continuing in the same State or Action, is only the present satisfaction in it; The motive to change, is always some *uneasiness*.... This is the great motive that works on the Mind to put it upon Action." At 1.3 he calls will and appetite the "springs[23] and motives" of actions, and of his ten uses of "motive" in the *Essay*, roughly half are identified with prior belief/appetitive states that figure as part of a strictly naturalistic, causal account of action.

For Locke, this is not the whole story, however, and although it may be a necessary condition of any free action that it be voluntary, it is not a sufficient condition. Free action requires in addition what Locke calls liberty.[24]

---

23 Locke's four other uses of "springs" in the *Essay* refer to the inner mechanisms of machines, so in coupling "motive" with "springs," Locke is using an innovative and live figure that should be taken seriously.

24 See the discussions of Peter A. Schouls, *Reasoned Freedom: John Locke and the Enlightenment* (Ithaca, NY: Cornell University Press, 1992), 117–144; Sheridan, *Locke*.

So that the idea of *liberty* is, the idea of a power in any agent to do or forbear any particular action, according to the determination or thought of the mind, whereby either of them is preferred to the other: where either of them is not in the power of the agent to be produced by him according to his volition, there he is not at liberty; that agent is under *necessity*. So that liberty cannot be where there is no thought, no volition, no will; but there may be thought, there may be will, there may be volition, where there is no liberty. (2.21.8)

After distinguishing mere volition from liberty, Locke goes on to consider several Frankfurt-style cases—the famous example of the man in the locked room—in which agents seem to will certain actions or to make voluntary choices that he thinks fall short of full-blown free or responsible actions in important ways (2.21.27). Thus, identifying or isolating the voluntariness of an action or choice is not sufficient, in his view, for capturing the criteria needed for determining whether actions are fully in the power of agents, hence an expression of their "liberty." To explain this further feature of free actions, Locke introduces the notion of "suspension":

we have a power to *suspend* the prosecution of this or that desire, as every one daily may Experiment in himself. This seems to me the source of all liberty; in this seems to consist that which is (as I think improperly) call'd *Free Will*. For, during this *suspension* of any desire, before the *will* be determined to action, and the action (which follows that determination) done, we have opportunity to examine, view, and judge of the good or evil of what we are going to do; and when, upon due *Examination*, we have judg'd, we have done our duty, all that we can, or ought to do, in pursuit of our happiness; and 'tis not a fault, but a perfection of our nature, to desire, will, and act according to the last result of a fair *Examination*. (2.21.47)

Locke claims that, although the will and human volitions are causally determined, yet we have a power to suspend volitions, and hence, in some (admittedly obscure) way, are at any time capable of suspending the causal force of prior stimuli and of rationally choosing between two alternative actions.

Gideon Yaffe, for instance, views Locke's account of our power to rationally suspend volitions as something causally suspicious—in his formulation, "a form of self-transcendence" and a way of "giving oneself over to God, and thereby freeing oneself from bondage to the self."[25] Yaffe is concerned to place Locke in a particular historical context and to acknowledge a precise strand of Christian theological argument that has its roots in Christian texts and ideology. However, I would argue that we have a better parallel, since Locke's account of "suspension" has an obvious Hellenistic philosophical pedigree. Moreover, it relies on the sort of optimistic faith in individual rationality that both Epicureans and Stoics attribute to unitary, rational, non-self-transcending agents; it reflects, that is, a particular picture of what on the one hand the Epicureans call *nephon logismos*, or sober reasoning, which they claim "tracks down the sources of every choice and avoidance and banishes opinions that beset souls with the greatest confusion" (Epicurus, *Letter to Menoeceus,* 132); and on the other, it mirrors a Stoic view of our rational ability to make decisions by giving or withholding assent to various impressions.[26] Moreover, Locke's emphasis on *judgment* as the crucial, final process in an agent's suspension and rational deliberation echoes Seneca rather directly.[27]

Of course, the Epicureans and Stoics themselves disagreed about whether our rational ability to suspend desires was best understood as being part of a causal or noncausal account of nature, so it should hardly

---

25 Gideon Yaffe, *Liberty Worth the Name: Locke on Free Agency* (Princeton, NJ: Princeton University Press, 2000), 6.

26 For the Stoic details, see the discussion of Brad Inwood, *Ethics and Human Action in Early Stoicism* (Oxford: Oxford University Press, 1985), 86.

27 See Brad Inwood, "Moral Judgment in Seneca," in Inwood, *Reading Seneca: Stoic Philosophy at Rome* (Oxford: Oxford University Press, 2005).

take us by surprise that Locke's modern interpreters differ over whether he takes himself to be offering a naturalistic or nonnaturalistic account of human agency. In either case, however, Locke seems to face a looming difficulty in his account of motives for action. This is because on the one hand as I have shown, he treats motives as "uneasinesses" and incitements to action. But on the other, his account of our ability to suspend the progress of desires and to coolly evaluate them is embedded in a teleological context in which motives are treated as intentional objects or ends of action. Happiness and virtue serve as crucial motives in this alternate sense. So, for instance, he calls pleasure the "motive" of our action at *Essay* 2.20; elsewhere he maintains that "the proper object and motive of our assent is probability" (4.16). Thus, while Locke speaks of "uneasinesses" as being motives, he also is clearly prepared to treat motives as intentional objects or teleological ends of action.[28] In the subsequent tradition of "autonomist internalism" leading to Kant, such motives as ends are typically treated as being different from causes, at least efficient causes; hence the reluctance of scholars like Yaffe to view Lockean agency as strictly naturalistic, inasmuch as it seems plausible to suppose that moral reasons and moral motives in this broadly teleological sense are not causes as such, at least of the sort amenable to investigation by the natural sciences. When coupled with Locke's further claim that autonomy consists in agents being able to step back and evaluate their inciting motives or uneasinesses along broadly ethical and prudential lines, the possibility of Locke's nonnaturalism seems to come even more clearly to the fore.

Locke's appeal to these two different conceptions of motive might therefore threaten to create a deep fissure in his account of agency,

---

28 See T. Cuneo, "A Puzzle Regarding Reid's Theory of Motives," *British Journal for the History of Philosophy* 19:5 (2011): 963–981, for a helpful discussion of the distinction between motives as ends for which we act and motives as mental states that incite us to act. I am indebted to his framing of the issues in what follows. Interestingly, Hobbes couples "motive" with "end" (see *Leviathan* 14) and in the four occurrences in *Leviathan* does not use "motive" as an inciting mental state. In appealing to both senses of "motive," Locke's example proved influential for the next generation of philosophers, though they worried, in a way Locke appears not to have, about the compatibility of these different conceptions.

since it appears that he assesses motives along two potentially conflicting dimensions: their rational authority and their pressing occurrent psychological strength.[29] Famously, Locke develops an agency-centered account that grounds many of his central metaethical claims about the nature of moral reality in a particular view of human agency. But while he deems autonomous actions to be those that are under the regulative control of the whole person or agent, his account of motivation based on the causal efficacy of the most pressing uneasiness would seem to shatter agency into a mere theater of impulses in the manner of Hume. To be sure, Locke identifies motives that are incitements as those that guide the voluntary actions of animals, children, and agents who have not rationally deliberated about their impulses. Actions that are the product of rational deliberation and judgment, conversely, display full human agency and derive from motives that have rational authority. But such a distinction between motives threatens to leave Locke with the potentially unpalatable result that when we are ordinarily motivated by our most pressing uneasiness, we are not engaged in a fully human action. By the same token, when we are motivated by rational principles and engaged in fully human action, incitements might seem to be left with no role at all to play in motivating us. We therefore seem doomed to fluctuate between two irreconcilable sources of motivation that in their own right never make contact.[30]

Locke claims, however, that there is a further important feature of rational agency. In evaluating desires in the light of their contribution to our virtue and final good, agents can change the agreeableness and disagreeableness of the things that desires aim at; that is, reason has the capability to, what Locke calls, "raise" desires after due rational consideration. We can calibrate, as it were, the motivational strength and the

---

29 See Cuneo, "A Puzzle" (2011).

30 See Cuneo, "A Puzzle," for an exceptionally clear statement of a parallel puzzle in Reid and his own suggested solution. See Inwood, *Ethics and Human Action in Early Stoicism,* 87, for a parallel discussion of controversies between Stoics and skeptics about the roles of impulse and suspension in generating action.

affective quality of our uneasinesses in the light of our authoritative rational motives and principles.

> Whether it be in a man's power to change the pleasantness that accompanies any sort of action? And as to that, it is plain that in many cases he can. Men may and should correct their palates and give relish to what either has, or they suppose has none. The relish of the mind is as various as the mind, and like that too may be altered; and it is a mistake to think that men cannot change the displeasingness or indifferency that is in actions into pleasure and desire, if they will but do what is in their power. A due consideration will do it in some cases; and practice, application, and custom in most. Bread or tabacco may be neglected where they are shown to be useful to health, because of an indifferency or disrelish to them; reason and consideration at first recommends, and begins their trial, and use finds, or custom makes them pleasant. That this is so in virtue, too is very certain. (*Essay* 2.21.71)

The general contours of Locke's account of motives and motivation would therefore appear to be as follows. He believes that we act from a great welter of motives—including those we have in common with children and animals—that typically propel us forward into action. What distinguishes us as rational agents, however, is our ability to pause and hold up for examination such motives and to regulate our conduct in the light of the two rational principles of motivation that function as our teleological goals: virtue and happiness. Indeed, it is our duty to ask ourselves whether any particular action truly contributes to our moral virtue and to our happiness. In a way that looks back to Hellenistic philosophers, but also forward to Kant, Locke argues that we are rational beings primarily because we can examine our various motives and impulses to act and judge them in accordance with the rational principle of moral law and, in Locke's case, in accordance with the demands of our happiness as well. We find these twin principles both motivating and obligatory, moreover, because of the very nature and structure of our reason. Although Schneewind argues that Reid and Kant were unique among the moderns in conceiving of morality primarily in terms of rational self-governance,[31] it is clear that Locke—relying on Stoics and Epicureans—should be included in their number and, indeed, strikingly anticipates Reid's more self-conscious discussion of the dual rational principles of morality and personal good and their mutual relation to self-governance. Unlike Reid and Kant, however, Locke does not establish the priority of morality. He thinks, like many ancient eudaimonists, that the virtuous experiences most suited to our nature must also contain the most enjoyment.

The overall picture that emerges, therefore, is that the right use of our reason enables us to discern the right course of action and to pursue both virtue and happiness in the right way. Such actions are paradigmatically both free and moral and in accord with the "perfection of our nature," while those that follow on hasty or precipitate judgment are morally defective and diminish our happiness. This use of our liberty is strictly in our power and on it depends the conduct of our lives and our endeavors to achieve happiness. We might object, of course, that if this account of Locke right, he is somehow failing to separate what his contemporary commentators have separated for him in attempting to account for his commitments to both moral law and to pleasure, that is, one ultimate source of moral motivation. Should we attempt to maximize pleasure or to follow the moral law when we suspend our desires and engage in rational reflection? If I am intent on listening to the call of the moral law, then, as Aristotle argued, are my pleasures not dependent on my prior beliefs about the law's value and, therefore, unable themselves to serve as the kind of prior independent standard of the good that is claimed for them by the hedonist?

---

31 J. B. Schneewind, *The Invention of Autonomy: A History of Modern Moral Philosophy* (Cambridge: Cambridge University Press, 1998).

One initial answer to this objection from a Lockean *eudaimonistic* hedonist might be that, given our natures, unless our beliefs about the moral law were truly pleasant, they would not track the truth. Locke certainly seems to think that the more truly agreeable the belief or experience, the more likely it is to be in accordance with virtue, and vice versa. But let me offer one final speculative historical suggestion. One possible trajectory of Locke's argument is that there is something distinctive in the affective experience of holding a particular belief or enjoying a particular action.[32] Such a claim is often hard won for contemporary defenders of hedonism, but Locke's account of "raising" desires suggests that holding and acting on the right moral belief is an experience more pleasurable than holding and acting on a mistaken one. This is because such beliefs answer to our specific rational nature. However, it is not just that the Lockean deliberator maintains various cognitive moral attitudes to the world that cause pleasure—this might arguably, as Aristotle claims, undercut hedonism—but that such virtuous beliefs and the actions they regulate are themselves justified by the particular sorts of pleasurable experience that God has affixed to them. We might, of course, be suspicious that Locke's theism dooms to success his attempt to harmonize the pursuit of both virtue and pleasure. By the same token, we might be equally suspicious of his claims that actions guided by moral law are themselves more pleasurable, not just for their further consequences but even as we engage in them, and that we can all come to recognize their superior agreeableness and cultivate it. However, such an account helps to explain why Locke moves so easily between pleasure and moral law when describing the *telos* of rational reflection throughout the *Essay*. In each case our goal is to live according to the demands of our rational nature, which for Locke means according to the dictates of both moral law and pleasure. Because of the nature of our rationality and the nature of our agency, we come to

---

32 See Roger Crisp, *Reasons and the Good* (Oxford: Oxford University Press, 2006), chap. 4, for an important discussion of felt-quality and attitudinal accounts of hedonism. See Sheridan, *Locke*.

discover these not as separate and competing ends, as the ancient Epicureans and Stoics thought, but in a way inseparably connected in the mind, with pleasure annexed to the idea of moral law.[33] Throughout the *Essay*, Locke puts only mathematical knowledge on an equal footing with moral knowledge. Even though there are no innate practical principles, we are still able to attain certain moral knowledge by coming to discover and to understand the relations among our moral concepts. Presumably, when we suspend the satisfaction of a present desire and rationally examine its good or evil, we come to see neither moral law nor pleasure, as Stoics and Epicureans thought, as being motivationally prior. Rather, we apprehend them together as a complex mode of ideas that answer to our rational nature and motivate us in "the conduct of our lives and the pursuit of pleasure."

Acknowledgments

I am grateful for helpful comments on earlier drafts of this essay to audiences at Queens University, Cornell University, the Graduate Center at City University of New York, and members of the Workshop titled "History of Moral Motivation," at City University of New York, October 2013.

---

33 See Sheridan, *Locke*, chap. 6, for a parallel discussion.

CHAPTER SEVEN

Hume on Moral Motivation

Jacqueline Taylor

INTRODUCTION: HUME'S SENTIMENT-BASED ETHICS

Hume aims in *Treatise* (T) book 3 to provide evidence that his "system of ethics" is true, or at least "satisfactory to the human mind, and might stand the test of the most critical examination" (T 3.3.6.1, 1.4.7.14). The particular hypothesis Hume sets out concerns our perception of moral right or wrong, virtue or vice, as a matter of sentiment, not of reason. After giving arguments against reason as the source of our perception of moral right and wrong, or virtue and vice (with opponents such as Samuel Clarke and William Wollaston in mind), he turns to set out the evidence that will support his hypothesis. We do not perceive moral right or wrong as mind-independent aspects of the world, graspable by reason or intellect alone, but we judge that actions are right or wrong, or characters are virtuous or vicious, by way of distinct sentiments of pleasure or pain in response to the traits of our own and others' character. These distinctive sentiments of moral approbation or blame require that we adopt a general or common point of view, from which we sympathize with those affected by a particular character. Sympathy with the agent's circle helps to correct for the distorting influences of self-interest, historical or physical distance from the agent surveyed, or attention to consequences rather than to character. Hume's task is thus primarily to *describe* how morality figures in our lives because of our capacity for sympathy, the principle that allows us to communicate our passions or opinions to one another, and the source of the moral sentiments that make us care about how one another's characters make a difference to the happiness or misery of mankind. So the focus is not in the first instance on moral motivation or the question of why we should be moral. Hume addresses the latter issue both in his account of why we should act justly and in the concluding paragraphs of the *Treatise*. An account of moral motivation, that is, of what motivates virtuous conduct, can be reconstructed by looking at Hume's account of motivation generally, as well as by examining the qualities we take to be virtues.

In the first part of this chapter, I set out Hume's *Treatise* account of motivation generally and then turn to look specifically at moral motivation, including justice, an artificial virtue, and the natural virtues. I also consider Hume's answers to the question of why we should care about being virtuous. I then turn to Hume's *Enquiry Concerning the Principles of Morals* (*EPM*), a work neglected until recently by philosophers, to examine his arguments for the essential role of reason if we are to evaluate or deliberate well. I will reconstruct an account of how we form moral commitments that can be brought to bear on practical deliberation and decision. In *EPM* and several essays, Hume makes the case that modern morality endorses communities that value humanity, justice, and benevolence and so contrasts appreciably with the morality of martial societies, particularly insofar as members of the modern society have greater opportunity to cultivate a sense of humanity that exerts a positive influence on both moral evaluation and moral motivation. In other essays, Hume elaborates how moral causes, which include institutional arrangements, such as forms of government, either delimit or provide opportunities for the kinds of character members of a society can cultivate and the kinds of values that they will tend to hold in esteem. In these later works, we find a unique normative dimension to Hume's ethics, with a focus on how character, as the source of our deliberation and motivation, is mediated in significant ways by the moral causes that influence how people conceive of their social and practical identities.

1. BELIEF AND PASSION: MUTUAL INFLUENCES

Critics of Hume's views on motivation typically focus on the argument in *Treatise* 2.3.3, where reason is assigned the role, "the slave of the passions," and serves to identify means to ends or to establish that a given object does meet the criteria of a desired end. According to the critics, Hume is either an instrumentalist (with a view equivalent to that of the contemporary Humean) or a skeptic about practical reason.[1] Some defenders of Hume also focus on *Treatise* 2.3.3 in order to show why the Humean reading of Hume's argument is mistaken.[2] Others argue that by considering the broader context of Hume's philosophy in the *Treatise*, we can find ample resources for reconstructing a substantive account of practical deliberation or moral motivation. I will begin by canvassing the main relevant parts of the *Treatise* to establish that Hume has an account more subtle than the instrumentalist's belief-desire model of means-end reasoning.

---

1 On instrumentalism see, for example, Michael Smith, *The Moral Problem* (Malden, MA: Blackwell, 1994). On Hume as a skeptic, see Christine M. Korsgaard, "Skepticism about Practical Reason," *Journal of Philosophy* 83 (1986): 5–25.

2 *Treatise* 2.3.3 continues to receive a lot of attention in the literature. For recent contributions see, for example, Elizabeth Radcliffe, "Moral Sentimentalism and the Reasonableness of Being Good," *Revue Internationale de Philosophie* 1 (2013): 9–27; Rachel Cohon, *Hume's Morality: Feeling and Fabrication* (New York: Oxford University Press, 2008); Cass Weller, "Scratched Fingers, Ruined Lives, and Acknowledged Lesser Goods," *Hume Studies* 30 (2004): 51–85; and Kieran Setiya, "Hume on Practical Reason," *Philosophical Perspectives* 18 (2004): 365–389.

In *Treatise* 2.3.3, Hume argues that only passion can directly influence the will. Reason alone can have no such influence. Reason's own influence is indirect, concerning the means to take to desired ends or establishing that an object does correspond to a desire or passion. So if someone has a false belief about a desired object or the means to it, "'tis not the passion, properly speaking, which is unreasonable, but the judgment" (T 2.3.3.6). But in *Treatise* 1.3.10, "Of the influence of belief," Hume examines how belief and passion *do* have a mutual influence on one another.[3] "The chief spring and moving principle" of the mind is the perception of good or evil, pleasure or pain. But it cannot be actual pain or pleasure alone that always moves us to action, since that would entail that we have actually to experience the pain or pleasure, without the means to avoid pain in advance or to take steps to experience pleasure. Nor can mere ideas serve to move us to action, since we frequently have fanciful thoughts about things that are good or harmful, and if the mind were actually moved to action by these "it wou'd never enjoy a moment's peace and tranquillity" (T 1.3.10.2). Belief or judgment about what does or will hold for us the prospect of pain or pleasure constitutes a "medium" between an existent pain or pleasure and an idle conception. Belief enlivens an idea, raising it "to an equality with our impressions" and bestowing on it "a like influence on the passions" (T 1.3.10.3). Beliefs about the prospect of good or evil influence the will by arousing a desire for a good or an aversion to an evil. In *Treatise* 2.3.3 Hume states: "when we have the prospect of pain or pleasure from any object, we feel a consequent emotion of aversion or propensity, and are carry'd to avoid or embrace what will give us this uneasiness or satisfaction" (T 2.3.3.3). Belief or judgment is thus a candidate for what presents "the prospect of pain or pleasure" and so for

---

3 Annette Baier points out that this section has been ignored by, among others, David Fate Norton, *David Hume: Common Sense Moralist, Sceptical Metaphysician* (Princeton, NJ: Princeton University Press, 1982), and J. L. Mackie, *Hume's Moral Theory* (London: Routledge and Kegan Paul, 1980). See Annette C. Baier, *A Progress of Sentiments: Reflections on Hume's "Treatise"* (Cambridge, MA: Harvard University Press, 1991), 309.

arousing the "emotion of aversion or propensity." As Rachel Cohon has pointed out, Hume's reworking of this section in his *Dissertation of the Passions* makes it clear that only beliefs about matters of fact *not* having to do with good or evil lack any influence on the will.[4] A lively belief about the prospects of pain or pleasure can influence the will "mediately," as Annette Baier puts it, by affecting the relevant passions.[5]

In their turn, passions influence belief. Hume gives us the example of the coward whose fear makes him believe that a perfectly safe situation holds danger for him. Someone with a cultivated empathy might be attuned to situations she encounters in such a way that she more readily forms beliefs about others' distress. We thus find a "mutual assistance" between belief or judgment and passion. There is also a mutual assistance between belief and the imagination: poetic descriptions that bear a semblance to reality prepare the mind to acquiesce and believe, while belief "gives vigour to the imagination." Hume observes: "a vigorous ands strong imagination is of all talents the most proper to secure belief and authority" (T 1.3.10.6–8).

2. INFLUENCES OF THE IMAGINATION ON THE MOTIVATING PASSIONS

In addition to the influence of belief, certain tendencies of the imagination and other passions have an influence on what Hume calls the *direct* passions, those that directly move us to action. In the concluding paragraphs of *Treatise* 2.3.3, Hume invokes a distinction between two kinds of motivating passions: the calm and the violent. The calm passions may be mistaken for the actions of reason since they "produce little emotion in the mind, and are known more by their effects [the

---

4 Cohon, *Hume's Morality*, 50.
5 Baier, *A Progress of Sentiments*, 159.

actions they produce] than by the immediate feeling." Some calm desires are original instincts, and these include "benevolence and resentment, the love of life, and kindness to children." Other calm desires constitute a "general appetite to good, and aversion to evil" (T 2.3.3.8). This general appetite for the good and aversion to evil help one form one's view of one's "greatest possible good," that which is genuinely in one's interest and the plans one makes for how one wants one's life to go. We might act against our greatest possible good when in the grip of a violent passion. On the other hand a calm and strong passion "can counter-act a violent passion" so that we prosecute our real "interests and designs," which shows that we are not simply moved by the "present uneasiness" of a violent desire. Both calm and violent passions influence the will, and which prevails depends on an agent's "*general* character or *present* disposition." When the calm passions more frequently guide a person's choices than the violent passions, she possesses strength of mind (T 2.3.3.10). Nevertheless, Hume observes that "when we wou'd govern a man, and push him to any action, 'twill commonly be better policy to work upon the violent than the calm passions, and rather take him by his inclination," than to rely on his calm appetite for the greater good (T 2.3.4.1). I will show shortly how magistrates appeal to the violent passion of interest in order to promote just conduct in citizens.

Hume notes that "what we commonly understand by *passion*, is a violent and sensible emotion of the mind, when any good or evil is presented.... By reason we mean affections of the very same kind with the former; but such as operate more calmly, and cause no disorder in the temper. Which tranquillity leads us into a mistake concerning them, and causes us to regard them as conclusions only of our intellectual faculty" (T 2.3.8.13). Many typically violent passions can become calm, and what are typically calm passions can be felt as more violent (particularly resentment or kindness to children). Custom, or repetition, has a calming effect on the passions, directing our actions and conduct without emotional agitation (T 2.3.4.1). If we act repeatedly from, for example, kindness, courage, prudence, industriousness, or frugality, custom bestows "a *facility* in the performance" of an action and subsequently "a *tendency* or *inclination* towards it"; we develop a habit of acting (T 2.3.5.1).[6] Repetition produces facility, which Hume calls "a very powerful principle of the human mind," because it is a source of pleasure. Facility's pleasure consists not in an agitation of the spirits but in "their orderly motion; which will sometimes be so powerful as even to convert pain into pleasure, and give us a relish in time for what at first was most harsh and disagreeable" (T 2.3.5.3–4). We need not simply be passive with respect to our experience of the passions but can cultivate certain passions, especially those that help us to pursue the ends we most value.

In addition to custom, our situation with regard to a desired object also influences whether the passion will be calm or violent. In particular, if a desired object is near, the passion tends to be more violent. As Hume explains, the imagination influences the passions by making them view their object in the present light, so that desirable objects near to us gain our favor even when they lack the "real and intrinsic value" of what really tends to our greater good: our passions "always plead in favour of what is near and contiguous," making us more likely to yield to their "sollicitations [*sic*]" (T 3.2.7.2). This tendency of the passions and their grip on the will constitutes a main reason that we act against our "known interest" or our greater good (T 3.2.7.3). When no desired object is near, we can consider at a distance the things that would best satisfy our greater good; that is, we mentally stand back from our passions and reflectively consider their objects and our real preferences. From this perspective, we find that "all their minute distinctions vanish, and we always give the preference to whatever is in itself preferable, without considering its situation and circumstances."

---

6 I do not mean to suggest that only passions directed toward one's own or another's good can be calm; as Hume observes, there can be a calm ambition, anger, or hatred that can "be very strong, & have absolute command over the mind." See "Hume's Letter to Francis Hutcheson, Jan. 10, 1743," in *The Letters of David Hume*, vol. 1, edited by J. Y. T. Greig (Oxford: Clarendon Press, 1932), 46.

This mental distance presents us with "the general and more discernible qualities of good and evil" (T 3.2.7.5). We may improperly think of this perspective as that of reason, since we are reflecting on what we want to do at some future time, and resolving to prefer that course of conduct that will be for our greater good, but the preference arises from that calm appetite for the good in general.[7]

Calm passions are thus typically *strong* passions and motives, able to prevail against an often more fleeting violent passion (a "momentary gust," as Hume puts it). In particular, it is those calm passions that, "when corroborated by reflection, and seconded by resolution," can most successfully counter our more violent passions. Through custom, and with reflection and resolve, a passion can "become a settled principle of action" and "the predominant inclination of the soul" (T 2.3.4.1). Echoing Joseph Butler's distinction between active, practical habits and passive ones, Hume argues that custom also increases our "*active* habits," so that the mind's tendency gives the "spirits" a "new force, and bends them more strongly to the action" (T 2.3.5.5). Some of our calm passions might also be considered as like reason not only because they are stronger than, and hence able to oppose, violent passions but also because they are *reflection-informed* responses that correspond to a *resolve* we have to act in a particular way (and that can include our moral commitments) and that give a *strength*, we might even say an *authority*, to our actions. This aspect of Hume's account of our dispositional motives deserves emphasis, for as Simon Blackburn has argued, Humean reasons are not merely wants but are deep-seated commitments to pursue or avoid, for example, certain objects or policies, and which give us reasons and prompt concern.[8]

---

7 See also Locke's detailed argument in chapter 21, "Of Power," in *An Essay Concerning Human Understanding*. Tito Magri nicely develops the implications of Hume's discussion in this part of the *Treatise*, in "Natural Obligation and Normative Motivation in Hume's *Treatise*," *Hume Studies* 22:2 (1996): 231–253.

8 Simon Blackburn, *Ruling Passions: A Theory of Practical Reasoning* (Oxford: Clarendon Press, 1998), 257.

3. Moral Motivation in the *Treatise*

After providing this broader context for motivation in general, I can now turn to consider moral motivation. I begin by looking at how various virtues inform our moral deliberation and contribute to our being moved to act well. Hume's focus in the *Treatise* remains primarily on the virtues (rather than on vices) because he draws important connections between virtuous conduct, others' moral approval (or approval of oneself through a mental self-survey), and taking pride in one's virtuous character or conduct. Pride, like love, is an *indirect* passion and a positive affective attitude we take toward ourselves in virtue of our accomplishments, advantages, or possessions; because pride has no end, it does not directly motivate. Nevertheless, Hume argues in the concluding paragraphs of the *Treatise* that taking pride in one's character makes up part of the "happiness" of virtue. Pride in virtue is both produced and sustained by our sympathy with the approval of others, and our own self-survey gives us a moral confidence and a sense of our own moral competence. Such pride reflects awareness of our ability to act well and to make a positive difference to our own and others' well-being. Pride thus lends support to those virtues that move us directly to action. And sympathizing with others' approval of the virtues that we all find valuable in turn sustains our sense of pride in being virtuous. Note, too, that "a due degree of pride," that is, a settled and stable sense of pride and valuing of ourselves "where we really have qualities that are valuable" is itself a virtue (T 3.3.2.8). Hume thus makes pride and self-confidence important characteristics of the virtuous person.[9]

Hume divides the virtues that move us to act into the artificial and the natural virtues. He discusses the artificial virtues first because the most important of these, namely, justice and the establishment of the rules for the possession and transfer of property, at the same time create

---

9 For further discussion, see Lorraine Besser-Jones, "Hume on Pride-in-Virtue: A Reliable Motive?," *Hume Studies* 36 (2010): 171–192. See also my "Moral Sentiments and the Sources of Moral Identity," in *Morality and the Emotions,* edited by Carla Bagnoli (Oxford: Oxford University Press, 2011), 257–274.

a society whose members take a *moral* interest in justice. In sharing a general sense of common interest, they acquire a sense of the *public* interest. Here I discuss the natural virtues first, since that will give us a general picture of how Hume conceives the nature of virtue and vice. Let us first briefly review Hume's claim in T 2.3.3 that it is "not contrary to reason to prefer the destruction of the whole world to the scratching of my finger" or "to choose my total ruin, to prevent the least uneasiness of an *Indian* or person wholly unknown to me" or to desire and choose my "acknowledg'd lesser good to my greater" as long as I am not in the grip of a false judgment about my preferences (T 2.3.3.6). Despite these infamous lines, what Hume does think about these three preferences is that they are vicious, arising from, for example, selfishness, imprudence, or folly. Vice is harmful to oneself or others but not irrational (although there is a sense in which we can find in Hume's moral philosophy a sense of reasonableness that does line up with being a virtuous person).[10] Reason alone does not require me to avoid my total ruin, but prudence does. If I possess prudence, and I can reason that relieving a stranger's mild distress would require me to sacrifice everything I have, then I can on reflection judge such self-sacrifice as imprudent and therefore wrong. My judgment that my desired course of conduct is imprudent and wrong is accompanied by an uneasiness that leads me to stand back from that action. Here my thinking becomes more practical as I reflect on the outcome of not helping the stranger. My usual calm desire to avoid action leading to my own destruction arises and can thus oppose the violent desire to assist the stranger at such great cost to myself.

A virtue is an enduring and useful or agreeable mental disposition, and the motivating virtues prompt us to act well in ways that are good for ourselves or others. They include the various traits making up "greatness of mind," such as courage and magnanimity, all of which

---

10 See, for example, Páll Árdal, "Some Implications of the Virtue of Reasonableness," in *Hume: A Re-Evaluation* (New York: Fordham University Press, 1976), and Baier, *Progress of Sentiments*.

derive a large part of their merit from pride (T 3.3.2.13). Other self-regarding virtues include such qualities as prudence and industry. We also can cultivate other-regarding virtues that Hume puts in the category of "goodness and benevolence," including generosity, gratitude, and equity. Traits that make up what in the *Enquiry* Hume calls *personal merit* include immediately agreeable mental qualities, such as wit, with no useful tendencies; talents that are mental qualities also contribute to someone's personal merit.

Character is what matters to us in terms of our responses to one another's conduct or attitudes. Character is made up of "durable mental qualities," settled habits of feeling and dispositions to respond and act in certain ways depending on the situation. These "durable principles of the mind," including justice and other social and self-regarding virtues, "extend over the whole conduct, and enter into the personal character" (T 3.3.1.4). Someone's reasons for acting typically reflect the characteristic way she responds to situations. Her actions or attitudes thus serve as "signs" and show us what kind of character she has. Character evokes certain moral responses, for example, approval or blame, independently of the consequences of the person's action. The relation between someone's character and the moral sentiments is crucial for Hume. As he puts it in *EPM*, moral taste gives us the sentiments of virtue and vice. It "has a productive faculty, and gilding or staining all natural objects with the colours, borrowed from internal sentiment, raises, in a manner, a new creation" (*EPM*, Appendix, 1.21). It is because we respond as we do, with approval or blame, to what we take to be someone's character that we recognize virtue and vice.

The artificial virtues are so called in the *Treatise* because we lack a natural motive to act as each particular virtue requires. For example, with respect to justice, we have no innate desire to respect the possessions of others; moreover, there is no such thing as property until its existence is established by a convention. Justice gets established necessarily when naturally sociable human beings realize both that their sociability is limited and that they nonetheless have a crucial interest in cooperating with one another, both to increase resources and for collective security. Lacking a universal benevolence that extends to all, at least some people see that conventions, such as those for the existence and transfer of property, will promote cooperation and so be in the interest of all. The first motive to justice is thus self-interest, not its "heedless and impetuous movement" but interest redirected by a natural sagacity and judgment (T 3.2.2.9). A more enlightened self-interest, one that reflects on the benefits of its own restraint, continues to prompt people to act justly, given the recognized payoff of doing so. Earlier we saw the importance of repetition in creating a facility of acting. With respect to justice, repeatedly conforming one's conduct to the rules of justice will in time become a habit of acting justly. In *EPM*, Hume emphasizes this point about habitually cultivating a regard for justice and blame of injustice (*EPM* 3.47).

We recognize a moral obligation to justice, that is, justice as a virtue and injustice as vicious, because of our natural capacity for sympathy. Sympathy, for Hume, is our capacity to share affectively the emotions and sentiments of others; we can also sympathize with others' opinions. Our capacity to sympathize with others often moves us to respond to them (for example, to help them), to consider the weight of their interests and opinions, or to praise or condemn them. More specifically, in the case of justice, the rules of justice govern the actions of a specific group of people in a specific place. These people form a shared interest in having everyone observe the rules of justice. A *public* interest reflects our recognition of the scope of these rules. According to Hume, it is sympathy with that public interest, or with the good of mankind, that leads us to disapprove of the violation of these rules. We should note that typically we might not explicitly approve of just conduct; at best our approval is tacit since there is near consensus that the public interest requires such conduct of one another. (In *EPM* Hume suggests an analogy with the convention regarding the rules of the road.) I here agree with James Harris, who in a recent article argues that just conduct does not, for most people, most of the time, arise from one specific virtue of character.[11] I will go further, however, and note that some people, at least some of the time, do cultivate virtues of justice and a more enduring commitment to justice for its own sake, which manifest themselves through, for example, acts of loyalty, patriotism, or judicial or political leadership. At one point, Hume suggests that most of us who have been raised well will make it a point of honor to regard justice as estimable and worthy (T 3.2.2.26). Moreover, a concern for our reputation and our desire "to live on good terms with mankind," which form part of "our interested obligation" to be virtuous, as Hume puts it in *EPM*, keep us from violating the rules of justice (T 3.2.2.27; *EPM* 9.10–11). And as Annette Baier has suggested, those who are charged with the oversight or prosecution of justice, such as magistrates, have a special reason to take pride in their work, given the importance of preserving social stability and order.[12] So while most people much of the time habitually observe the rules of justice from a calm, enlightened self-interest or respect for convention, some people will have a genuine calm and strong passion for justice. One can here recall the point made earlier about how reflection and resolution can give an authority to the calm passions, in this instance in connection with the maintenance of justice.

4. THE *ENQUIRY*: HUME'S MATURE MORAL PHILOSOPHY

In *EPM*, Hume gives an account of moral evaluation and moral deliberation that has a greater sophistication than that of the *Treatise*. It gives a crucial role to reasoning well, such that habits of doing so are virtues of good evaluation and deliberation. Hume also identifies *different kinds* of moral sentiment, including the sentiment of humanity, which favors the useful virtues that make our lives go better. In *EPM*,

---

11 James A. Harris, "Hume on the Moral Obligation to Justice," *Hume Studies* 36 (2010): 25–50.

12 Annette C. Baier, "Master Passions," in *Explaining Emotions*, edited by Amelie O. Rorty (Berkeley: University of California Press, 1980), 403–423; see also Baier, *Justice: The Cautious Jealous Virtue* (Cambridge, MA: Harvard University Press, 2010).

part of Hume's task is still to settle the controversy concerning the foundation of morality, whether grounded in reason or taste and sentiment, but his approach is quite different, beginning with our actual practice of moral discourse about the "mental qualities" that make up someone's personal merit or demerit, and only returning to the respective roles of reason and sentiment in the first appendix.[13] He begins with the socially useful virtues of benevolence and justice. After introducing the socially useful qualities, he can make the case for self-regarding traits that are useful for the individual. Finally, he looks at those traits or aspects of traits that are immediately agreeable. The standard of virtue is now based on "general usefulness" and established through the moral conversation, debate, and negotiation of those taking up the common point of view. How an agent's character affects himself or others still matters, for it is our sympathy with others that leads us to care about the happiness of mankind, but the responses of those others no longer establish the standard of virtue, as Hume had argued at T 3.3.1.30 (see also T 3.3.1.18). Those who cultivate the virtues of reasoning well and a sense of humanity have an observable "great superiority" over others with respect to evaluation and deliberation (*EPM* 5.39). Hume notes that the sentiment of humanity especially characterizes members of modern societies that prize justice and benevolence. Moral discourse has a larger role in *EPM*, which accommodates the reality of our often having to debate or negotiate our evaluations of character and nicely highlights how moral knowledge can be a collective resource accruing through a social process. Finally, Hume takes account of how historical and cultural context matter for the recognition and valuation of character traits.

---

13 I believe Hume also corrects for certain inadequacies in the *Treatise* account of moral evaluation; while he shows in that work how we make our sentiments more impartial, he fails to discuss the role of good reasoning in moral evaluation. The virtues he identifies that are part of good moral evaluation in *Enquiry Concerning the Principles of Morals* also inform his account of moral deliberation. For more on these changes see my "Hume on the Standard of Virtue," *Journal of Ethics* 6 (2002): 43–62, and "Hume's Later Moral Philosophy," in *The Cambridge Companion to Hume*, 2nd ed., edited by David Norton and Jacqueline Taylor (Cambridge: Cambridge University Press, 2009), 311–340.

In cultivating the virtues of good judgment we can properly exercise our sense of virtue or *moral taste* as well as more consistently deliberate and choose well. Here Hume gives an essential role to good reasoning. To pave the way for the moral sentiments or to act from the appropriate virtue, and properly discern their objects, "we find, that much reasoning should precede, that nice distinctions be made, just conclusions drawn, distant comparisons formed, complicated relations examined, and general facts fixed and ascertained" (*EPM* 1.9). With the more complex orders of beauty, "it is requisite to employ much reasoning, in order to feel the proper sentiment; and a false relish may frequently be corrected by argument and reflection"; moral beauty as well "demands the assistance of our intellectual faculties, in order to give it a suitable influence on the mind" (*EPM* 1.9). We must exercise due diligence in gathering relevant facts: "we must be acquainted beforehand with all the objects, and all their relations to each other; and from a comparison of the whole, fix our choice or approbation.... All the circumstances of the case are supposed to be laid before us, ere we can fix any sentence of blame or approbation" (*EPM,* Appendix, 1.2). And if some "material circumstance be yet unknown or doubtful," then we must suspend our moral decision, although this may not be possible in cases in which we must act immediately (*EPM,* Appendix, 1.11). A cultivated sense of humanity may improve moral taste and give someone "a warm concern for the interests of our species" and a more "delicate feeling of all moral distinctions," which will inform both moral evaluation and deliberation (*EPM* 5.39). As Hume notes, some will be better at moral evaluation than others, but all possess some "spark" of humanity (unless their tempers have been corrupted by an overriding passion such as malice or envy) that leads to at least a "cool preference" for other's happiness over their misery (*EPM* 5.39). On the other hand the moral sentiments of those with a cultivated sense of humanity can take the form of regard or friendship, which are themselves virtues.

Regarding moral deliberation, Hume writes: "When a man, at any time, deliberates concerning his own conduct, (as, whether he had better, in a particular emergence, assist a brother or a benefactor) he must consider these separate relations, with all the circumstances and situations of the persons, in order to determine the superior duty and obligation" (*EPM*, Appendix, 1.11). In contrast to the mathematical reasoner, who infers an unknown relation from those already known, the moral deliberator "must be acquainted before-hand, with all the objects and all their relations to each other, and from a comparison of the whole, fix" his choice or approbation (*EPM*, Appendix, 1.11). There is no new fact or relation to be ascertained; he makes a choice based on his knowledge of all the relevant circumstances. Hume's example concerns the benevolent agent, whose sense of compassion or generosity makes him sensitive to the salient circumstances and informs his choice, moving him to offer assistance to the person he judges to be in most need. His humanity favors the choice that will be most useful and beneficial (*EPM*, Appendix, 1.3).

In the second part of section 9 of *EPM*, Hume examines what he calls our "interested obligation" to virtue or merit. The system of personal merit he has set out—focusing on the four kinds of qualities, useful or agreeable to oneself or others—gives us reason to believe that, as agents, cultivating the social virtues contributes to our own "happiness and welfare" (*EPM* 9.14). Cultivating the social virtues is not an onerous duty, and Hume has represented virtue "in all her genuine and most engaging charms," such that we "approach her with ease, familiarity and affection." Unlike some theological moralities, Hume's virtue asks for no denial or suffering. The aim is to make others and ourselves, "if possible, cheerful and happy." The only thing virtue demands is "just calculation, and a steady preference of the greater happiness" (*EPM* 9.15). Dropping the "figurative expression," Hume also makes the case more systematically. Those traits that are useful or agreeable to the agent should also be desired from self-interest, given their role in helping us to form and prosecute those plans and projects that help our lives to go well. The "companionable virtues," such as good manners and wit, earn us the company and admiration of others

(*EPM* 9.18). And in "the confederacy of mankind," the "enlarged virtues of benevolence, generosity, and humanity also contribute to *our* happiness and so are also desirable from the point of view of self-interest. Possessing the social virtues is agreeable for *us*, for they are felt as "sweet, smooth, tender, and agreeable." They give us a "pleasing consciousness," keeping us in a "humour" with ourselves and others. We find it agreeable to reflect on having done our part for mankind. In cultivating the social virtues, we find united "an agreeable sentiment, a pleasing consciousness, and a good reputation" (*EPM* 9.21).

Although the social virtues contribute to our own happiness, they are not forms of self-interest. In appendix 2, Hume explicitly argues against the selfish hypothesis, although an appropriate self-interest helps us to cultivate self-regarding virtues. Traits such as benevolence or friendship motivate us to act for the good of others when we find them in need or distress or because we recognize our natural duty to care for them. Hume argues that we distinguish between the "niggardly miser," whom we do not regard as praiseworthy, and the bravest hero, whom we do, typically on the basis of our own experience of generosity and courage in ourselves or others (*EPM*, Appendix, 2.2). Both our felt sentiments and the language of virtue and vice reflect the distinctions we make between the two, seeing them as two fundamentally different characters with quite different motives. We think that only the miser is moved by an excessive avidity. We *observe* dispositions toward friendship, benevolence, and compassion in ourselves and in other animals. People's actions, attitudes, and what they say all disclose to us the kind of character they have so that we can infer what motivates them to act as they do. The arguments to reduce all motivation to self-love are too subtle and intricate to convince us to abandon our observations of genuine sociability. (Hume makes a point of commenting on the honor of Epicurus and his sect, on the friendliness of Atticus and Horace, and on the "irreproachable lives" of Hobbes and Locke; *EPM*, Appendix, 2.3.) Borrowing an argument from Joseph Butler, Hume argues that just as hunger has eating for its end but can give rise to a secondary desire for the pleasure of particular foods, so too can benevolence and friendship have the good of others as their primary end but also give rise to a pleasure that contributes to our happiness. Benevolence *and* the pleasing consciousness and reflection on doing our part can combine to motivate us to promote the well-being of others (*EPM,* Appendix, 2.12).

5. JUSTICE AND HUMANITY IN THE *ENQUIRY* CONCERNING THE PRINCIPLES OF MORALS

Hume suggests that given what he has urged about the social virtues and their contribution to our own happiness as well as that of others, we can have no "pretext" for choosing vice over virtue, from the point of view of self-interest, "except, perhaps in the case of justice, where a man, taking things in a certain light, may often seem to be a loser by his integrity" (*EPM* 9.22). A sensible knave, for example, may hold as a general rule that "honesty is the best policy" but thinks that he can act unjustly for his own gain (*EPM* 9.22). Even the typically just person may sometimes find it difficult to act as or agree with what justice requires, given that not every instance of just conduct *by itself* promotes the well-being of society. We find it hard to be glad that the court awarded the inheritance to the debauched bachelor when a hardworking and loyal neighbor and his family would make much better use of the money. Unless we keep firmly in mind what justice requires, some individual decisions will seem to us uncompassionate or imprudent. The matter is different with the natural virtues that are not established by convention. If someone is in distress, I can exercise my benevolence to promote her well-being. My industriousness daily moves me closer to achieving my goals for my work. But with justice, it is not the individual acts that matter but the whole scheme, the steady following of the universal and inflexible rules that serve to maintain order and security for all. Hume acknowledges he has no reasoning for this view that could convince a knave whose heart does not "rebel against such perniciousness," who has no need for the pleasing "consciousness of integrity," and seems not to care about risking "a total loss of reputation, and the forfeiture of all future trust and confidence with mankind" (*EPM* 9.23–4).

He does think that most of us do care about "inward peace of mind, consciousness of integrity, a satisfactory review," of our own character and conduct, given what he has said about the role of virtue in contributing to our happiness (*EPM* 9.23). We can buttress the case for why most of us do adhere to the rules of justice most of the time by considering Hume's case for the relation between the sentiment of humanity and the virtue of justice. In *EPM* Hume argues that our sense of humanity prompts us to approve of justice and benevolence because they are useful virtues, and that our recognition and approval of utility does not derive solely from self-love. Close attention to the text in sections 5, 6, and 9 shows that for Hume, the principle or sentiment of humanity, insofar as it issues in moral approbation or blame, is a sympathy-based response to the happiness or misery of others when their condition is caused by their own or others' *useful* or *harmful* character traits. In section 9, Hume maintains that the sentiment of humanity allows us to see ourselves as members in the party of humankind, united in our love of or regard for virtue and our abhorrence of vice.

While Hume does not posit a strict hierarchy of virtues (and no unity of the virtues), the evidence suggests that the sentiments arising from the principle of humanity give the traits that are their object a greater moral significance for us. This is particularly the case for justice. Utility is a "considerable part" of the merit of the virtues of benevolence and the self-regarding virtues (which also have immediately agreeable aspects), but it is the *sole* source of the moral approval of justice, veracity, fidelity, honor, and integrity. Hume writes: "The necessity of justice to the support of society is the *sole* foundation of that virtue; and since no moral excellence is more highly esteemed, we may conclude, that this circumstance of usefulness has, in general, the strongest energy, and most entire command over our sentiments"

(*EPM* 3.48).[14] Since human society, which all individuals need, cannot "subsist" without justice, it should make "inviolable" our regard for the duty to be just (*EPM* 3.39). Alluding to his experimental methodology, he concludes: "It is entirely agreeable to the rules of philosophy, and even of common reason; where any principle has been found to have a great force and energy in one instance, to ascribe to it a like energy in all similar instances. This indeed is Newton's chief rule of philosophizing [in *Principia*, book 3]" (*EPM* 3.48). Usefulness, especially when consideration of it enjoins conduct to meet a need as important as social order and the security of the people, leads us to regard as more morally significant the useful over the agreeable traits of character, and a regard for justice as most useful of all. Correspondingly, we regard violations of justice as most blameworthy. An unjust injury to an individual creates both a public wrong, because the rules of equity have been violated, and a private harm, by disappointing the legitimate expectations of the injured individual. As Hume points out, the second consideration is only possible because the first is in place, "but where the greatest public wrong is also conjoined with a considerable private one…the highest disapprobation attends so iniquitous a behavior" (*EPM*, Appendix, 3.11).

Annette Baier has argued for the importance of Hume's introducing in *EPM* the passion of resentment in relation to justice. Resentment is not a form of hopelessness but a *power* of rational creatures of equal strength, insofar as they can make others feel the force of their resentment for injury and wrongs. Baier sees resentment as potentially a good, a protomoral sentiment that motivates avenging oneself against wrongdoers. She also sees it as the natural watchdog of pride, since opportunities for pride are threatened in those who are the victims of injustice and other wrongdoing, including oppression. In essays such as "Of the Populousness of Ancient Nations" or "Of Polygamy and Divorce," Hume examines how both pride and resentment are sometimes

---

14 Hume capitalizes "sole"; I have italicized it to capture the emphasis.

fragile goods, ones that can be extinguished by extreme inhumanity, as he thinks happens in slaveholding and polygamous societies.[15] In the *Essays: Moral, Political, and Literary,* Hume considers another form of humanity as a motivating virtue and inhumanity as a vice. Inhumanity is a vicious motive to treat others cruelly, callously, or with indifference. Its opposite is humanity as a virtue that moves us to treat others decently. In other essays, particularly "Of the Rise and Progress of the Arts and Sciences" and "Of Refinement in the Arts," Hume details how certain modern societies, in which industry flourishes and justice and government provide greater civil liberties, will also encourage the cultivation of both the sentiment and motive of humanity. There is, moreover, a mutual influence between humanity the virtue and justice, since the former can prompt social and political reforms that benefit more members of society. Hume's examination, in his role as historian and social theorist as well as political philosopher, of how institutions such as the law, government, or economy influence the tempers and characters that motivate particular actions and ways of living adds another important normative dimension to his moral philosophy.[16]

6. Conclusion: Pride and the Protection of Character

Hume's emphasis on the moral sentiments as responses to character, and the subsequent pride or humility of an agent who sympathizes with and is sensitive to others' responses to her, points to the reality of human interdependence and how we are deeply identified with others and with social expectations, including moral expectations. I find a similarity here between Hume's view and that of Bernard Williams

---

15 See David Hume, *Essays: Moral, Political, and Literary,* Eugene F. Miller, ed. (Indianapolis: Liberty Classics, 1985).

16 This is especially evident in "Of the Rise and Progress of the Arts and Sciences" and "Of Refinement in the Arts"; see Hume, *Essays.*

with regard to the ancient Greeks. Williams notes that on the view of the modern Kantian, the Greeks' internalization of shame in response to (sometimes imagined) others' blame, makes them, in Kantian language, socially heteronomous.[17] The Kantian may well think the same about Hume's account of pride and humility (or shame) as sympathetic responses to the moral approval or blame of others.[18] But Hume suggests that moral evaluation is a social practice and that our participation in it helps to establish as a collective resource moral knowledge about our general preferences for what has utility. The standards of merit and demerit require conversation, debate, and mutual intelligibility. The Humean agent does not take pride in her virtue simply because others approve of her (nor does she act simply to get their approval). Rather, others approve of her because she has traits that they find valuable and praiseworthy. Their approval reflects their sense of her value insofar as she possesses a praiseworthy trait, and her sympathetically engendered pride in virtue reflects her affirmation of that value and her self-worth. Our ongoing approval or blame of one another thus sustains a sense of pride or of shame that makes us aware of ourselves in particular ways. Shame can move us to change our ways or improve ourselves, and as we saw earlier, pride contributes to a sense of confidence and ethical competence.[19]

I make one final point about Humean pride and its relation to moral motivation and character. Bernard Williams makes the case that shame is protective of character. In contrast to guilt, only shame gives one

---

17 See Bernard Williams, *Shame and Necessity* (Berkeley: University of California Press, 1993), 98. And as Williams also notes, the Greek emphasis on shame—and we can add Hume's on pride and humility—contrasts appreciably with the contemporary emphasis on blame and guilt by philosophers such as Alan Gibbard or R. Jay Wallace. Indeed, Hume's view emphasizes the importance of moral approval to our sense of agency.

18 Christine Korsgaard takes just this view toward Francis Hutcheson and Adam Smith as well as Hume. See her "Creating the Kingdom of Ends: Reciprocity and Responsibility in Personal Relations," in Korsgaard, *Creating the Kingdom of Ends* (Cambridge: Cambridge University Press, 1996), 188–223.

19 I discuss pride's role in relation to ethical competence further in "Moral Sentiment and the Sources of Moral Identity."

insight into one's wrongdoing and helps one "to rebuild the self that has done these things and the world in which that self has to live." Shame "embodies conceptions of what one is and of how one is related to others."[20] Hume at one point does observe that shame can be useful, writing: "a sense of shame, in an imperfect character, is certainly a virtue; but produces great uneasiness and remorse."[21] Hume emphasizes pride much more than humility or shame. In his *EPM* discussion of pride, he connects pride to the importance of human dignity and indicates that this virtue also protects our character, especially with respect to how we conduct ourselves and in our dealings with others: "We never excuse the absolute want of spirit and dignity of character, or a proper sense of what is due to one's self, in society and the common intercourse of life. This vice constitutes what we properly call *meanness*; when a man can submit to the basest slavery in order to gain his ends; fawn upon those who abuse him; and degrade himself by intimacies and familiarities with undeserving inferiors. A certain degree of generous pride or self-value is so requisite, that the absence of it in the mind displeases" (*EPM* 7.10). Earlier, I agreed with Simon Blackburn's point that the Humean can have deep commitments that give her reasons to act and keep her focused on those things she thinks it right to be concerned about. Blackburn also notes that we can locate "value in those concerns that we intend to foster and to guard against threat or change."[22] While shame can certainly reveal to us, when we act against our moral commitments, the betrayal of those concerns, it is a virtue of the generous pride and self-value that Hume speaks about that it is plausibly a more useful and agreeable way to guard against such betrayals of the moral commitments that motivate us to act well.

---

20 Williams, *Shame and Necessity*, 95.

21 Hume, *Essays*, 180.

22 Blackburn, *Ruling Passions*, 257.

CHAPTER EIGHT

Kant and Moral Motivation

THE VALUE OF FREE RATIONAL WILLING

Jennifer Uleman

This chapter is shaped by a kind of incredulity. For Kant, I was taught, a conception of right, or law, or duty—which one depended on who was teaching—comes before any conception of the good. A conception of the good did not drive Kantian morality. There was, of course, text to underwrite the claim. In the 1788 *Critique of Practical Reason*, Kant writes: "instead of the concept of the good as an object determining and making possible the moral law, it is on the contrary the moral law that first determines and makes possible the concept of the good" (KpV 5:64).[1] In the 1785 *Groundwork of the Metaphysics of*

---

1 References to Kant's works are by title initials (from the German originals, listed here) with volume and page number from the standard Akademie edition: *Kants gesammelte Schriften*, ed. Königlichen Preußischen [later Deutschen] Akademie der Wissenschaften (Berlin: Georg Reimer [later Walter de Gruyter], 1900–). The exceptions are citations to Kant's *Critique of Pure Reason*, which give page numbers for both the A (1781) and B (1787) editions, e.g., A301/B358 (where a passage occurs in only one edition, only one is given, e.g., B131), and to Reflexionen, which include Reflexion numbers. Translations are from the English editions listed here unless otherwise noted. The square-bracketed number following the publication date here is the Akademie volume number.

Morals, Kant urges "the renunciation of all interest" in moral willing, that is, "in volition from duty" (G 4:431). Kant, the argument seemed to be, carves out a space for rightness, or lawfulness, or moral obligation, or "volition from duty," that is independent of a story about goodness. Kant is concerned with formal principles, not conceptions of the good life; or, Kant requires a kind of rule-governed reasoning, not a determinate outcome; or, most extremely, for Kant, morality just consists in volition from duty, for its own sake.

This picture, in any of its versions, did not make sense. Why would we want to do right, or be in the right, or be principled, or lawful, or do our duty, or pursue morality at all, however you put it, unless the right, or the law, or duty, or morality, were somehow *good*? Whatever else was the case, it seemed to me, *will* could only be expected to engage, could only be motivated, when it took something to be good. This last thought is, of course, present in the first line of Aristotle's *Nicomachean Ethics* and is endorsed by the many after him who, like me, are persuaded on the conceptual point—we make things objects of our wills if and only if they seem to us in some way good. The thought that a morally proper will was precisely one that eschewed attention to the good seemed to me impossible.

A/B   *Kritik der reinen Vernunft* (1781/1787) [Ak 3, B ed.].
      Critique of Pure Reason, trans. Paul Guyer and Allan Wood (Cambridge: Cambridge University Press, 2000).

G   *Grundlegung zur Metaphysik der Sitten* (1785) [Ak 4].
      Groundwork of the Metaphysics of Morals, trans. Mary Gregor (Cambridge: Cambridge University Press, 1997).

KpV   *Kritik der praktischen Vernunft* (1788) [Ak 5].
      Critique of Practical Reason, trans. Mary Gregor (Cambridge: Cambridge University Press, 1997).

KU   *Kritik der Urtheilskraft* (1790) [Ak 5].
      Critique of the Power of Judgment, trans. Paul Guyer and Eric Matthews (Cambridge: Cambridge University Press, 2000).

MS   *Metaphysik der Sitten* (1797) [Ak 6].
      Metaphysics of Morals, trans. Mary Gregor (Cambridge: Cambridge University Press, 1991).

R   *Reflexionen (handschriftliche Nachlaß)* (1750–1790s) [Ak. 14–19].
      Notes and Fragments, ed. Paul Guyer, trans. C. Bowman, P. Guyer, and F. Rauscher (Cambridge: Cambridge University Press, 2005).

ZeF   "Zum ewigen Frieden: Ein philosophischer Entwurf" (1795) [Ak 8].
      "To Perpetual Peace: A Philosophical Sketch," in *Perpetual Peace and Other Essays*, trans. Ted Humphrey (Indianapolis: Hackett, 1983).

I understood the nonconsequentialist claim, that is, the claim that for Kant aim matters more than actual results in determining moral worth. But I could not understand the claim that moral worth depends somehow on a form of reasoning that *had no aim*. But yes, no, I was given to believe, it is so with Kant—we must pursue duty *for its own sake*, not because of some ulterior motive, like a mere feeling that the demands of duty are good. Eyebrows up, internally, anyway. It seemed, incredibly and as Bernard Williams has put it, that for Kant, "there can be no reason for being moral, and morality itself presents itself as an unmediated demand, a categorical imperative."[2]

The possibility that this was Kant's view also worried many of his friends. Schiller's 1794 *Letters on the Aesthetic Education of Man* sought to make clearer to a skeptical public wherein the ennobling power and appeal of Kant's moral view lay.[3] At present, thanks significantly to work by Barbara Herman and Paul Guyer, characterizations of Kant's work as purely formal are out of favor. The moral law *has* an end, a value that grounds it, their work has insisted.[4] The account I offer here

---

2 Bernard Williams, *Ethics and the Limits of Philosophy* (Cambridge, MA: Harvard University Press, 1985), 55.

3 Friedrich Schiller's 1794 *On the Aesthetic Education of Man in a Series of Letters* sought to do this even as Schiller authored this famous satirical verse, which mocks the Kantian moralist:

Gewissensskrupel
Gerne dien' ich den Freunden, doch tu' ich es leider mit Neigung.
Und so wurmt es mir oft, daß ich nicht tugendhaft bin.
Decisum
Da ist kein anderer Rat, du mußt suchen, sie zu verachten,
Und mit Abscheu alsdann tun, wie die Pflicht dir gebeut.

[Scruple of Conscience]
Gladly I serve my friends, but alas I do it with pleasure.
Hence I am plagued with doubt that I am not a virtuous person.

[Ruling]
Surely, your only resource is to try to despise them entirely,
And then with aversion to do what your duty enjoins you.

Friedrich Schiller, *Xenien* (1797), collected in Goethe, *Werke I*, edited by Erich Trunz (Hamburg: Christian Wegner Verlag, 1949), 221; this translation (apart from English headings, which I've added) appears in H. J. Paton, *The Categorical Imperative: A Study in Kant's Moral Philosophy* (London: Hutchinson, 1947).

4 See Barbara Herman, "Leaving Deontology Behind," in Herman, *The Practice of Moral Judgment* (Cambridge, MA: Harvard University Press, 1993), 208–240. See Paul Guyer, "Kant's Morality of Law and Morality of Freedom," in Guyer, *Kant on Freedom, Law, and Happiness* (Cambridge:

builds on this work and also, thereby, seeks to address the worry that Kantian moral subjects are motivationally opaque, if not, as some have also charged, perverse.[5]

This chapter has two sections. The first defends a claim that, for Kant, moral attitudes and actions are precisely those motivated by respect for and commitment to actively promote the activity of free rational willing itself. The second addresses the question that lingers even once this has been established, namely, what motivates this respect and commitment? What, in other words, motivates the moral Kantian? Here, I seek to make explicit those aspects of free rational willing that motivate moral subjects to respect and actively promote free rational willing; free rational willing promises release from the mechanism of nature and from both interpersonal and inner turmoil, forms of intellectual and moral self-sufficiency, and experiences of self and others as universal, necessary, infinite, and creative (among other things). Many of these echo merits advertised by other moral theories, though in Kant they find distinctive derivation and expression. Noticing them, I claim, not only begins to answer critics who worry that there is no reason to be Kantian, but may also remind us of the power and appeal of Kant's view.

1. KANT ON MORAL MOTIVATION

This section sketches Kant's basic view of moral motivation. It begins by asking what is distinctive about that view, indicating why characterizations of the view as "nonconsequentialist" and "deontological" both fail to adequately capture it. The section then turns to the mechanics of Kantian willing itself, articulating both "bare" and "full" senses of the will's

Cambridge University Press, 2000), 129–171. Herman characterizes the end of morality as rational nature; Guyer characterizes it as freedom. I prefer "the activity of free rational willing," for reasons that will become clear. My view is initially worked out in Jennifer Uleman, *An Introduction to Kant's Moral Philosophy* (Cambridge: Cambridge University Press, 2010). This chapter extends that work.

5 See Schiller's satirical verse; see also, for instance, Ermanno Bencivenga, "Kant's Sadism," *Philosophy and Literature* 20:1 (1996): 39–46.

freedom and rationality. Understanding these distinct senses will be important for understanding the motives available to a Kantian will. The section ends by showing that the specifically moral Kantian will is one motivated by a respect for and commitment to actively promote fully free rational willing itself. This sets the stage for section 2, where I ask the further question of what might motivate such respect or commitment.

What Is Distinctive about Kant's View of Moral Motivation?

Everyone knows part of the answer here: for Kant, the will's motives, and not its effects, are decisive in determining whether an agent has acted in a way that is morally worthy. This is Kant's well-known "nonconsequentialism," his refusal to locate a story about moral worth in the effects or consequences of willing, the way a Humean or a utilitarian would. Here, as he knew, Kant has commonsense on his side. Familiar forms of moral judgment and moral practice are focused on motive and intent, on what an agent wills and why, and they assess responsibility and award moral (as well as legal) praise and blame on these bases. For Kant, motives and intentions are what matter,[6] morally speaking, and truly good ones pave the road not to hell but to perpetual peace.

But nonconsequentialism for its own sake is not driving Kant. Kant seriously does want worldwide perpetual peace and thinks the moral law will help us achieve it.[7] His 1797 *Metaphysics of Morals* lays out the basic principles for a morally successful human society, including principles of external (political, legal) governance and of internal (psychological, self) governance. Kant's commitment to finding bases for human *hope*,

---

6 I here run roughshod over technical distinctions between motives (*Bewegungsgrunde*), incentives (*Treibfedern*), aims or intentions (*Absichten*), and interests (*Interesse*), distinctions Kant and his commentators sometimes find it very helpful to make. For my purposes here, these distinctions are less important than the fact that all name reasons or grounds (*Grunde*) for acting. I take the question about motive in this volume to be an overarching question about what can move us to action.

7 See Kant's essay "Perpetual Peace" (ZeF). Also see Kate Moran, *Community and Progress in Kant's Moral Philosophy* (Washington, DC: Catholic University Press, 2012). Moran makes an important case for the roles played in Kant's moral thought by ideals of progress and of realizable moral community. See also David Cummisky, *Kantian Consequentialism* (Oxford: Oxford University Press, 1996).

that is, grounds for optimism that the arrangements of the world will increasingly conduce to human well-being, makes clear that he is not Stoically indifferent to consequences, nor does he think the rest of us could, should, or will be (see, for instance, A805/B833; KpV 5:129–130; ZeF). So while there is something right, there is also something inadequate in the claim that Kant is a nonconsequentialist.

Similarly, there is something right but also something inadequate in the claim that Kant is a deontologist, that is, that he understands morality to consist just in conformity with a set of rules or roster of duties. It is true that the surest way to find one's moral footing, for Kant, is to consult the "fundamental law of pure practical reason" (KpV 5:30), which serves as "the canon of moral appraisal of action in general" (G 4:424). But this law is not, like one of the Ten Commandments, handed us from on high or otherwise simply given, something to be adhered to without rationale. The Kantian moral law is something we give ourselves, and (presumably) we give it to ourselves because we value and respect what it promotes. It is also true, as those calling Kant a deontologist will note, that Kant confines moral worth to actions undertaken *out of duty* (G 4:397–398). An action that conforms, externally, to moral requirements but is performed for "non-dutiful," that is, base or anyway ulterior, motives deserves no special moral praise. But it is misleading to characterize Kant's view as ultimately about duty for its own sake, leaving matters there; this characterization muzzles itself on the question of why we would be motivated to act out of duty, that is, on the moral law. It seems to insist that we do the right thing just because it is right, where rightness is arbitrary and opaque.

Kant opens the first section of the *Groundwork* by announcing: "it is impossible to think of anything at all in the world, or indeed even beyond it, that could be considered good without limitation except a *good will*" (G 4:393; Kant's emphasis). Kant there proceeds to unfold an account of the thing that, in us, is subject to motivation—the will—and of those motives that alone can make it morally good, indeed the only unconditionally good thing "in the world, or indeed even beyond it"

(G 4:393). Kant's moral philosophy, I now turn to argue, revolves around this good. Yes, intentions matter more than consequences for Kant; and yes, morally worthy actions are morally worthy in virtue of their accord with a particular kind of law. But there is more to be said than nonconsequentialism or deontology can say about what makes the unconditionally good will so good. I turn now to the mechanics of Kantian willing, asking what that will is, explaining its freedom and rationality, and describing the motives available to it.

What Is the Will, That Is, What Is the Thing That Is Motivated, for Kant?

For Kant all living things (even plants, it seems) have a faculty of desire.[8] This faculty, as Kant carefully puts it, is "a being's faculty to be by means of its representations the cause of the reality of the objects of these representations" (KpV 5:9n). A faculty of desire, in other words, is a capacity to turn ideas into realities, thoughts into things, or at least to try to (success is not guaranteed). To have this capacity is precisely to be able to want something and act toward its realization.

A faculty of desire is, as Kant's careful definition makes clear, a form of causality.[9] As a form of causality, a faculty of desire is always both a source of effects and something that works according to a principle.[10] These features will become important shortly.

In human beings, the faculty of desire has a special name, the *will*.[11] Will is distinct from other faculties of desire (e.g., those in

---

8 The capacity for desire is, for Kant, characteristic of life itself. We routinely think of plants as living, but it is hard to tell from Kant's comments whether he really means to extend the capacity for desire to plants as well as animals. Insofar as a plant pursues ends (sunlight, water) and "senses" the environment, it may perhaps be said to "act in accordance with its representations," which capacity, Kant writes, "is called life" (MS 6:211; see also KpV 5:9n).

9 Specifically, a *teleological* or *final* form of causality (see G 4:436n; KU 5:359–360 and 369–370).

10 Readers who imagine they can desire without effect should consult Kant's discussion of how even mere *wishing* makes the blood rush and the heart pound at KU 5:177–178n; see also MS 6:356–357.

11 Attentive readers of Kant, and of the Kant literature, will know that Kant uses two relevant cognate terms: *Wille* (usually translated "will") and *willkür* (usually translated "capacity for choice"). Here, I understand by "will" what Kant understands by *Wille,* namely the whole faculty of practical reasoning, including the specifically human faculty of desire with its power or capacity for (free) choice.

animals) in being both rational and free. Crucially, it is rational and free, for Kant, in two importantly different senses. In the first, bare senses, any human will is always already rational and free; its rationality and freedom are inevitable and thoroughgoing, not something we can avoid even if we want to. In the second, full senses, rationality and freedom are achievements of a will, achievements that are far from inevitable, that admit of more and less, and that can be forfeited all too easily. To make better sense of this, let us look at rationality and freedom each in turn.

In a first, bare sense, rationality is an inevitable and thoroughgoing feature not only of human will but of human mental life in general. Rationality here comprises our use of concepts to determine objects and their relations and to compare what is given to standards; rationality in this minimal, bare sense is employed whenever we make judgments of any kind, however routine or unconscious. Specifically practical reason—the species of reason proper to will—also has a minimal or bare version. Whenever I will, I will for reasons (however bad, of whatever origin, however unconsciously endorsed). Where I am *not* willing for reasons, the things I do are not properly *actions* or willed at all but mere physical events that take place in or with my body: driving to Brooklyn is a willed action; digesting my lunch is not. My will is thus rational in a bare sense whenever I make any prudential or means/ends calculations, whatever the end, whatever the source or moral status of the end, whatever the wisdom of the course or of my calculations. In this minimal sense, then, the will's rationality is inevitable and thoroughgoing.

In the second, full sense, the will's rationality is an achievement. Will is fully rational only when its reasons for willing are endorsed by reason qua reason—that is, only when its reasons are *not* serving as prudential Humean slaves to the passions but are serving reason on its own behalf, as it were. As I will show, the only reasons that reason qua reason can endorse are reasons of its own, that is, reasons for willing that have their origin not in sensuous desires or inclinations but in the interests of reason itself. The will is thus rational in this second, full sense only when it is moved by reasons of reason's own. It is moved by reasons of reason's own only through effort and commitment, and only the will that is rational in this second sense is fully moral.

In the same way, there are two senses in which will can be free. The first, bare sense picks out something inevitable and thoroughgoing, and the other sense picks out a precarious, morally praiseworthy achievement. For Kant, all freedom consists in not being determined by something external, whether that external thing is nature, God, or another's will; freedom is self-determination. In the first, bare, inevitable, and thoroughgoing sense, will is free insofar as it is not, like a cog in a machine, forcibly sprung into organism-galvanizing action by sensuous desires. There is a gap, always, between the desires I have as a sensuous creature and my choice of whether to be determined, that is, moved to action, by them. This distinguishes human will from the faculties of desire in plants and animals; they just go whenever a relevant inclination or stimulus is present.

We are free in this first, bare sense whenever we choose what to will, whether we choose willing determined by nature, God, another's will, or ourselves. We are thus *always* free in this sense, because we always do *choose*. Thus does Kant hold that we can be held responsible for all our actions (though not of course for all the motions of our bodies, some of which, as I have shown, are not actions). We always have the capacity to choose what reason for acting will move us, and so we are always responsible for the actions we undertake. The metaphysics required for this claim will need to be left for another time; the upshot here is that there is a first, bare sense in which the Kantian will is always free, in a way that is inevitable and thoroughgoing.

In the second, full sense, will is free for Kant when it chooses to will in a way that sustains its own freedom. It does this whenever it chooses to will on a reason that is fully its own—not one given by nature, or God, or another's will. A reason that is reason's own is one that belongs to reason qua reason. Only when will chooses in favor of such a reason is it *fully* self-determined—only thus are both the *choice* of reason and the *reason* itself fully its own—and so only here is the will's freedom sustained throughout determination. Full freedom, like full rationality, cannot be taken for granted but is an achievement; and, like full rationality, it is a precarious one.

Now, because will is always and inevitably rational and free in the bare senses, it always wills on a principle, or maxim. "Maxim" is the term Kant uses for the "subjective" or local and actually operative principle adopted by an individual will. To adopt a maxim is to represent it to oneself (however unconsciously) and to choose (again, however unconsciously) to be guided by it. In the *Critique of Practical Reason*, Kant discusses a case in which I have "made it my maxim to increase my wealth by every safe means" (KpV 5:27). Earlier in the *Critique*, Kant considered the maxim "Let no insult pass unavenged" (KpV 5:19). These maxims, like the maxims considered and rejected in the four famous *Groundwork* examples,[12] turn out to be morally problematic, but Kant elsewhere offers examples of maxims that are morally sound. One can make "pursuit of morality itself" one's maxim (MS 6:392), along with, "love of one's neighbor in general," "love of one's parents" (MS 6:390), and "the happiness of others" (MS 6:393). Maxims thus come in many syntactic shapes and sizes and vary widely in specificity. What they have in common is that they are the local laws or principles that govern or determine actual wills, and that do so just in virtue of having been chosen by the subject.

Why choose one maxim rather than another? Maxims also have in common that they all advert to an end or ground, that is, to an ultimate reason for acting. This end or ground constitutes the reason the

---

12 The maxims are: (1) "From self-love I make it my principle to shorten my life when its longer duration threatens more troubles than it promises agreeableness" (G 4:422), (2) "When I believe myself to be in need of money I shall borrow money and promise to repay it, even though I know that this will never happen" (G 4:422), and (3) "Let each be as happy as heaven wills or as he can make himself; I shall take nothing from him nor even envy him; only I do not care to contribute anything to his welfare or to his assistance in need!" (G 4:423). Kant, in his fourth example, does not formulate the subject's maxim as such, but we can reconstruct it as (4) "because I prefer to give myself up to pleasure, I will not trouble myself with enlarging and improving my talents" (G 4:422).

principle is chosen or adopted.[13] Maxims, in other words, advert to possible motives.

What Kinds of Motives Are There, for Kant?

For Kant, there are two fundamental motives: in a given case, we opt to will in accord with nature or to will in accord with reason. Each of these two motives is contained in a corresponding kind of maxim.

We opt to will in accord with nature when we choose to act on a maxim that is grounded in self-preservation, sensuous pleasure, or some combination of both (they often coincide) whether the terms of these are set by the organism, God, or another's will. We pursue self-preservation and pleasure by pursuing particular local ends or states of affairs, of course, but the idea here is that, for this set of maxims, the underlying motive is provided by nature via the inclinations of the organism. Kant describes all such willing as willing on the principle or law of self-love. The precise content of a maxim grounded in this law, depending as it will on the given natural constitution and situation of the organism in question, will always be empirical. But, whatever the local content, whenever I choose to will in ways grounded in the law of self-love, I choose to let my will be determined by a law that is given from without and to which I am passively subject. I am motivated by self-love, not by reason. Willing on maxims grounded in self-love, though free and rational in the bare senses described earlier, is thus neither fully free nor fully rational. Such willing does not sustain my freedom through determination, nor does its motive reside within reason itself.

In contrast, when we choose to will on a motive that resides within reason itself, we achieve both full rationality and full freedom. Reason as such is not motivated by self-preservation or sensuous pleasure (though it may be instrumentally interested in these, insofar as they serve its purposes). If we can, for Kant, identify a purely rational motive and the principle grounded in it, and if we choose determination by

---

13 For a more fine-grained account, see Uleman, *An Introduction to Kant's Moral Philosophy*, 41–48.

that principle, then we choose to will in a way that is fully free and fully rational. We accomplish fully free rational willing.

What, Then, Is the Purely Rational Motive?

How are we to identify a purely rational motive, something in which reason as such has an interest? There are several ways to go here. I could just cite text where Kant tells what such a motive would be: "Now I say that the human being and in general every rational being *exists* as an end in itself, *not merely as a means* to be used by this or that will at its discretion; instead he must in all his actions, whether directed to himself or also to other rational beings, always be regarded *at the same time as an end*" (G 4:428; italics in original). All rational beings as such are, for Kant, ends in themselves (G 4:431). How does this constitute a purely rational motive? "All objects of the inclinations have only conditional worth," Kant writes, but rational beings as such have unconditional or "absolute" worth (G 4:428). Rational beings are characterized by what Kant calls "rational nature" or, in us, "humanity" (G 4:428–431), that is, the capacity to will in ways that are at once inherently free and rational in the bare senses described earlier, and potentially free and rational in the full senses. Kant's claim in the passages just cited is that we must take an interest in this; rational being constitutes a necessary end, one we must embrace independent of sensuous inclination. My explication could end here: will can and should, for Kant, be moved by reason itself to make free rational willing as such always an end, and so to adopt maxims that serve this end.

But it may be more helpful to get to this claim the way Kant does. Kant looks at the kind of thing that determines a will, namely a principle, and asks what principle there could be that abstracts from all empirical, inclination-based, natural motives. This is the strategy that inspires Kant's detractors, as well as those sympathizers who characterize him as nonconsequentialist and deontological, so it is worth working though.

Kant offers an argument from elimination, asking us to imagine a practical, or action-guiding, law that abstracts from all empirical content, that is, from all sensuous ends. When we do so, we are left just with *features of the form of law itself*, namely, with universality and necessity themselves. How does this get us to a practical law, to a rule for willing? It does so by revealing the demand that we must will *in a universalizable way*, that is, on universalizable maxims and, what will amount to the same thing, that we must will in a way that serves a necessary, nonempirical end.

This is a neat trick, but it is not just a trick. In moving from the fact that any law, as a law, must be universal to the demand that we freely adopt a law that itself demands universalizable maxims, Kant accomplishes something profound. If I restrict myself to willing on universalizable maxims, I make willing in ways that others could endorse a priority. I privilege, in other words, free rational willing (my own and others') itself over any particular empirical end. Kant is no fool when it comes to either human conflict or the diversity of human desires, commitments, and forms of life, but he is guardedly optimistic that human beings can, if we try, find a common framework for leading lives that, broadly speaking, cooperate. Willing only on universalizable maxims pledges allegiance to that ideal by pledging allegiance to a framework that is grounded not in this or that contingent and possibly idiosyncratic empirical end but in a form of willing that is in principle respectful of everyone else's willing.

A universal law not only holds necessarily but also, if it is a practical law, is grounded in a necessary end. Focus on the form of law reveals reason's demand for an end or ground it can regard as unconditioned or necessary. Self-love only ever proposes conditioned, contingent ends. But a practical system that is not grounded in an unconditioned good or necessary end can never give final answers about what matters (G 4:428); willing, in the absence of such answers, risks perpetual idiosyncrasy and ultimate pointlessness. Kant, by looking just at the form of law, has discovered a demand for universalizability that itself serves a necessary end by demanding respect for and promotion of free rational willing itself. Kant gets from the form of law to its content.[14]

Why should we care about this content? As subjects with free rational wills, we are interested not only in satisfying inclinations but also in free rational willing as such, and in sustaining our freedom and rationally by willing in ways that are fully free and rational. At work is a kind of "self-interest" that is not that of the natural organism but of the free rational self itself, the same self that is potential creator, sustainer, and respected member of a moral order. Kant thinks we will recognize this self and its capacities for free rational willing as both intrinsically and supremely valuable. We are free to make the mistake of thinking that pleasure, or self-preservation, or anything other than free rational willing, is the ultimate end after which we should strive. But it would be a mistake. The ultimate good in line with which all our ends should fall is precisely a kind of volitional activity, the kind that is free and rational and that sets and pursues ends consistent with free rational willing itself. Hegel thus aptly captures the structure of Kant's moral philosophy when he describes it as a system based in "the free will which wills the free will."[15] We might recall the opening of the *Groundwork* and rephrase Hegel's remark, describing Kant's as a system in which the good will wills the good will. To unpack a bit more: a will, for Kant, is unconditionally good when it is fully free and fully rational, and it is fully free and rational when it is moved to respect and promote free rational willing, and it is moved to respect and promote free rational willing when it is motivated by the unconditional goodness of the good will.

In the next section, I consider why a Kantian subject might be motivated thus. The question is pressing because Kantian subjects face a

---

14 A much more detailed version of this account can be found in Uleman, *An Introduction to Kant's Moral Philosophy*, especially chaps. 3 and 6 (39–61 and 111–143).

15 Or in Hegel's German, "der freie Wille, der den freien Willen will." G. W. F. Hegel, *Grundlinien der Philosophie des Rechts* (*Werke* 7) (1821) (Frankfurt: Suhrkamp Verlag, 1970), sec. 27; translation from *Elements of the Philosophy of Right*, trans. H. B. Nisbet, edited by Allen Wood (Cambridge: Cambridge University Press, 1991), 57.

choice. Nature appeals to us to make ends of objects that promise pleasure, self-preservation, or both, whether or not they respect or promote free rational willing. The reasons to adopt these ends are no mystery and the appeals are clear. It is more puzzling, on the face of it anyway, that we should pursue the end given by pure practical reason, the end of free rational willing itself, especially as it will often enough demand that we sacrifice pleasure and sometimes even self-preservation.[16] Why would we be motivated to it?

2. WHAT MOTIVATES THE KANTIAN?

I look here at aspects of free rational willing that might help explain why Kant thinks we are motivated to respect, promote, and otherwise aim to both serve and instantiate it. I look at aspects, in other words, that help address the question of what motivates the Kantian. The aspects that I think elicit respect for and commitment to actively promote fully free rational willing include release from the mechanism of nature, release from both interpersonal and inner turmoil, forms of intellectual and moral self-sufficiency, and experiences of self and others as universal, necessary, infinite, and creative. None of these is a separable *consequence* of fully free rational willing; in being motivated by these, one is not motivated to use morality, so to speak, as an instrument to their attainment. Rather, being motivated by these is just part of what it is to respect and want to actively promote fully free rational willing. Making them explicit begins to break the grip of the prejudice that Kantian moral agents are motivationally opaque or perverse and shows the limitations of deontological and nonconsequentialist characterizations of Kant. It also shows how a Kantian can satisfy the Aristotelian demand that there *be* a good animating the will.

---

16 See Kant's famous *Critique of Practical Reason* example of the man commanded by his sovereign to bear false witness against an innocent man on pain of death. Morality demands he refuse and face death (KpV 5:30).

Making these aspects explicit also connects Kantian morality to other traditions. The aspects just mentioned should sound familiar. Kant is not the first or last to think that we value release from the mechanism of nature as well as from turmoil, that we long to transcend particularly, contingency, and limitation, or that we value the coherence, harmony, and consistency that come from rational self-control. Nor is he unique in privileging forms of intellectual and moral self-sufficiency. The Stoics of course come to mind, among many others. Kant is not alone in imagining we deeply admire universality, necessity, infinity and creativity; all, after all, are traditional perfections of God. But this is as it should be. Kant understands his innovation to lie in the metaphysics and the account of practical reasoning that allow us to securely access moral truth—he thinks he has finally got the philosophy right. He does not understand himself to be challenging the basic moral truths and strivings people have pursued all along.

So what motivates a Kantian? To begin, fully free and rational Kantian willing elevates a person above the natural or sensible world. This may not sit well with contemporary naturalism, but comments to this effect are everywhere in Kant's texts. Duty's root or origin, Kant writes in the *Critique of Practical Reason*, "can be nothing less than what elevates a human being above himself (as a part of the sensible world), what connects him with an order of things that only the understanding can think and that at the same time has under it the whole sensible world and with it the empirically determinable existence of human beings in time" (KpV 5:86–87). This root of duty, Kant goes on to say, must be "*personality,* that is, freedom and independence from the mechanism of the whole of nature" (KpV 5:87; italics in original). What Kant here calls "personality" is precisely our capacity for fully free rational willing, that is, our capacity for fully free rational self-determination. The sensible world, "and with it the empirically determinable existence of human beings in time" (KpV 5:86–87), is the Kantian world of appearances or phenomena. Moral willing allows us to leave this world.

What is so attractive about leaving this world? Why should we sign on to a project that promises this? Kant's detractors as well as some of his naturalistically inclined friends claim precisely that this supposed deliverance from nature is neither wonderful nor coherent. But to leave the sensible world is, most generally, to leave a shape of existence and self-understanding in which we are mere cogs, animated by forces beyond our control. Physical laws push our bodies around. We are pulled internally by inclinations, which represent our constantly changing, contingent reactions to what is in front of us. Even our considered judgments, if we do not ground them in something that transcends nature, are just complex slaves to our sensuous inclinations. This can leave us feeling out of control. Moreover, inclinations form a necessarily incoherent and contradictory set, as they come from diverse natural sources and aim at diverse natural ends. Unless we attach to a good and a principle of action not beholden to inclinations, they are liable to pull us in contrary directions, leaving us at war with ourselves. In a dramatic passage about the burdensome confusion of even pleasant feelings (a passage often seized on by Kant's critics), Kant writes: "Even [the] feeling of compassion and tender sympathy, if it precedes consideration of what is duty and becomes the determining ground, is itself burdensome to right-thinking persons, brings their considered maxims into confusion, and produces the wish to be freed from them and subject to lawgiving reason alone" (KpV 5:118).

The moral law that formalizes respect for free rational willing is clear about what trumps what, and tames our "propensity to rationalize" (G 4:405). "Common human reason," Kant writes, is impelled to step into moral philosophy not only in order to learn the "source" and "correct determination" of the principle of duty but also "that it may escape from its predicament about claims" (G 4:405). Adherence to the moral law "is the sole condition under which a will can never be in conflict with itself" (G 4:437). Thus, moral willing brings not only transcendence but also peace.

Willing in service to the nonsensuous good of free rational willing is also the only way to deal with the competing claims made by different people. The claims of the sensible world, by themselves, can only result in "a harmony like that which a certain satirical poem depicts in the unanimity between a married couple bent on going to ruin: '*O marvelous harmony, what he wants she wants too*' and so forth, or like what is said of the pledge of King Francis I to the Emperor Charles V: 'What my brother Charles would have (Milan), that I would also have'" (KpV 5:28). The only source of peace—or "omnilateral concord" (KpV 5:28)—is respect for a good that has the capacity to subordinate inclination-based claims.

Release from the controlling, tumultuous, and competing demands of the sensible world is thus accomplished by committing our wills to the good respected and promoted in and by the moral law. Commitment to this good and this law also constitutes us as members of a supersensible world, a world of Kantian intelligibilities or noumena or, to put it in a way that may frighten fewer, a world structured by and understood in terms of active respect for fully free rational willing. In this world, as *personalities*, forms of intellectual and moral self-sufficiency, as well as experiences of self and others as universal, necessary, infinite, and creative, are made available.

Take self-sufficiency first. For Kant, practical reason acts independently of sensibility's input in framing fundamental principles and in forming the "practical elementary concepts" of good and evil, which "have as their basis the *form of a pure will* as given within reason and therefore within the thinking faculty itself" (KpV 5:65–6; italics in original). We do not need to rely on external resources to come to know good and evil or the law that tells us how to pursue the first and avoid the second. Practical reason, in drawing up its basic policies, is intellectually self-sufficient. Fully free rational willing also promises *moral* self-sufficiency: agents who choose to will in ways that are fully free and rational are self-sufficient in their moral worth. "To satisfy the categorical command of morality is within everyone's power at all times" (KpV 5:36–7). Even a person, Kant famously claims, whose efforts are stymied "by a special disfavor of fortune" can be morally good, since goodness is a question not of his effects but of the quality of his will, which is his, not fortune's, to control (G 4:394). Indeed, in acting on the moral law, we *are good wills*; this goodness is something we can effect without the cooperation of nature or anything else in the external world.[17] Free rational willing makes us self-sufficient both in authoring moral concepts and laws and in realizing moral goodness itself, saving us from the vagaries of moral luck.

What about universality and necessity? Recall that when I will in a way that is fully free and rational I will with or through the moral law, which, qua law, is a principle that carries with it universality and necessity. When I opt to will in a way that is fully free and rational, I thus will "with universality and necessity" in several senses. I will on universalizable maxims, and so am willing in a universal, because universalizable, way; I will on maxims that could hold universally. I am "necessitated" or obligated to will as I do because such willing is directed at a necessary end, free rational willing itself; my interest in willing on the law, though sometimes inadequate to motivate me, is not contingent. Finally, insofar as I am *author* of the moral law, my connection to the world structured by the moral law is "not merely contingent…but universal and necessary" (KpV 5:162). In legislating a universal and necessary law, I participate in the space of universal reason and contribute activity that is necessary if there is to be moral law, and hence a morally structured realm, at all.

Why or how might such involvement with universality and necessity contribute to motivating the Kantian? The moral law that the fully free and rational will makes is the same law all would make; it would be universally endorsed, as would any maxim that can be universalized. For this reason, the fully free and rational will legislates universally. It

---

17 Anyone in possession of practical wisdom "can suffer no loss by chance or fate, since he is in possession of himself and the virtuous man cannot lose his virtue" (MS 6:405).

is entitled to this because the faculty it uses, reason, and the perspective it adopts in using it are both universal; the legislation is not justified in terms of private, idiosyncratic interests. What is motivating about this? Willing this way allows us to abandon a view of ourselves as mere accidents of self-interest, positionality, or personal preference and experience ourselves as "bigger" than all that. In being "universal"—that is, fully rational—I am also, for Kant, simultaneously my "proper self" (G 4:458) and the self most connected to, most "in common with," others. Goods we might call those of communicability and community are made available here.[18]

What about necessity? As I have shown, the moral law carries necessity; in Kant's expression, it "necessitates," it unconditionally demands our allegiance, because it is grounded in a necessary end for us. Beyond this, it is necessary *that the law be*—without it, there would be no specifically moral realm, no way of thinking about the world in terms of any but contingent values. This renders our lawmaking activity *itself* necessary. Why should this motivate? We are here assured not only that moral willing pursues something of unqualified worth but also that our own activity as morally motivated wills itself *instantiates* this worth and is itself crucial to constituting the fiber of the moral world. We can see ourselves, in these regards, as necessary, and therefore as significantly more significant than we could if we could only conceive of ourselves as contingent comings-together of passive atoms in an impersonal Newtonian void.

Perhaps even more grandly, fully free rational willing implicates us in *infinity*. The moral law, Kant writes, "begins from my invisible self,

---

18 Paul Guyer, "Kant on the Theory and Practice of Autonomy," in Guyer, *Kant's System of Nature and Freedom: Selected Essays* (Oxford: Oxford University Press, 2005), 131, brought the following note from the *Reflexionen* (probably 1776–1778) to my attention: "Freedom is the original life and in its connection the condition of the coherence of all life; hence that which promotes the feeling of universal life or the feeling of the promotion of universal life causes a pleasure. Do we feel good in universal life? The universality makes all our feelings agree with one another, although prior to this universality there is no special kind of sensation. It is a form of *consensus*" (R 6862, 19:183). Although strange in many ways, the note is certainly suggestive that we feel motivated to universality/universalization. For further discussion see Guyer, "Kant on the Theory and Practice of Autonomy," 115–145.

my personality, and presents me in a world which has true infinity" (KpV 5:162). This view of myself, Kant continues, "infinitely raises my worth as an *intelligence* by my personality, in which the moral law reveals to me a life independent of animality and even of the whole sensible world, at least so far as this may be inferred from the purposive determination of my existence by this law, a determination not restricted to the conditions and boundaries of this life but reaching into the infinite" (KpV 5:162). As fully free rational wills, we are unbounded, "not restricted to the conditions and boundaries of this life" (KpV 5:162). This is enormously significant; it means that as long and insofar as we are moral wills, we are not limited by space or time, by foreign desires, or by empirical facts. What I, as a natural being, can actually do in the world of space and time is of course limited, but my will itself, insofar as it is free and rational, is not. We can see ourselves as (thus) unlimited and can aim at whatever we can imagine, setting ends and designing projects that go beyond what exists in the world.

A final motive to Kantian morality, creativity, is intimately implicated in and dependent on many of the motives mentioned already. The claim that the free rational Kantian will is creative seems to me uncontroversial but is nonetheless rarely made as such.[19] This is especially surprising as it is perhaps the most characteristic and radically Kantian reason to be Kantian, that is, the most radically Kantian aspect of what makes fully free rational will the ultimate good for Kant.

By "creativity," I have in mind the human activity of intentionally introducing new aspects and arrangements into the world. Artistic creation is a species of this activity but not the only species. New ways of building roads, or treating anxiety, or sentencing misdemeanors, or

---

19 Friedrich Schiller is one thinker who made this connection explicitly (Schiller, *On the Aesthetic Education of Man in a Series of Letters*). More recently, the point has been made by Susan Neiman, *The Unity of Reason: Rereading Kant* (Oxford: Oxford University Press, 1994). Arendt's discussion of "natality" and the unique newness each person's birth promises resonates deeply, I think, with what I am calling Kantian creativity. Hannah Arendt, *The Human Condition* (Chicago: Chicago University Press, 1958).

cooking trout are all creative. Random mutation is not creative, but sudden, as well as hard-won, solutions to problems on which one has been working are: creativity is doing or making something in a way that is new and different on purpose.

For Kant, we are creative, that is, we intentionally introduce new aspects and arrangements into the world, precisely insofar as we will and act freely and rationally. Kant writes in many places about the natural world gaining "intelligible" or "supersensible" form through the free rational activity of moral agents (see, e.g., KpV 5:43–48, G 4:438). This is true both when our actions are aimed at specifically moral ends and when they are simply aimed at innovation. The natural world is rationally "informed" or reshaped whenever we can say of something that it was produced by us under the guidance of reason rather than nature or instinct. Under reason's guidance, we have created not just the many physical artifacts that are peculiarly human products but also the institutions and relationships within which much of what matters in our lives takes place. We have created and will continue to create a world full of and informed by ideas and meanings that are not from nature, as Kant understands it.

This capacity for rationally informing nature—for devising plans and carrying them out, for aspiring to things we make up, and for continually reinventing our empirical selves and the world around us—is truly creative. We do not create "the raw material" (whatever it is) of the phenomenal world, nor do we control the ways our cognitive faculties intuit and categorize it. But artifacts are ours, and, more important, the entire world of moral value is a creature under our control, and profoundly so: the laws of freedom, and the objects and concepts that derive from them, are the inventions of reason, acting independently of nature, that is, are the inventions of free rational will. This places us, as free wills and as rational cognizers, at the authorial center of a very important universe, namely the moral one. If Copernicus's Copernican revolution dislodged us, as inhabitants of earth, from the center of the physical universe, Kantian moral philosophy returns us to its moral center. This distinguishes Kant's view from any that locate the source of moral value outside of reason itself. It also makes Kant's methodological innovation evident, explaining his insistence that we get to know the moral law before we go looking for the good. Free rational willing, as the good motivating morality, is not something we can understand independently of understanding the activity of free rational willing itself. It is a good the possibility of which we create through the activity of free rational willing itself. No view places our creative activity so squarely at the heart of morality as Kant's.

CONCLUSION: THE VALUE OF FREE RATIONAL WILLING

Bearing creativity in mind may put Kant's thought back on the table for some who have otherwise written it off. Kant is frequently dismissed by thinkers who see in his commitments only the punishing rationality of a hyperactive superego or guarantees of a formal, barren freedom. Kant himself sows the seeds for this picture, of course. But the picture is nonetheless partial. Reason grounds community, making us legible to each other, giving us something in common; freedom opens possibility, letting us get outside what is given about ourselves. Focus on the goods of free rational willing, and especially on its creativity, can remind us of these aspects.[20]

Thinking about creativity can also, as just noted, help us focus on what makes Kant's view Kantian. Characterizations of his view as "deontological" and "nonconsequentialist" still circulate widely, and while they contain grains of truth, they obscure that moral willing for Kant is very much for the sake of something we can understand and contributes to states of

---

20 In an earlier extended discussion of creativity, I look at phenomenologies of creativity provided by Virginia Woolf in *To the Lighthouse*, sec. 3 (New York: Harcourt Brace Jovanovich, 1981) and *A Room of One's Own* (New York: Harcourt Brace Jovanovich, 1981), and Adrian Piper, in *Out of Order, Out of Sight* (Cambridge, MA: MIT Press, 1996), xxxiv. I suggest that many of the stranger aspects of free rational willing discussed here, such as being universal, necessary, and infinite, seem less strange in the contexts they provide. Uleman, *An Introduction to Kant's Moral Philosophy*, 167–171.

affairs that are good (for instance, the state of world peace Kant hopes we will attain).[21] My aim here has been to challenge those readings by showing that the ultimate moral motive for Kant is found in the good of free rational willing as such. True, this good is not realized when we create this or that specifiable-in-advance state of affairs; rather, it is realized when we engage in the continuously creative activity of fully free, fully rationally guided striving, whatever we create. It is realized whenever we will whatever universal reason, apart from contingent inclinations, would demand in the case at hand, which is the same as willing a course of action that will respect, instantiate, and promote free rational willing.

There are many things a chapter on Kantian moral motivation might have done. It might have carefully distinguished my reading from the readings of leading commentators. It might have spent more time on species of nonconsequentialism and deontology. It might have given a fuller picture of what, exactly, fully free rational willing is, of the kinds of things it does and why, of what it is like, compared with other forms of willing. All of these would have been worthwhile, but I have opted instead to do the two things that seem most pressing and that together address the charge that Kantian moral subjects are fundamentally motivationally opaque, if not perverse. The first thing was to begin to establish that Kantian morality is grounded in free rational willing's interest in its own self-preservation, that is, in willing in ways and toward arrangements that instantiate and promote fully free rational willing itself. The second was to show that free rational willing's interest in this is not just an abstract form of self-interest but an interest in a host of aspects that cannot be separated from fully free rational willing itself.

There are things we might wish were different in Kant's moral theory. But one thing we need not lament is a lack of plausible motivation to endorse and act on Kant's moral law—the motivation to be moral, as Kant understands morality, is there. It is a serious mistake to

---

21 Again, see Moran, *Community and Progress.*

think Kant wanted us to be moral for no reason, or for no reason other than that being so is moral, according to Kant. It is a mistake, in other words, to think that the motive to Kantian morality cannot be scrutinized and unpacked, and of course critiqued. A full account of what motivates the Kantian needs to go beyond abstract recognition of the rationality and freedom built into Kant's moral law and begin to look to the host of reasons the complex activity that is fully free rational willing has a motivating hold on us.

ACKNOWLEDGMENTS

I am grateful for thoughtful comments on an early draft offered by other contributors to this volume; their enthusiasm and interest were invaluable. I am also grateful to Iakovos Vasiliou for skillful, patient shepherding throughout. Errors and shortcomings of course remain my own. I am acutely aware that I do not begin to do justice here to the embarrassment of riches that is contemporary scholarship on Kant, and I beg indulgence for all the failures-to-mention and unacknowledged debts.

CHAPTER NINE

Moral Motivation in Post-Kantian Philosophy

FICHTE AND HEGEL

Angelica Nuzzo

My topic in this essay is the discussion that shapes the notion of "motive" in German post-Kantian philosophy—in Fichte and Hegel in particular. Since the concept is not yet terminologically fixed and does not display a specific technical meaning in these authors, I bring to the forefront the conceptual constellation covered by the problem of the motive for action: the terms *Absicht, Bestimmung, Trieb, Triebfeder, Vorsatz, Motiv* all coalesce around this issue.[1] My analysis is framed by the central challenge that the post-Kantian discussion inherits from Kant's practical philosophy. This concerns the way post-Kantian philosophy makes the concept of motive functional to the solution of what is perceived as a fundamental flaw of Kant's position, thereby accomplishing the shift from the notion of motive as determination of the

---

1 Thus, I use "motive" in a general sense, as referring to all these German terms; when I indicate, more specifically, one or the other German concepts (*Absicht, Bestimmung, Triebfeder, Vorsicht*) I make it explicit.

agent's will and source of her moral worth to the idea of motive as the value-determination of the action in relation to which the agent's will ought to be appraised. The problem to which Fichte and Hegel respond can be summarized as follows: While for Kant the will's motive is the exclusive source of the *moral* validity of the action, the moral motive (being the pure, a priori law of reason) does not properly *appear in the action* itself (and properly does not even *appear to the will* in its own determinate state at a particular time). Although central in the practical evaluation of the action, the moral motive, being a noumenal and merely formal determination of the will, remains, as it were, phenomenologically inscrutable and cognitively unknowable, that is, ultimately disconnected from the actuality of the action. Seeing in this disconnect the unsolved problem at the heart of the Kantian position, Fichte and Hegel aim—albeit on different grounds—at (re)connecting the subjective motive to the objective realization of the action and only on this basis at making the will's motive a criterion for the action's practical evaluation. Responding to this challenge, the motive displays a double character. In order to be a determination of the will (i.e., to actually move the will to action), the motive must become a determination of the action itself, that is, must drive the action to its realization and be discernible in the action's material and intersubjective appearance. In order to function in this way, however, in contrast to Kant's position, (moral) motives must leave their formality behind and become "impure," that is, concrete and particular. They must be transferred from the invisible space of the will's noumenal determination to their appearance in action, thereby showing how they can be intersubjectively shared, and how they are contextually determined by the social, political, and juridical institutions from which they derive their motivational force. Ultimately at stake in this discussion is a shift in the perspective in which the practical validity of actions is evaluated: the shift leads from pure, personal morality to the intersubjective, social context of ethical life. To put it in Hegel's words: "morality" must yield to "ethical life." Kant's pure moral philosophy is overcome by Fichte's system of "concrete ethics," presented in texts such as the 1798 *System der Sittenlehre* and the 1800 *Bestimmung des Menschen*, and by Hegel's expressivist and contextualist theory of action,[2] which is the center-piece of his "philosophy of spirit"—in particular of the development of the last stage of subjective spirit in the 1830 *Encyclopedia*, and of the development of action in the 1821 *Grundlinien der Philosophie des Rechts*.

In what follows I concentrate on some paradigmatic passages from these texts in order to bring to light the problematic constellation in which Fichte and Hegel, respectively, develop the concept of motive in the space that connects the determination of the will to the determination of the action and that connects moral decision-making to the evaluation of the agent's deeds. At issue herein is a fundamental extension and differentiation of the validity of motives, which, for Kant, seems to fall within the exclusive alternative that separates moral and nonmoral intentions. In Kant's aftermath the problem of moral motivation does not regard, directly, the choice of individual actions but concerns instead the principles or sets of norms under which motivation is regarded and appraised. First I sketch out the Kantian framework against which Fichte and Hegel place their respective account of practical motivation. My aim is to outline what the post-Kantians take to be the open questions left for them to address. Turning then to Fichte, I show how in order to be a determination of the action, the motive (all motives, including the moral ones) must speak to the agent individually and personally, hence lose the abstract universality that for Kant the *moral* motive must instead display. For Fichte motivation requires the individualization of abstract norms. As the motive's value lies no longer in its subjective source (i.e., reason versus desire) but in its capacity to lead the agent to action, the individuality of the motive opens up to the dimension of its concrete and shared universality.

---

2 See Robert Pippin, *Hegel's Practical Philosophy: Rational Agency as Ethical Life* (Cambridge: Cambridge University Press, 2008).

(Herein Kant's requirement of universalization can be found restated yet significantly modified.) This position characterizes Hegel's practical philosophy, which I discuss in the third section. While motives do motivate because of their individual appeal, they are valuable and actually valued only insofar as they are displayed in the concrete practices from which they gain intersubjective, "ethical" validity. I bring to the fore the connection between practical motivation and the idea of freedom's realization in the social and political world (or the transition from a merely "moral" to a fully "ethical" motive). This is the fundamental step beyond Kantian morality (*Moralität*) into Hegel's ethical world (*Sittlichkeit*).

1. LEAVING KANT'S PURE MOTIVES BEHIND

In the *Critique of Pure Reason*, in the transition from the paralogisms to the antinomies, Kant accomplishes the crucial shift that leads from the I as *object* of cognition to the I as *subject* of action.[3] The subject is now presented as "*acting* subject" or "*active* being,"[4] and receives a characterization that the "I think" of speculative reason could never attain. In fact, only the acting subject is truly and irreducibly "subject." For to be subject of knowledge—that is, to know external objects and to know oneself as object—characterizes a position that still concerns the I only as a phenomenal *object*, that is, as an appearance causally determined in space and time. To be "subject" in the proper sense is, for Kant, to be subject of action or to be agent. Agent is the subject who is

3 See Angelica Nuzzo, *Ideal Embodiment: Kant's Theory of Sensibility* (Bloomington: Indiana University Press, 2008), chap. 4. Immanuel Kant, *Critique of Pure Reason* B 428. Henceforth the *Critique of Pure Reason* is cited according to the customary abbreviation KrV followed by the page number in the A (1781) and B (1787) editions; the *Critique of Judgment* is cited referring to section number; Kant's other works are cited according to *Kants gesammelte Schriften*, Hrsg. v. der Preußischen Akademie der Wissenschaften (Berlin: de Gruyter, 1910) (AA) followed by volume and page number; Fichte's works are cited following the edition *Fichtes Werke*, edited by I. H. Fichte, vols. 1–8 (Berlin: de Gruyter, 1971) (SW); Hegel's *Philosophy or Right* is abbreviated as R followed by section number; the *Encyclopedia* as *Enz* followed by section number.

4 Kant, KrV B 569/A 541.

actually determined or moved to action by a "determining ground." That which the determining ground determines is the subject's will; motive is that determining ground which, among many possible grounds, actually moves the will to action. Only when determined by a noumenal ground—that is, by an internal motive that does not itself appear in space and time—is the will free, for in this case determination is spontaneous. Spontaneous determination is autonomous self-determination. Only in this case is the motive a *moral* motive.

If Kant's position is viewed in relation to the successive developments of the problem in Fichte and Hegel, its characteristic features can be brought back to Kant's distinctive answer to the following questions.[5] (1) The first, formal question regards *how* the motive motivates or actually moves the will to action. This entails an account of the modality of the determination to which the will is subject. (2) The second, content-based question concerns *what* can have the capacity of moving the will to action and leads to a differentiation in the types of motives determining the will. From these questions two issues arise. (3) How does the difference in motives yield the different evaluation of the action? Question 3 is immediately connected to the final question: (4) how does one differentiate the class of subjects able to respond to respectively different motives? I shall consider each question in turn.

(1) Kant maintains that the motive operates intentionally and causally and that the causality of the motive is the causality of purposes, that is, is the practical causality of representations or concepts insofar as the representation of the object (or the state of affairs to be produced) is regarded as the object's cause.[6] Moreover, the motive exerts its force *internally*, and this is the case even when its origin may be external to the will (as when the motive, as *Trieb,* is an external stimulus). However, when the will's determination is free, the force of the motive is properly neither internal nor external but placed outside the

---

5 In what follows, Kant's position is reconstructed in light of the post-Kantian reading of Kant's texts.
6 See Immanuel Kant, *Critique of Judgment* § 10.

spatiotemporal continuum of phenomena in which determination only occurs necessarily. In this case, the motive's causality is *free* causality, is *original* self-determination or *spontaneity*. (2) Kant's take on the second issue reveals the peculiarity of his *transcendental* discussion of practical motivation. Historically, it famously measures his distance from Wolff as well as his disagreement with Hume. On Kant's view, since Wolff's aim was to develop a "universal practical philosophy" concerned with "willing as such" and not with a particular kind of volition, Wolff's investigation had to take into account *all* the conditions and the motives capable of influencing the will. Hence such investigation was an empirical moral psychology, which differentiated motives only on the basis of their material and empirical constitution, that is, on the basis of the "relative strength or weakness" with which they act on the will and succeed in determining it.[7] Kant, by contrast, distinguishes motives on the basis of their *transcendental source* in one or the other mental faculty with whose transcendental principles his critical philosophy is concerned. Thus, the motives determining the will are for Kant fundamentally heterogeneous, as they do not differ *empirically*, that is, according to their material constitution or psychological strength or weakness, but *transcendentally*, that is, on the basis of whether their origin lies respectively in reason or sensibility. The transcendental perspective implies that both reason and sensibility have the power to directly motivate the will to action (i.e., to be "practical"). Herein lies Kant's well-known objection to Hume's denial that reason can in fact move us to action. Reason is practical, as it motivates the will through its a priori law; sensibility instead motivates through empirical stimuli, drives (*Triebe*), and desires acting as motive force (*Triebfeder*). In the former case (i.e., for practical reason), motivation has the force of an *obligation,* and the motive is "pure" or moral. Once possible contents are transcendentally brought back to the mental faculty from which they receive their motivational force, the difference is drawn be-

---

7 This is Kant's rendering of Wolff's position in *Groundwork*, AA 4:390–391.

tween "formal" and "material" motives for action. This is a stark alternative that allows for no gradual transition and accounts instead both for the heterogeneity of motives and for the different modality according to which those two faculties respectively motivate: reason motivates a priori and formally, sensibility a posteriori and materially. It follows that Kant's transcendental account of moral motivation is framed by an alternative that restricts the inquiry to a "*special kind* of will," namely the "*pure* will," which is defined as a will determinable a priori by a "pure" (and purely formal) motive.[8] Whatever the action to which they give rise, or, alternatively, whatever the action in which they appear, motives are moral for Kant only if their *transcendental source* lies a priori in practical reason. Fichte and Hegel react precisely to this restriction, and they do so by fundamentally transforming the more general framework that leads Kant to limit what counts as a moral motive to pure a priori motives legislated by practical reason.

(3) Kant's position on the difference between moral and nonmoral action implies that the appraisal of moral motives is always *formal* (since the moral principle motivates on the basis of its "form" alone, i.e., the form of "duty"). In whichever way motives may be embodied in action, their evaluation should be brought back to the transcendental source from which they derive their motivational force. For Kant, moral evaluation—and even self-evaluation—is neither a matter of empirical (i.e., psychological) inquiry nor a matter of intersubjective, collective discourse and negotiation.[9]

(4) The transcendental distinction of heterogeneous types of motives leads to the distinction of different kinds of agents. Not all kinds of will can be determined by a priori motives (*arbitrium brutum,* or the animal will, cannot), just as not all kinds of will can be motivated by sensible drives (*arbitrium sanctum,* or the holy will, cannot). Placed between the two, the human will has the capacity of being determined either way (*arbitrium liberum*)—hence

---

8 Kant, *Groundwork*, AA 4:390 (my emphasis).
9 See Kant, *Groundwork*, AA 4:407.

is free to choose whether to be determined freely or unfreely, to be moral or nonmoral. As Fichte and Hegel revisit the issue of the distinction among different kinds of motives, their views of the willing human subject, of the nature of moral motivation, and of the appraisal of free action change with regard to Kant's position in a substantial way. Before discussing their positions, however, I want briefly to dwell on the general systematic transformation that this Kantian framework undergoes in Fichte and in Hegel.

The most relevant modification concerns Kant's transcendental tenet according to which the difference between motives and their evaluation depends on their source alternatively in reason or sensibility. While Hegel rejects this tenet *tout court*, Fichte undermines Kant's radical distinction of the faculties but still holds on to the transcendental framework. The crucial point is that both for Fichte and for Hegel, motives determine the agent's will on the basis of their material constitution, that is, *a parte post*, on the basis of what they enjoin the will to do or to refrain from doing; they do not receive their determining force formally and *a parte ante*, from the mental faculty through which the will is ultimately moved. Although it may seem, in this regard, that Fichte and Hegel endorse a position closer to Wolff, it should be noted that for them the issue at stake is no longer the topic of moral psychology but of a social philosophy. Since motives are "contents" of volition and since they motivate the will to action and are evaluated in action in force of their materiality, all motives (including the moral ones) are ultimately "impure." Contents motivate to moral and ethical action because of their social, intersubjective constitution, that is, because they are motives that we share with other agents. Both for Fichte and for Hegel the notion of a purely formal motive is, in the end, an oxymoron: a purely formal prescription cannot move the will to action, hence cannot be properly motive. Indeed, a formal principle may obligate but not motivate. The point is that since the radical separation of the two sources drawn by Kant—namely, practical reason for intelligible motives and sensibility for material motives—is now rejected,

and since, for Kant, it is this distinction that grounds the moral validity (and the purity) of motives, the criterion of moral validity is now
placed in a different context constituted by different connections
among the elements. This context is the intersubjective ethical world
of spirit. The relation between the motive of the will and the validity of
the action is maintained; but since the moral motive is no longer
brought back to a purely noumenal source outside the world of experience, it can now be set in relation to its actualization in the world.
Thus, as motives appear and become actual in the world, they are
judged accordingly. Kant's connection between motives and their
transcendental source in the mental powers is replaced with the connection that anchors the motive to the process of its realization. This
leads Fichte and Hegel to rethink not only the practical validity of actions
but also the position and nature of the subject of practical motivation.
Kant's abstract personalistic view of the moral subject ultimately yields
to Hegel's idea of (objective) spirit, that is, to a collective, historical
subject to which ethical motives can now be attributed.

2. OBLIGATION AND MOTIVATION: FICHTE'S IDEA
OF MORAL MOTIVATION

By claiming that "the human being…is absolutely one,"[10] against
Kant's split between sensibility and understanding, theoretical and
practical reason, sensuous desires and intelligible motives, Fichte positions the issue of practical determination/motivation (*Bestimmung*) in
a new context. Crucial to Fichte's idea of motivation is the rejection of
the split between spontaneity and receptivity that for Kant matches
the separation between the intellectual and the sensible faculties as
sources of practical motivation. On Fichte's account, since everything
ultimately has its source in the *activity* of the I, the determinability
(*Bestimmbarkeit*) characterizing the subject is not receptivity to sensible

---

10 Johann Gottlieb Fichte, *SW* 2:255.

stimuli or mere passivity and is not the opposite of free self-determination. In fact, there is properly no receptivity or sheer passivity within
the I. Fichte eliminates from the subject all trace of passivity, hence all
dependence on a given datum capable of affecting sensibility. For him
all determination is, in the end, practical and is free self-determination: sensible motives are no longer the irreconcilable opposite of
moral motives.[11] The movement of "determination" is crucial to Fichte's
account of the activity of "willing": "an act of willing is an absolutely
free transition from indeterminacy to determinacy, accompanied by a
consciousness of this transition."[12] Fichte deems "the concept of the
will *as such*"—or the faculty of willing as a mere indeterminate power
or potentiality—to be philosophically and phenomenologically useless because merely "abstract" and unable to capture the real activity of
willing. For "willing is not completed, indeed there is no willing at all,
if no determination is present."[13] This means that the will is "real" only
as "*a* will, a *determinate* will," or as a will that is always already determinately motivated to a particular action. And since only the will can
provide itself with "the object" or the determinate motive of its willing,
the will is always "free in the material sense of the term." The natural
drive may provide the object of desire or longing. This, however, has no
true motivational power—is not properly "motive"—unless the will
makes the desired object into its own motive, that is, into "the object of
a determinate decision to realize such an object." And in this respect,
Fichte argues, "the will gives itself its object absolutely. In short, the
will is purely and simply free, and an unfree will is an absurdity."[14]
Indeed, if the will is real only as a determinately motivated willing, and
if all motive is self-given motive, then the will is free. Yet the point is

---

11 Or, to put the point with Kant, the will is not free when it is autonomously motivated by the moral
law and unfree when it follows heteronomous motives given by sensibility.

12 Fichte, *SW* 4:158. See Francesco Moiso, "*Wille* e *Willkür* in Fichte," *Revue Internationale de Philosophie* 191 (1995): 5–38.

13 Fichte, *SW* 4:158.

14 Fichte, *SW* 4:159.

that not everything—not all contents and not all concepts—can be endorsed by the will as *moral* motives; not everything can become an actual determination of the I and display moral validity. Hence the central question Fichte raises at the outset of *Die Bestimmung des Menschen* (1800) is: What is *my determination*?[15] In posing this question, Fichte's use of the term *Bestimmung* hints at a problem that is more far-reaching than the practical issue of the will's motivation (or its movement from indeterminacy to determinacy). The issue of practical (and specifically moral) motivation is connected with the cosmological issue of man's position in the world. In this framework, what can (and should) motivate or determine me to action is that through which I can realize my "vocation" (*Bestimmung* as *vocatio*) within the natural and social world.[16]

For Fichte, the way in which the human being must determine herself depends on the determinate place that humanity occupies within the order of nature. Fichte turns the connection between nature and freedom, man's position in the world and his moral "vocation" within it, into an argument against Kant. On Fichte's view, Kant's ideas of duty and freedom are not sufficient to ground man's true vocation. In its formality, duty is indeed the necessary basis of moral *obligation* but is not sufficient to account for man's practical *motivation*. In Fichte's view, Kant has conflated obligation and motivation and implied that since the moral law obligates on the basis of its formality it also motivates the will to moral action. The two, however, are not identical: motivation requires material conditions of determination. Now, in order to really function as "my determination," that is, to be endorsed as *my motive* and to move me to action, a content must be able to speak *to me* individually and to *actually determine* me. This means that no content

---

15 Fichte, *SW* 4:169.

16 The question of what is my determination/vocation in the world as human being has, as general candidates for an answer, possibilities such as: *knowing* nature and myself as part of the natural world; *acting* in connection with others in a world of persons like myself. My particular choices fall within these general ways of regarding the "vocation" to which all my actions respond.

that is either purely formal or generically universal and abstract can become my actual motive and move me to action. Motivation is always and necessarily individual, concrete, and itself determinate as the action it produces. Thus, I can endorse the form of duty as my motive only insofar as this abstract form connects to my personal condition becoming my vocation.

In the *System der Sittenlehre* (1798), in discussing the principle of an "applicable ethics," Fichte expresses the moral command in this way: "*Fulfill your determination in every case.*" However, he also immediately acknowledges the insufficiency of this formulation, thereby hinting at the further task that occupies *Die Bestimmung des Menschen.* Thus expressed, observes Fichte, the moral command "still leaves to be answered the question: *What then is my determination?*" In other words, the moral command obligates me (it tells me *that* I ought to) but does not motivate me to action until the material question of *what* my determination is, is answered as well. (The question is, "*what* is it that we purely and simply ought to do?"—it is only this "what" that provides the motive for action.)[17]

On a general level, for Fichte determination is necessarily both content-based and referred to the concrete individual. It has a practical normative validity—that is, ultimately, truly and really determines—if and only if it displays motivational force, if it commands a determinate action and is addressed to a determinate individual (not to the abstract idea of humanity, not even to the idea of humanity in myself) so that the individual is moved to actualize her determination in the world. Determination as motive is a practical concept that necessarily possesses applicability, hence reality. "To say that a concept possesses reality and applicability means that our world—that is to say the world...of consciousness—is in some respect determined by this concept."[18] Motives not only determine the agent to action but in so

17 Fichte, *SW* 4:65.
18 Fichte, *SW* 4:63.

doing they shape our world as they are made real in the world through action. Only under these conditions does determination really *determine* or *motivate*, that is, is actual ground for action, and is self-determination, that is, freedom. "*When applied to an empirical human being,* the domain of the moral law has a *determinate starting point*: the determinate state of limitation in which every individual finds himself.... It also has a *determinate goal*, which can never be achieved: absolute liberation from all limitation. Finally, it guides us along a *completely determinate path*: the order of nature."[19] This is Fichte's full account of how the motive for action works. He argues "that for every determinate human being, in each situation, *only one determinate something is in accord with duty*, and one can therefore say that this is what is demanded by the moral law as it applies to this temporal being."[20] While the moral law in its formality does not directly motivate to action, in the order of phenomena the individual agent can always "find" but truly give to herself the concrete motive for action that corresponds to the moral command, that is, that actualizes the command in the sensible world. In this way, content-determination and application are one with the moral principle—they do not indicate a successive moral task consisting in specifying (or indeed determining) the empty formality of duty. In fact, it is from its "applicability," that is, from its capacity to become concrete motive for action, that the principle receives true reality (not vice versa). Fichte's premise is relevant here: at stake is the *application* of the domain of the moral law *to that empirical individual which I myself am*. It is only within this framework that freedom becomes not only possible for a human "subject" in general but realizable, actual, and determined through and through at every step for me as an individual and concrete agent. Thus, the concept of *Bestimmung* as moral motivation is the crucial mediating link whereby duty's application is established.

---

19 Fichte, *SW* 4:166 (my emphasis).
20 Fichte, *SW* 4:166 (my emphasis).

For Kant the moral law is the normative source of the will's moral determination; such determination, however, is merely formal, that is, is not motivation to particular empirical actions. Duty is that which formally posits an obligation for the will; but the purely moral motivation never appears in a particular action. The form of duty is not immediately "applied" to empirical actions: with regard to content, it remains necessarily *indeterminate* (which constitutes its formality). On Fichte's view, however, the gesture that distances the form of duty from its application or appearance in particular actions is responsible for the fact that Kant's duty does indeed obligate but does not truly motivate the will. The shift that the connection between duty and determination undergoes in Fichte can be summarized as follows: while Kant unsuccessfully attempts to make the formality (indeterminateness) of duty into the will's motive, for Fichte only that which can function as my concrete determination or motivation can become my duty. Duty, for Fichte, is based on the capacity that a content has to morally motivate me (or to be carried out in the intersubjective world), not vice versa. For Kant the normative force lies in the *universal form* of duty—duty determines the *form* of what ought to be done, but in order to do this it must remain indeterminate with regard to content, and as a consequence it ultimately lacks motivational force. For Fichte, the normative validity lies in the *content-based*, *individual* character of determination working as concrete motivation—determination commands that which is my duty. Duty is always and necessarily applicable and real— even though its complete fulfillment remains an infinite task.

This is the context in which the quest for my determination/vocation is developed in *Die Bestimmung des Menschen*: "What am I and what is my determination?" This question means: I am setting out to find that content-based, individual determination which alone can be *my moral motivation*, namely, that which alone can speak *to me* and *determine* me, that is, can exercise the normative force of a duty, make me into a true individual, and relate me to a world that has meaning for me, a world of other human beings in which I participate as an active and worthy member. This and this only can be the moral motive for action; to pursue and actualize this motive is "my vocation."

3. ACTUALIZED FREEDOM AS MOTIVE OF THE WILL: HEGEL'S OVERCOMING OF "MORALITY" IN "ETHICAL LIFE"

In the *Encyclopedia*, Hegel first tackles the problem of the will's motivation in the last section of the Philosophy of Subjective Spirit, in the Psychology.[21] Herein he presents the movement that leads from "practical spirit" to "free spirit," from which he then accomplishes the transition to the sphere of objective spirit.[22] At stake in this movement is the idea of freedom, the development from the merely subjective and individual notion of the will's autonomous self-determination in its confrontation with the external world, to the actual realization of freedom in spirit's intersubjective and social world. Significantly, when compared to the positions discussed above, for Hegel the will's motivation and action at the level of "practical spirit" are considered outside the sphere of moral evaluation, whereas in the realm of objective spirit strictly moral motives are confronted with and expanded into the more complex dynamic of ethical life. Systematically, the issue of motivation arises first as the topic of psychology and only in its further development leads to a properly moral philosophy; this, however, is only part of Hegel's more comprehensive "philosophy of right."

It is as "will" that spirit first becomes actual. The will is not a merely potential faculty or the power of ineffectual intentions but the active link that roots thinking (or theoretical spirit) into the world, making thinking itself real. The reality that spirit displays through the will is the concrete and individualized existence of the subject. Thereby it is immediately set in opposition to the universality attained in the

---

21 See Adriaan Peperzak, *Hegels praktische Philosophie* (Stuttgart: Frommann, 1991).
22 G. W. F. Hegel, *Enz* §§ 469–482.

"concept" by theoretical knowledge.[23] Like Fichte, Hegel sees the will as "free"—this, Hegel claims, is the "determinate concept" of the will—because the will is nothing but spirit's activity "to give itself a content."[24] Such a content is the will's motive. The will is identical with and nothing other than the motive that sets it into action. To this extent, the will is "determined" by its motive not only in the sense of being moved by it (as for Kant and Fichte) but also in the sense that it is the motive that qualifies and makes the will what it is (and it is not the type of will that selects or can be moved only by a particular type of motive). The will is always motivated, concretely (self-)determined will; and it is self-determined even when it takes its contents outside of itself because only the will can make such contents into "motives." In its first appearance, however, the will is finite because it is merely formal. Significantly, for Hegel, the "formalism" of the will does not consist in the lack of content (for the will as such always has a content) but in the lack of identity that separates the particular subjective will, defined in its particularity by the pursuit of motives that are "its own" motives, from "actualized reason,"[25] that is, from the broader context in which rationality is objectively embodied in intersubjective, institutional practices of the social world.

Hegel's distance from Kant's and Fichte's positions should be underscored here. For Kant, a motive is rational and moral when it determines the will formally and universally and is devoid of subjective conditions (it is not strictly *my* motive); while for Fichte a content determines the will only when it is embraced as *my* subjective motive, thereby shedding the form of abstract universality. Moreover, at stake for both Kant and Fichte is the indication of what counts, distinctively, as *moral* motive. Hegel holds the different, developmental position

---

23 Hegel, *Enz* § 469: "as will, spirit enters reality; as knowing, it is in the sphere of the concept's universality."

24 Hegel, *Enz* § 469; recall Fichte's claim that "an unfree will is an absurdity" (*SW* 4:159).

25 Hegel, *Enz* § 469.

whereby the will, which is initially only formally free, achieves fully actualized freedom only under the condition of bringing out its own particular motive within the space of actualized reason. The will's motive ceases to be merely abstract and formal only when it is realized and shared in the realm of actualized reason (i.e., ultimately, within the sphere of ethical life). It is not, however, a moral judgment that requires such development. (There is no "ought to" underlying such movement.) Nor is it Hegel's task to construct an axiological scale of values against which motives are ranked. On his view, it is the very concept of the will that in its immanent dialectic drives the particular motive to its ethical actualization; it is the dialectical nature of the will to actualize its own personal motives in the reality of a shared world, thereby revealing that personal motives are truly always socially mediated—or ethical—motives: they are my motives because they are instituted as valid recognizable motives by the community in which my action takes place. At the level of objective spirit, the discrepancy that initially separates the formality of the merely subjective will from actualized reason yields the conflict between allegedly individual motives (with their intransigent claim to absolute "goodness" or morality) and collective norms. Objective, rational freedom consists in the capacity to overcome the "contradiction" produced by this actualization.[26] (Kantian) morality and the alleged "purity" of moral motives is, for Hegel, a transitional stage in the actualization of the free will. In its claim to absoluteness, morality is a position that is internally undermined by the dialectical tension between the formalism of the will's intention (the motive of the "good") and the "impurity" of the realized deed that never entirely matches the purity of the motive. Ultimately, the contradiction is overcome in the mediation process made possible by the structures of spirit's ethical world. It is here—in the relation, for example, between the activity of the individual in the family or civil society and her membership in the state—that individual, subjective

---

26 See G. W. F. Hegel, *R* § 28.

motives are mediated and reconciled in the concrete universality of the ethical whole. I now turn, in my analysis, to select moments of this development.

In presenting the concept of "practical spirit," Hegel lays out the trajectory that the development of the subjective will follows in order to gain the dimension of its objectivity: "The determination of the will that is *in itself* consists in bringing freedom to existence in the *formal* will, and thereby in bringing to existence the purpose of the latter [the formal will]—this purpose is to fulfill itself in its concept, i.e., *to make freedom into its own determinateness, into its content and purpose as well as into the form of its existence*."[27] Thereby Hegel outlines the development of the will from its subjective formality to its fulfilled freedom by pointing to the way the will's motive changes on the basis of the inner dialectic belonging to it. While the will is formally free precisely because it gives itself a motive (i.e., because it can transform whatever content it finds into a motivation for action), the crucial point—or the fulfilled idea of its freedom—consists in making freedom itself and its actualization into a motive. In other words, while the will is formally free for the simple fact of willing, it is free in a realized objective sense only when it embraces the realization of freedom in the world as its own motive and purpose. Hegel expresses this by saying that freedom becomes the will's determination, content, purpose, and very way of existence. This is the path that leads to the sphere of objective spirit. Since Hegel maintains that the "concept of freedom" that the will assumes as its chief motive and goal "is essentially only as thinking," it follows that "the path of the will that makes itself into *objective* spirit" consists in raising itself to "thinking will," that is, to the will that has as its determinate motive only contents that are the object of thinking in its universality and necessity (and not merely contingent feelings, sensations, natural desires).[28] Hence the "actually free will is the unity of

---

27 Hegel, *Enz* § 469 (my emphasis).

28 Hegel, *Enz* § 469.

theoretical and practical spirit,"[29] is the spirit that "knows itself as free" and acts accordingly.[30] With this position, Hegel reverses Kant's argument for the morality of motives. Freedom is not the capacity of the will to be determined a priori by a purely rational, moral motive—a motive that can never fully appear in reality as what it is in thinking, hence is never truly objective but always implies an unfulfilled, open-ended "ought to" (*Sollen*). Freedom, for Hegel, is not coextensive with morality. Freedom is the realized motive of a will that in its activity brings the universal contents of thinking to appear in the actuality of the world; freedom is the express motive of a will that assumes as its moving purpose the construction a world that is the world of spirit's actualization. In this process, the will endorses freedom as its properly "ethical" motivation. "*True* freedom," Hegel maintains, "as ethical life [*Sittlichkeit*] consists in this, that the will is not subjective or selfish, but has the universal content as its purpose."[31]

In the introduction to the *Philosophy of Right* (1821) Hegel outlines the role that willing plays in the development of objective spirit.[32] "The will that is free is the starting point" from which the realm of "right" in its broadest extension is established. Hegel repeats at this point that the will is free when "freedom constitutes its substance and determination,"[33] that is, when that which moves the will and constitutes its substantial reality is the actualization of freedom, or when the will expressly wants the actualization of freedom. The "system of right is the realm of freedom's actualization."[34] Thus, we can say that at the level of objective spirit, in exploring the expanse of the "system of right" in its inner articulation (Abstract Right, Morality, Ethical Life), Hegel assumes as his topic the free will's motive (i.e., freedom), viewing it from the side of its actualized

---

29 Hegel *Enz* § 481.

30 Hegel, *Enz* § 482.

31 Hegel, *Enz* § 469 Remark.

32 See Hegel, *R* §§ 4–29.

33 Hegel, *R* § 4 and Addition.

34 Hegel, *R* § 4.

objective existence. In other words, if compared with Kant's critical moral theory, in which motives of free action are considered exclusively within the space of the will's self-determination, what Hegel explores in the *Philosophy of Right* is the opposite side of the will's motive, when such motive is freedom itself in the process of its actualization. From this development I want to select two moments. First, I briefly dwell on Hegel's general presentation of the dialectic of moral motivation in the sphere of Morality (*Moralität*).[35] Then I turn to a moment of Ethical Life (*Sittlichkeit*), to civil society, in which the conflict between personal motivation and collective ends is staged and solved in a paradigmatic way.

Moralität is the sphere of the will's subjectivity and personality. The "moral standpoint" characterizes the will in its attempt to bring its personal ends into the world—a world that is already the objective world of spirit in which juridical and ethical norms and institutions constitute the backdrop of the subject's activity. Morality is the standpoint of finitude and inadequacy for which the action in its particularity seems never to match the alleged loftiness and purity of the self-ascribed intention. While the subjective intention is never entirely fulfilled but remains a mere "ought to" or an infinite task,[36] it is in the subjective "purpose" (*Vorsatz*) (which is *my* particular purpose) and in the "intention" (*Absicht*)[37] (which is *my* intention) that the action finds its value. The action has value as the affirmation or "expression" in reality of subjectivity and its motives. The intention gives to the action a "relative value," which consists in its "relation to me."[38] The content that expresses the purpose of "my particular subjective existence" is my "welfare."[39] Once such content, taken in the interiority that characterizes

35 For a reading of this part of the *Philosophy of Right* in the direction of Hegel's theory of action, see Michael Quante, *Hegel's Concept of Action* (Cambridge: Cambridge University Press, 2004); and more generally Adriaan Peperzak, *Modern Freedom: Hegel's Legal, Moral, and Political Philosophy* (Dordrecht: Kluwer, 2001).

36 See Hegel, *R* § 108, § 111.

37 Hegel, *R* § 114.

38 Hegel, *R* § 114 Addition.

39 Hegel, *R* § 113.

the motive, is raised to the form of universality and, despite its interiority, to the claim of objectivity, it becomes the "absolute end of the will," that is, "the good" as the highest moral motive, and its opposite, "evil" and "conscience."[40]

While Kant and Fichte follow the movement that goes from the will's intention-motivation to its realization in action, Hegel works methodologically backward in the opposite direction. Endorsing as his point of departure the standpoint of the realized action that is fully displayed in the objective world, Hegel characterizes the "moral standpoint" through the attempt to bring the *value* of the action back to the subjective motivation that has produced it. In the section "Intention and Welfare," for example, Hegel derives the "intention"—*die Absicht*—from a consideration that retrospectively moves from the scattered multiplicity of individual factual connections in which the action appears in its particularity to the unity of the subjective intention of a "thinking agent" who has allegedly generated it. It is in the intention that the particularity of the action claims the moment of "universality."[41] In fact, what Hegel pursues in this way is the dialectical strategy that exposes the fundamental inconsistency of Kant's (and Fichte's) position, namely, of the claim that it is the subjective intention or motivation that lends exclusive moral value to the action. For, the inference that goes from the actual deed to its alleged intention is always and necessarily an arbitrary—even a hypocritical—one. Who can tell whether my not overcharging my customers stems indeed from my conception of the good and is not, rather, a self-interested action? Hegel shows that within the standpoint of morality, subjective motivation displays a dialectical articulation that (1) starts in the formality of the purpose (*Vorsatz*); (2) lends to the action a "relative value" by referring it back to my intention (*Absicht*); and finally (3) claims for the action an "absolute value" once the action is referred to the idea of the

40 Hegel, *R* § 114.
41 Hegel, *R* § 119.

good as the highest motivation.[42] In this way, Hegel's dialectical un-
folding of the notion of subjective motive is a *reductio ad absurdum* of
the claim of "morality" according to which the value of the action lies
in the motive that has produced it. By endorsing the perspective of the
realized action, the moral standpoint is shown to be untenable. For,
what this movement reveals is rather the opposite of what morality
claims. It reveals that the subjective intention is ultimately unable to
truly motivate and produce particular actions unless inscribed in the
broader context of ethical life. Herein lies Hegel's critique of Kant's
moral formalism.[43] Subjective motives do not arise in a vacuum but are
themselves shaped and justified—precisely in their motivational validity for the subject—by the intersubjective context in which norms
are actually enforced in social and collective practices. Hence the opposite of the moral standpoint is the case: intentions gain their subjective value from the ethical context in which they are *de facto* concretely
enacted; they receive their value from the action itself because action is
always and necessarily inscribed in the broader framework of socially
accepted values and practices. To be sure, in Hegel's view, my action of
not overcharging my customers should not be judged within the restricted moral alternative proposed by Kant: either motivated by the
moral imperative or self-interested. Hegel's point is that my action as a
shopkeeper is ultimately dictated by the fact that my motives are
formed in connection with the broader economic dynamics and trans-
actions in which I am one of the many participants. It is only within
this context that my choices can be explained as meaningful. This is

---

42 The distinction between *Vorsatz* and *Absicht* poses a problem for the interpreters. Hegel himself
does not strictly separate the two notions (see for example Hegel, *R* § 114 Remark). See Quante,
Hegel's Concept of Action, chap. 4; Allen Wood, *Hegel's Ethical Thought* (Cambridge: Cambridge University Press, 1990), 141.

43 I will not discuss Hegel's critique of Kant's moral formalism in further details here (for this issue
see my "Contradiction in the Ethical World: Hegel's Challenge for Times of Crisis," in *Freiheit*, Akten
der Stuttgarter Hegel Kongress 2011, edited by G. Hindrich and A. Honneth [Stuttgart: Klostermann,
2011], 627–648) but will concentrate on the more limited point concerning moral motivation. Hegel's
critique, however, is implied in what I just presented.

the argument that guides Hegel's "transition" from *Moralität* to *Sittlichkeit*.[44]

I turn now briefly to a passage that shows the force of such transition as it brings to light what it means that subjective (even selfish) motives are socially mediated, hence ethically enforced, even when strict morality is either lacking or not intended. Hegel argues that in the sphere of ethical life the "idea of freedom as the living good" has become the actual motive for self-consciousness's action. Freedom is the content and form of self-consciousness's "knowledge and volition," is its concrete purpose and the form of its existence. Freedom is *actualized* freedom, since "the concept of freedom has become the existing world and the nature of self-consciousness."[45] This is what it means, for Hegel, that freedom is both the highest motive of action and the realized action itself. The second sphere of ethical life is "civil society." Its first division, the "System of Needs," presents the economic relations among individuals. To introduce the mechanism of the market as a sphere of ethical life means that economic relations are neither self-sufficient nor self-regulating but are part of an organic unity that provides the condition for their actuality and rationality. Relevant is the *subjective* condition that for Hegel supports the economic life of individuals. Within civil society the "ethical disposition" that informs the individual's action is "rectitude and the honor of one's estate." These moral feelings are tied to the role that the individual plays within the broader context in which economic relations are specified. Accordingly, to be a citizen of civil society is to be motivated by such feelings as rectitude, honor, and justice, to be active as a member of a corporation and estate, and "to be recognized in one's own eyes and in the eyes of all others" as a subject who embodies such an ethical disposition.[46]

---

44 See Angelica Nuzzo, *Rappresentatione e concetto nella logica della Filosofia del diritto di Hegel* (Naples: Guida, 1990), chap. 3; Ludwig Siep, "Was heisst: 'Aufhebung der Moralität in Sittlichkeit' in Hegels Rechtsphilosophie?," *Hegel Studien* 12 (1982): 75–96.

45 Hegel, *R* § 142.

46 Hegel, *R* § 207.

Significant in Hegel's argument is not only the socially mediated character of our access to ourselves but also the assumption of a fundamental *visibility* of moral motives to the eye of society. This contrasts with Kant's claim that even our own motives are "invisible" to ourselves. (They are absolutely impenetrable to others.)[47] The point, for Hegel, is that only through society can we gain access to our own motivations. In other words, I am motivated the way I am not in force of some original and a priori condition rooted in reason, but simply because all the other participants in the economic life of which I am part are motivated in a similar way. My motivations and my purposes are constituted in connection with and in response to the motivations and purposes of others. This is what it means to be agent in the sphere of ethical life, that is, a member of a family and of civil society, and an active citizen.

Unlike the abstract "person" subject of rights and the moral "subject," the "citizen" of civil society is a "concrete" subject. It is here, Hegel explains, that we encounter for the first time the *"human being—Mensch."*[48] As "human being," the citizen of civil society stands in reciprocal dependence with all others, whereby she displays an aspect of "universality as *being-recognized*" by others. "Recognition" confers to the agent's needs, motivations, and sentiments a specifically "social" character. That recognition is constitutive of one's motives and needs means that "I have to orient myself according to the others"; that in order to act on my motivations and to satisfy my needs "I have to take the other's opinion" into account.[49] The individual's motivation is here socially mediated not only because it matters to the agent how her motives are regarded by others in this sphere (I have to view my own motives with the eyes of others) but also—and crucially—because the others' opinion becomes for me a source of "need": I seek

47 See Kant, *Groundwork*, AA 4:407.
48 Hegel, *R* § 190.
49 Hegel, *R* § 192 Addition.

the satisfaction of the opinion of others and this becomes my motive for action, that is, the way others appraise my motives, and the motivational contents that others read in my intentions influence and shape my own motives for action. The agent of civil society is a particular, "concrete person" characterized by a totality of needs, selfish motives, and arbitrary volitions. However, it is only through her relation to other individuals that she is able to fulfill her volitions and satisfy her needs. This interaction is the basis of the peculiar "universality" that characterizes this sphere.[50] Although individual ends are "selfish," based on merely personal interests and motivations, they are also social and intersubjectively mediated, hence somehow universal. Individual ends are conditioned by the universal context of reciprocal interaction because this context alone allows for those ends to be realized. Subsistence, welfare, and rights of the individual are interwoven with and dependent on the subsistence, welfare, and rights of all.[51] Furthermore, within civil society selfish motivations are acted on because they display a *reflective* universality that is due to their belonging to an individual *only through* their belonging to any other person. The individual is here one of the many abstractly equal individuals.[52] Her motivations are *legitimate* motivations in their selfish character because they are selfish motivations of all other individuals. In order to act as a citizen of this sphere, the individual is required to recognize this double character of her volitions—the *selfish* motivation must be recognized as a *shared selfish* motivation. In sum, in this argument we find Hegel's reply to the formalism of Kant's morality of intentions. In the sphere of civil society we have an example of selfish motivation that acquires a binding universality that is not moral and not abstractly formal but is the concrete instantiation of the actualization of freedom in the ethical world.

---

50 Hegel, *R* § 182.

51 Hegel, *R* § 183.

52 Hegel, *R* § 187.

By way of conclusion, let me sum up the systematic and methodological points that emerge from this discussion. I have shown how Fichte and Hegel differently develop their views on the will's motivation to action against the backdrop of Kant's critical philosophy. Systematically, while Kant reclaimed the place of moral motivation in a transcendental moral philosophy, rejecting the placement of the topic within psychology, Hegel takes up again the psychological dimension of the will's motivation but does so in order to set the issue within the broader context of a social and political philosophy. Fichte retains Kant's transcendental framework, although he, with Hegel, concentrates his attention on the intersubjective implications of action. He draws to the center the "applied" dimension of the will's motivation whereby motives are always and necessarily detected in the action's realization. Here, however, we encounter the crucial methodological difference between Kant's and Fichte's transcendental approach, and Hegel's dialectical and developmental account of motivation. While Kant and Fichte proceed, phenomenologically, from the motive to the realized action and place in the intention the source of the action's moral value, Hegel's dialectic critically reverses this relation. Hegel shows that once we proceed from the realized action to its subjective motivation, far from being the source of the action's moral value, the intention owes its value and its motivational force to the broader ethical context in which individual motives are always and necessarily inscribed. Both points, the systematic and the methodological, are crucial in order to understand the link between the notion of motive and the idea of freedom.

Reflection

MORAL MOTIVATION AND THE LIMITS OF MORAL
AGENCY IN LITERARY NATURALISM

DREISER'S *SISTER CARRIE*

Anne Diebel

❧

With the rise of deterministic thinking in the nineteenth century, novelists in the realist tradition—that is, novelists who aspired to represent the world as it is—had to redefine some of the most basic aspects of their form: character, plot, and the relationship between the two. If our bodies and minds are governed by forces beyond our control, could our moral beliefs then be a significant source of motivation and cause of action?

The 1880s were a critical moment in the redefinition of the novel, as English and American novelists, following Émile Zola's lead, sought new ways of representing the relationship between humans and their environments. Whereas realists took for granted the existence of conscious, autonomous subjects, naturalists argued that consciousness and autonomy were impossible in a universe controlled by impersonal forces. Not only could "consciousness" be reduced to biochemical processes, but individual action came to be seen as the product of historical, economic, and social conditions. Whereas the plots of realist novels hinged on characters' individual decisions and the motives underlying them, the plots of naturalist novels were structured by overriding trajectories—rises and falls, triumphs and declines—that had little or nothing to do with the characters' choices, much less their moral beliefs. Work, sex, and death gained new thematic prominence as the essential processes of life; so too did the category of the unwilled, our instinctive, reflexive behaviors. Darwin's theory of natural selection is keenly felt in Edith Wharton's novel *The House of Mirth* (1905), where the beautiful but hopelessly snobbish Lily Bart is described as socially maladaptive, never to find a husband in the modern marriage market: her "inherited tendencies had combined with early training to make her the highly specialized product she was: an organism as helpless out of its narrow range as the sea anemone torn from the rock."

The question of moral agency is given thorough consideration by Theodore Dreiser in his novel *Sister Carrie* (1900), a grim depiction of urban capitalist modernity in turn-of-century America. By the time he began the novel in 1899, Dreiser was under the sway of Herbert Spencer, whose universal theory of cosmological, biological, and social evolution forced the young writer to abandon "all that [he] had deemed substantial"—"man's place in nature, his importance in the universe and on this too too solid earth"—and to reconceive of man as servant, not master, of his own destiny. Dreiser was similarly enamored of the mechanistic ideas of Jacques Loeb, who saw moral behavior as no less automatic or "tropistic" than any other behavior. Loeb tried to reconcile mechanism with morality by arguing that *only* a "mechanistic conception of life" could lead to "an understanding of the source of ethics."

Fittingly, then, at the center of *Sister Carrie* is a moment of apparent choice: George Hurstwood, an unhappily married Chicago restaurant manager who has fallen in love with the much younger Carrie Meeber, is performing his nightly duties when he discovers that the restaurant's safe has been left open. He removes the money, counts it ($10,000!), and stands there deliberating whether to take it and run away with his new lover. A bit tipsy, he wavers for several minutes, one moment sure that he can get away with it, the next moment fearing scandal. Finally, he decides to return the money to the safe and does so, only to realize that he has put the sums in the wrong boxes. Just after he retrieves them for sorting, the door of the safe closes and the lock clicks (see figs. 3–5).

This scene of "decision" is in fact a scene of *indecision*, and the question of Hurstwood's moral motivation, for taking the money or for returning it, becomes irrelevant the moment the safe door swings shut. What difference does it make that Hurstwood tries to do what he thinks is right, only to be thwarted by an accident of physics? That he then flees with the money, rather than explaining the situation to his boss? That, having fled to Montreal, he then mails back a large portion of the money to his former employers in order to repair his reputation and (unsuccessfully) to regain his job? The novel's deterministic framework would suggest that,

FIGURES 3–5 Laurence Olivier as George Hurstwood in *Carrie*, William Wyler's 1952 film adaptation of Dreiser's novel.

FIGURES 3–5 Continued.

despite his feelings of guilt, Hurstwood bears no responsibility for what has occurred, a point reinforced by the narrator's commentary on humans' limited understanding of what at any moment, and particularly at moments of "conscious action," they are actually doing.

Yet the narrator's didactic intrusions make it easy to miss the subtle moral dimension of this scene. In the novel as a whole, characters are motivated by desires for material objects (an umbrella, new shoes, a nice dinner) and by vague longings for wealth and fame. But is urban capitalist modernity the sole explanation for and exculpation of all action, or is there room to appraise actions in terms of the agent's particular motive? In the scene of Hurstwood and the money, Dreiser seems to treat the very notion of determination with a certain irony, and thus to open up the possibility of understanding Hurstwood's motives as ineffective in the world yet an important source of sympathy for the reader. The absurdity of the situation, in which a man's fate is sealed by a Newtonian accident (as if through a literalization of the concept of "force"), prompts us to examine all the more closely the moral considerations he makes before his dilemma is abruptly resolved for him.

The narrator even warns the reader not to judge Hurstwood for his uncertainty. "To those who have never wavered in conscience, the predicament of the individual whose mind is less strongly constituted and who trembles in the balance between duty and desire is scarcely appreciable, unless graphically portrayed. Those who have never heard that solemn voice of the ghostly clock which ticks with awful distinctness, 'thou shalt,' 'thou shalt not,' 'thou shalt,' 'thou shalt not,' are in no position to judge."[1] According to the narrator, what needs to be "graphically portrayed" is Hurstwood's inner conflict, the tick-tock of the clock, rather than the moment when that conflict is mooted by the click of the lock. Hurstwood

---

1 Theodore Dreiser, *Sister Carrie* (New York: Norton, 2006), 184.

has motives for stealing the money: he could divorce his wife, and he could "get Carrie" and live comfortably with her for years. He also has motives for *not* stealing it: "Think of what a scandal it would make. The police! They would be after him. He would have to fly, and where? Oh, the terror of being a fugitive from justice!"[2] That Hurstwood hesitates because he fears getting caught, rather than because he wants to do right, does not diminish the significance of his imagining himself, however foolishly, as a moral agent. Indeed, it is this man's confused moral sense that Dreiser ranks more worthy of "graphic portrayal" than the clearest conscience. A novel, Dreiser suggests, should not be so heartless as the universe. *Sister Carrie*'s premise is naturalistic, but its ends are humanistic.

Dreiser and other naturalists did not eliminate motive but instead challenged the realist assumption that we can always see actions in terms of motives and vice versa. Hurstwood chances to have a "sensitive, highly organised nature," but his moral conflict is the expression of a tendency Dreiser sees as innate to humanity. As Dreiser writes, with his characteristically awkward mingling of sentiment and hard fact, "the dullest specimen of humanity, when drawn by desire toward evil, is recalled by a sense of right.... We must remember that it may not be a knowledge of right, for no knowledge of right is predicated of the animal's instinctive recoil at evil. Men are still led by instinct before they are regulated by knowledge."[3] Many characters in naturalist novels lack the intelligence to think morally at all; they seek animal satisfaction in food, warmth, sex, sleep. Even when these characters (such as Hurstwood) have some moral conviction, their attempts to act on their beliefs are often superseded by morally indifferent scientific laws. And yet, while their agency is limited, their dim accumulation of knowledge is a counterforce to the brutality of impulse and happenstance.

---

2 Dreiser, *Sister Carrie*, 185.

3 Dreiser, *Sister Carrie*, 184.

CHAPTER TEN

Consequentialism, Moral Motivation, and the Deontic Relevance of Motives

Steven Sverdlik

Some people believe that these two statements might both be true: if Jane informs the police of the location of the fugitive Smith *out of revenge*, she acts wrongly; but if Anita informs the police of the location of Smith *out of public spirit,* she acts rightly. To suppose that both of these statements might be true is (probably) to suppose that motives are relevant deontically. To suppose that motives are relevant deontically is to suppose that the motive of an action can affect whether it is morally right or wrong.

The classical consequentialists from Jeremy Bentham to G. E. Moore were, in my opinion, understandably skeptical about whether the motive of an action ever could be relevant deontically. I begin this chapter with a historical sketch of their thinking about this question. But I go on to argue that there is room in consequentialist theory for saying that motives can occasionally affect whether an action is right or wrong. Furthermore, the consequentialist account that I sketch can,

I believe, give a plausible account of those rare cases where motives do affect whether an action is right or wrong.

I think moral common sense is of two minds about whether motives ever are relevant deontically. On the one hand we say that it is possible to "do the right thing for the wrong reason." This suggests that motives (which could be taken to be an agent's reasons for acting) are irrelevant deontically. But actions like informing out of revenge probably do strike some people as being wrong in virtue of their bad motives.

The issues here are related to the concept of moral motivation. I interpret that concept to pick out the motive or motives that an ethical theory takes to be morally valuable or praiseworthy. Consider a case where an agent is thought to have done the right thing for the wrong reason. This would occur if, say, Jane gives money to a charity only from self-interest. To be led by moral motivation to give to the charity, someone might say, would be to give from sympathy for the recipients of the charity's activities, or from a sense of duty, that is, from a desire to do what is right. I will describe three criteria that the classical consequentialists proposed for which motives are praiseworthy. I will show how the issues of deontic relevance and praiseworthiness can intersect.

The idea of deontic relevance will be one of my main concerns here. It can be explained more fully as follows. There are three deontic concepts or categories, which are applied to actions: the obligatory (required, a duty); the wrong (prohibited, forbidden); and the "merely permissible." To say that an action is merely permissible is to say that the agent is neither morally required to perform it nor morally prohibited from performing it. In one important sense of the deontic terms—the "all things considered" sense—it seems that all particular actions are either morally wrong, morally obligatory, or neither (that is, merely permissible): the three concepts are mutually exclusive and jointly exhaustive of all actions. In this sense, no action is, for example, both obligatory and wrong.[1]

---

[1] See my *Motive and Rightness* (Oxford: Oxford University Press, 2011), 3–4.

To give a more precise explanation of the idea that motives are relevant deontically, we can then say this: "There is an action type X such that if a token of X were performed from one motive it would fall into one deontic category, and if another token of X were performed from another motive it would fall into a second deontic category in virtue of this difference in motives." In other words, if motives are relevant deontically then there are cases where the motive of an action makes a difference in whether it is obligatory, wrong, or merely permissible.

I

This section surveys the most important consequentialist treatments of the deontic relevance of motives in the early period of the theory's development (1789–1912). After that period the theory went into eclipse until the 1950s. There were certainly important ideas about the deontic relevance of motives that were developed after its revival in the 1950s.[2] However, I think that the basic consequentialist claims and distinctions were established in the earlier period. The consensus of consequentialist thinkers in the period I examine, I argue, is that motives are irrelevant to the deontic status of actions. I will also examine consequentialist ideas about moral motivation. In later sections I will criticize some of the arguments I present here.

The consequentialist approach to rightness and the other deontic categories, as it is currently understood, might be stated as follows. The fundamental claim of "act" consequentialism is this: at a given time an agent is morally obligated to choose the action open to her that will have the best consequences. In other words, the right act is the one that

---

2 R. M. Hare, *Moral Thinking* (Oxford: Oxford University Press, 1981), chaps. 2, 3; Derek Parfit, *Reasons and Persons* (Oxford: Oxford University Press, 1984), 24–43; Peter Railton, "Alienation, Consequentialism, and the Demands of Morality," in *Facts, Values, and Norms* (Cambridge: Cambridge University Press, 2003), 151–186; David Brink, *Moral Realism and the Foundations of Ethics* (Cambridge: Cambridge University Press, 1989), 216–217, 256–262. Robert M. Adams, "Motive Utilitarianism," *Journal of Philosophy* 73 (1976): 467–481, comes at the issue in a fundamentally different way.

will produce the best consequences. Any action that she chooses that has less than the best consequences is wrong. Utilitarianism is historically the main form that consequentialism has taken. The utilitarian version of act consequentialism is based on a hedonistic theory of value. This theory asserts that the only thing that is intrinsically valuable is happiness—which was itself conceived of by the early theorists as a large surplus of pleasure over pain. The only thing bad in itself is pain. Thus, the act utilitarian theory of rightness is that at a given time an agent is morally obligated to choose the action open to her that will produce the most happiness. Any action that she chooses that produces less than the most happiness is wrong.

These statements leave some questions open, as I will show. Furthermore, there are various other forms of consequentialism that make somewhat different claims. It is clear even from these statements that in consequentialism motives do not figure in the theory at the most basic level. But there is the possibility that they are deontically relevant in some derivative way. Nonetheless, it is easy to see why consequentialists would tend to doubt that motives are relevant deontically. If the consequences of an action are better than those of any alternative, it is plausible to think it would be right no matter what motive it were performed from. So if Jane and Anita were to inform the police about Smith's whereabouts, it hard to see how Jane's motive could alter the calculation that determined whether her action has the best consequences. But at this point we should turn our attention to the actual reasoning of the early consequentialists.

Bentham

Jeremy Bentham's *An Introduction to the Principles of Morals and Legislation* (1789) is largely concerned with the project of designing legal institutions, especially the criminal law, along utilitarian lines. Bentham begins the book by announcing what he calls the Principle of Utility, which is actually not stated in the same way as I stated the basic claim of act utilitarianism.[3] Bentham proceeds to apply the principle in a methodical way, pausing over many analytic questions. Chapter 10 is devoted to the nature and evaluation of motives. This is the most searching treatment of motives ever written by a consequentialist.

Bentham states that the word "motive" can have a number of meanings (*IPML* 96–100). The sense that is closest to what we mean by the term he calls "the internal motive in *esse*" (IPML 98). Bentham conceives of motives in this sense as being the pleasure that accompanies the anticipation of acting in a certain way. This sort of pleasure can trigger the will into initiating an action. The fact that motives in this sense are pleasures leads Bentham to say: "There is no such thing as any sort of motive that is in itself a bad one" (*IPML* 100; compare 114). However, Bentham generally ignores the fact that motives have some small value in themselves: "If they [motives] are good or bad, it is only on account of their effects: good on account of their tendency to produce pleasure or avert pain; bad, on account of their tendency to produce pain or avert pleasure" (*IPML* 100). Most of the chapter is devoted to considering the effects of motives, which is to say, the effects of the actions they give rise to. One central claim of the chapter is that any given type of motive, like the love of reputation, can give rise to a variety of actions, some that are socially beneficial and some that are not (*IPML* 100–116).

Bentham seems to think that motives can have these variable effects for three reasons. First, agents can be placed in different circumstances. This means that in one situation the motive of self-preservation, say, might lead an agent to kill another person, while in a second situation it might lead her to save another person's life.[4] Second, an agent's propensities to expect pleasure and pain, that is, her motives, always work

---

3 Jeremy Bentham, *An Introduction to the Principles of Morals and Legislation,* edited by J. H. Burns and H. L. A. Hart (London: Methuen, 1982) (hereafter *IPML*), 11–12. For discussion of whether Bentham meant to endorse a moral principle somewhat like the central claim of act utilitarianism, see the introduction by Hart, xlix–lii.

4 Bentham, *IPML,* 112–113, which oddly instances only actions that work to the detriment of others.

in conjunction with certain beliefs that she has. This means that an agent in a given situation would be moved to do one thing by a certain motive if she had certain beliefs but would be moved to do another if she had other beliefs. For example, if someone were pleased to do God's will, which action she would choose to do would depend on what she believed God's will to be (*IPML* 123; compare 126). In making this point Bentham is in effect recognizing something like the practical syllogism. He is noting that having a motive by itself cannot lead a person to act. She also needs a belief, which functions as a minor premise. This belief states how she can realize the goal that her motive in effect sets for her. Third, certain motives, like the central one of benevolence, admit of varying scopes. Bentham contrasts "enlarged" and "confined" benevolence (*IPML* 128; compare 116–118). Partial benevolence might move a person to do something that benefits her family; a more extensive benevolence might move her to do something else.

Bentham goes on to give utilitarian evaluations of the different types of motives that people typically act from. One such evaluation considers the general tendencies of certain types of motive to increase or decrease the amount of happiness of other members of society; a second considers the general tendencies of certain types of motive to increase or decrease the amount of happiness of all members of society, including the agent (*IPML* 114–122). He expends more effort on the former endeavor. "Good will," especially enlarged benevolence, is adjudged the best motive; "dissocial" motives like revenge are the worst.

Since no type of motive has uniformly good or bad effects, even a dissocial motive like revenge can lead to actions that are right in utilitarian terms, and a good motive like enlarged benevolence can lead to an action that is wrong. Bentham's legal orientation seems to explain his stress on the good consequences of initiating criminal prosecutions, even if the motive is dissocial, and however much popular condemnation they attract (*IPML* 124; compare 133, 154, note o). Given all these facts, Bentham asserts that the legal (and presumably, moral) evaluation of a motive must consider what its effects are "in each individual instance" (*IPML* 116). "An act of injustice or cruelty, committed by a man for the sake of his father or son, is punished, and with reason, as much as if it were committed for his own" (*IPML* 118; compare 128–9).

Austin

John Austin's *The Province of Jurisprudence Determined* (1832) is also focused on legal questions, especially analytical ones. But in developing his account of human and divine law Austin devotes some space to expounding utilitarianism as a moral theory. In Lecture 4 he addresses some misconceptions about the theory. The first of these involves confusing a "standard or measure" of conduct with "a motive or inducement" to conduct.[5] Apparently echoing Adam Smith, he states that a man who "delves or spins" does so in order "to put money in his purse." But by doing so "he adds to the sum of commodities," so that his action "conforms to utility considered as the standard of conduct," even though "general utility is not the motive to [his] action" (*PJD* 107). Austin continues with this striking example:

Of all pleasures bodily or mental, the pleasures of mutual love, cemented by mutual esteem are the most enduring and varied. They therefore contribute largely to swell the sum of the well-being, or they form an important item in the account of human happiness. And, for that reason, the well-wisher of the general good, or the adherent of the principle of utility, must, in that character, consider them with much complacency. But, though he approves of love because it accords with his principle, he is far from maintaining that the general good ought

5 John Austin, *The Province of Jurisprudence Determined,* edited by H. L. A. Hart (New York: Noonday, 1954) (hereafter *PJD*), 105. A similar distinction was earlier made by William Godwin in a pamphlet published in 1801. Godwin distinguished "the motive from which a virtuous action is to arise, and the criterion by which it is determined to be virtuous." See William Godwin, *Enquiry Concerning Political Justice, with Selections from Godwin's Other Writings,* edited by K. Codell Carter (Oxford: Oxford University Press, 1971), 322.

to be the motive of the lover. It was never contended or conceited by a sound, orthodox utilitarian, that the lover should kiss his mistress with an eye to the common weal (*PJD* 107–108).

Austin seems to be claiming that the lover acts rightly in kissing his mistress.[6] This entails that an act that is morally obligatory in utilitarian terms need not be done from a sense of duty or obligation, that is, from a motive that aims to do what is morally right. Nor need an act that is morally obligatory in utilitarian terms be done from a desire to produce the most happiness or pleasure for all concerned. Indeed, Austin argues that most people have a very limited understanding of other people's interests, so that if they are motivated to further the general interest they will often fail to do so. "The principle of general utility imperiously demands" that an ordinary person commonly "shall attend to his own rather than to the interests of others" (PJD 106).

Mill

Perhaps the most famous treatment by a utilitarian of the deontic relevance of motives occurs in John Stuart Mill's *Utilitarianism* (1861). In this brief passage the claims of earlier utilitarians are put into their most general form. Mill, like Austin, insists that we must distinguish "the very meaning of a standard of morals," which provides "the rule of action," from the motive of the action. He continues: "utilitarian moralists have gone beyond almost all others in affirming that the motive has nothing to do with the morality of the action, though much to do with the worth of the agent. He who saves a fellow creature from drowning does what is morally right, whether his motive be duty

---

6 Austin is here apparently criticizing the utilitarianism of Godwin's *Enquiry Concerning Political Justice* (1793). Godwin was understood to be claiming that rational benevolence should always be a utilitarian's motive for acting. See J. B. Schneewind, *Sidgwick's Ethics and Victorian Moral Philosophy* (Oxford: Oxford University Press, 1977), 136–137; 153–154. Godwin later disavowed this idea. See the pamphlet of 1801, in Godwin, *Enquiry Concerning Political Justice, with Selections from Godwin's Other Writings*, 321–322.

or the hope of being paid for his trouble; he who betrays the friend that trusts him is guilty of a crime, even if his object be to serve another friend to whom he is under greater obligations."[7] We can reasonably take Mill here to be asserting here that motives are always irrelevant deontically. That is, whether an action is right or wrong is never dependent on facts about the motive it is performed from. It is a fair interpretation to say that Mill's "morality of the action" is another way of speaking about its deontic status, since he goes on to speak of "what is morally right." Mill also makes another important distinction between the deontic relevance of motives and their relevance to character or virtue judgments about the agent. They are presumably also relevant to judgments about whether the agent is morally praiseworthy or blameworthy for so acting. Mill claims that the judgments that we make about an agent's character do sometimes depend on facts about what motive moved her to perform a given action. But he insists that the rightness or wrongness of the action never does so depend. Note that Mill in effect agrees with Bentham that a good motive can, on occasion, lead a person to act wrongly: he asserts that a wrongful act can be done from friendship.

Why is the motive of an action irrelevant deontically? The passage is not clear. Mill seems to have relied on two lines of thought. The first is the one suggested by the passage just quoted from the first edition of *Utilitarianism*. The second is developed in a long footnote that was added to later editions. Here Mill responds to two counterexamples to the claim about motives put to him by a critic (*U* 18, note 2). I believe the material here is less persuasive.[8] In any case, Mill must have continued to think of the material in the first edition as persuasive, since he did not withdraw it but only added to it.

---

7 John Stuart Mill, *Utilitarianism,* edited by George Sher (Indianapolis: Hackett, 1979) (hereafter *U*), 17–18.

8 On this note see Jonathan Dancy, "Mill's Puzzling Footnote," *Utilitas* 12 (2000): 219–222; Michael Ridge, "Mill's Intentions and Motives," *Utilitas* 14 (2002): 54–70; Steven Sverdlik, *Motive and Rightness*, 47n17.

The following argument may well go beyond what Mill meant, but it has appeared in the literature.[9] For a utilitarian the rightness of an action depends only on its consequences; the right act is the option that produces the most happiness. But motives are not consequences. (Mill himself thinks of a motive as a "feeling" [*U* 18, note 2], somewhat as Bentham did.) The motive of an action is one of its causes. Thus, at the time that an action is performed, its motive is water that has just passed under the bridge. A completely "forward-looking" theory of rightness like utilitarianism cannot allow that the antecedent of an action affects its rightness. Consider Mill's case of saving the drowning person. Suppose that Jane and Anita on separate occasions have the option of saving someone from drowning. In each case the best consequences will result if they do so. The fact that Jane would be acting from a higher motive and Anita from a lower motive cannot alter the fact that saving the person has the best results.[10]

Sidgwick

Henry Sidgwick's *The Methods of Ethics* (1874) is the most careful and comprehensive treatment of ethical theory by a classical utilitarian. He discusses the moral significance of motives at a number of points.[11] Sidgwick recognizes that "low" motives like malevolence can lead to socially beneficial results if, for example, they prompt a person to act "in aid of justice" (*ME* 371). And when he speaks most abstractly about the moral significance of motives he echoes Austin and Mill: "the doctrine that Universal Happiness is the ultimate *standard* must not be understood to imply that Universal Benevolence is the only right or always the best *motive* of action. For, as we have observed, it is not necessary that the end which gives the criterion of rightness should

---

9 Julia Driver, *Uneasy Virtue* (Cambridge: Cambridge University Press, 2001), 68–70.

10 I will set aside a case that Mill describes, where a person saves another from drowning only in order to torture her when they reach the shore.

11 Henry Sidgwick, *The Methods of Ethics* (hereafter *ME*), 7th ed. (Indianapolis: Hackett, 1981), 202–210; 217–228; 362–372; 413.

always be the end at which we consciously aim: and if experience shows that the general happiness will be more satisfactorily obtained if men frequently act from other motives than pure universal philanthropy, it is obvious that these other motives are reasonably to be preferred on Utilitarian principles" (*ME* 413; compare 202–210, esp. 202–204). Sidgwick seems here to deny that motives are ever relevant deontically. He does not explicitly make the other distinction that Mill does, but he seems inclined to accept Mill's claim that facts about the motive from which an action is performed are only relevant to judgments about the character or virtue of the agent.[12] Again, these judgments can be thought of as concerning, in part, which motives are most praiseworthy morally.

The most interesting feature of Sidgwick's thinking is the way that he took issue with Kant, who was now being studied carefully by British philosophers. Sidgwick disputes the Kantian claim that the motive that is most praiseworthy morally is the concern to do one one's duty. Some virtuous actions, Sidgwick says, are "made better by the presence of certain emotions in the virtuous agent" (*ME* 222; compare 204–205). "We recognize that benefits which spring from affection and are lovingly bestowed are more acceptable to the recipients than those conferred without affection, in the taste of which there is admittedly something harsh and dry" (*ME* 223). But Sidgwick seems to think that these important points are only relevant to judgments about character or virtue, or, presumably, moral praiseworthiness, and have no bearing on whether an action is right or wrong.

Moore

G. E. Moore developed one of the first important pluralistic forms of consequentialism. In *Principia Ethica* (1903) he defends the view that morally obligatory actions produce the greatest amount of

---

12 See *ME*, 221–228, but Sidgwick nowhere says this explicitly.

good.[13] But he claims that more than one type of state of affairs has intrinsic value. The two types of states of affairs that have the greatest intrinsic value, according to Moore, are complex "organic unities," namely, the enjoyment of beautiful things, and personal affection (*PE* 183–208). Moore also says that certain psychological attitudes have intrinsic value. He holds that "a love of some intrinsically good consequence which he [the agent] expects to produce by his actions" is intrinsically good, as is "a hatred of some intrinsically evil consequence he hopes to prevent" by his action.[14] "The emotion excited by rightness as such" is also intrinsically good (*PE* 177; 179). On the other hand the love of what is evil or ugly and the hatred of what is good or beautiful are intrinsically bad (*PE* 208–211).[15] The importance of these claims lies in the fact that these desires and emotions can be motives that lead an agent to act. Moore thus seems to leave room for saying that the intrinsic value of a motive can change the intrinsic value of an action. This seems to mean, in turn, that the intrinsic value of an action could change the intrinsic value of its consequences, construed broadly. In the next section I will expand on these points.

However, in *Ethics* (1912) Moore explicitly denies that motives are relevant deontically. He devotes some space to the consideration of this question.[16] He first makes the point often made by utilitarians that an agent may act from wrongly from "the best of motives" (*E* 78). But the main reason that he rejects the possibility that motives are deontically relevant is based on a set of distinctions. More carefully than Mill, or any previous philosopher, Moore distinguishes the question of whether the rightness of an action depends on its motive from other moral judgments that we make concerning motives: (1) whether the

---

13 G. E. Moore, *Principia Ethica* (Cambridge: Cambridge University Press, 1903) (hereafter *PE*), 25; 106; 147.

14 This sort of "recursive" structure is developed in depth in Thomas Hurka's *Virtue, Vice, and Value* (Oxford: Oxford University Press, 2001).

15 Moore also accepts the hedonistic claim that pain is intrinsically bad. Moore, *PE*, 211–214. In contrast, he thinks that pleasure as such has very little intrinsic value; 92–96.

16 G. E. Moore, *Ethics* (Oxford: Oxford University Press, 1965) (hereafter *E*), 77–80.

motive is itself intrinsically good or bad; (2) whether a motive tends generally to produce right actions; and (3) whether the agent deserves moral praise or blame for performing the action from that motive.

With regard to the first type of judgment, Moore claims that even if motives do have intrinsic value this cannot affect the value of an act's consequences (*E* 78–79). I will show that this is false.

The second distinction adds nothing to points already made by Bentham, but the third is of some interest. Moore here seems to be addressing the issue of moral motivation. He argues that the question of whether an action is right or wrong is distinct from the question of whether the agent deserves praise or blame for performing it. He supports the existence of this distinction as follows: "When we say that an action deserves praise or blame we imply that it is right to praise or blame it; that is to say, we are making a judgment *not* about the rightness of the original action, but about the rightness of the further action which we should take if we praised or blamed it. And these two judgments are certainly not identical" (*E* 79).

This concludes my historical survey. I will take stock first of consequentialist thinking about the deontic relevance of motives. All of the leading consequentialists in this period tended to believe that the motive of an action never has any bearing on whether it is morally right or wrong. Only Mill and Moore make this assertion explicitly. But the others seem clearly inclined to accept it. I have attributed to Mill, with some hesitation, an argument for this claim, but the same train of thought may well be operating in other writers like Bentham. Many of them note that any given type of motive, including even the one most often rankest highest, "enlarged benevolence," can sometimes have good effects, and sometimes bad. And we find them developing a set of distinctions—between the standard of rightness and an action's motive, and between rightness and the worth of character, or rightness and the desert of praise or blame—that tend to support the claim that motives are never relevant to the issue of an act's rightness or wrongness.

I will now consider moral motivation. At least three different consequentialist criteria for when a motive is praiseworthy can be found in the material I have presented. Bentham often seems to lean toward the view that the types of motive that are most praiseworthy morally are the ones that most commonly lead people to act rightly. Sidgwick sometimes seems to agree with this (*ME* 413). One often-noted problem with this claim is that it leaves open the possibility that self-interest is a morally praiseworthy motive, which seems to be false in most cases, if not all. A sophisticated second approach to moral praiseworthiness, which is designed to address this difficulty, is found in Sidgwick and Moore. They distinguish between the usefulness of a motive or character trait and the usefulness of praising it. Certain motives like self-interest, although very useful to society, are usually present and operative in human beings, and there is little need to praise people who act from it. Other motives, though also useful, are less common, and these are the ones a utilitarian ought to praise (*ME* 428; *PE* 172).[17] Moore seems to make a third proposal in *Principia Ethica*: the motives that are most praiseworthy are the ones that are intrinsically valuable. Moore thinks that the motives that are intrinsically valuable are the ones that constitute correct responses to other, more basic values such as beauty. Consequentialists used all three of these criteria to argue for the praiseworthiness of motives like love and extended benevolence.

2

Moore argued that certain desires have intrinsic value but denied that they are ever relevant deontically. In this section I show that he made a mistake about the concept of an act's consequences that is appropriate for consequentialism.

---

17 This point was earlier suggested by Joseph Butler. See "A Dissertation upon the Nature of Virtue," in *Five Sermons*, edited by Stuart Brown (Indianapolis: Library of Liberal Arts, 1956), 86.

An act is not a consequence or effect of itself. Nonetheless, consequentialism has to include any intrinsic value that the action itself has in the calculation that determines its deontic status. This is because the choice to do one action rather than another will mean that the world will differ not only with respect to the consequences of the two actions but also with respect to the fact that one action rather than another is performed. The total difference in the world that an action makes must reckon on the difference the act itself makes. Moore takes note of this point in passing (*PE* 25).

We therefore need to clarify the notion of consequence in the statement of act consequentialism. Above it was stated as follows: at a given time an agent is morally obligated to choose the action open to her that has the best consequences. I will begin by distinguishing between the "narrow" and the "broad" consequences of an action. Narrow consequences include only those events that occur after an act, qua intentional bodily movement. "Narrow consequences" thus include two kinds of events (or facts): first, the causal effects of an action, considered as an intentional bodily movement, and second, any states of the world following the action that would have been different had the agent chosen to act differently. If S shoots and kills T then the death of T is a narrow consequence of S's action. Likewise, if S sees T drowning and chooses not to rescue T then the death of T is also a narrow consequence of S's action (that is, her intentional inaction). This sort of conceptual inclusiveness is commonly accepted, I think, by consequentialists. The notion of a broad consequence is more inclusive still. Broad consequences include all narrow consequences, as well as the properties of the act itself. The terminology here is my own, but all consequentialists should agree that deontic status is determined by the value of the broad consequences of actions. That is, they should agree that if an action X has properties that have any intrinsic value, or if the act itself does, then this value must be included in the moral calculation that determines if X is right. I have shown that this point has some significance in Bentham's approach to the question, since he seems to think that motives themselves are pleasures. If so, a utilitarian should include their magnitude in the calculation of the broad consequences of actions. Bentham himself seems to ignore this point.

Moore's form of consequentialism opens up the possibility that motives could be relevant deontically in a different way than utilitarianism could allow them to be. Some motives themselves have intrinsic value, Moore's views imply, and this value is not due to the fact that they are pleasures. It is due instead to the fact that they are correct responses to values. Other motives, like malevolence, are incorrect responses to values. These values or disvalues should theoretically be reckoned into the value of an act's broad consequences. If a particular action is performed from, say, self-interest, this motive has no intrinsic value. On the other hand if another token of this type of action is performed from a love of rightness, then the motive has intrinsic value. Thus, even if these two action tokens have narrow consequences that have exactly the same total intrinsic value, their broad consequences would differ in intrinsic value. That means that one action could be right and the other wrong. Consider this chart, where the numbers represent units of intrinsic value. We are comparing the options of two individuals, S and T, where both of them can perform a certain type of action X or not.

	S's options		T's options	
	Do X	Not-X	Do X	Not-X
Act	0	0	3	0
Narrow consequences	10	12	10	12
Total	10	12	13	12

We are supposing that S will perform X from a motive that has no intrinsic value and will perform not-X from a motive that has no intrinsic value. T, however, will perform X from a motive that has three units of intrinsic value and will perform not-X from a motive that has no intrinsic value. The narrow consequences of the two actions will be the same for both agents (ten if either of them does X, twelve if either does not-X). But the value of the broad consequences of doing X differs for S and T, precisely because T will be doing X from a motive that has intrinsic value, while S will not. Given these assumptions, a consequentialist like Moore should say that doing not-X is right for S, but doing X is right for T. And this is to say that the motive for doing X makes a difference to its rightness. So Moore's pluralistic form of consequentialism suggests that motives are deontically relevant.

3

In this section I will investigate further the problem of the deontic relevance of motives. I will look more closely at the central argument I hesitantly attributed to Mill. There are two defects in this argument that consequentialists themselves must recognize.

The Value of Motives Themselves

The first defect has already been noted. The Millian argument assumes that the deontic status of an action is determined only by the value of its consequences. But we have seen that all consequentialists must count any intrinsic value that the act itself has in the calculation that determines the value of its consequences. And I have shown that there are different reasons why a consequentialist could hold that motives themselves sometimes have intrinsic value, which would thereby give some intrinsic value to actions. In this way, the motive of an action could make a difference to the act's deontic status. The Millian argument ignores these points.

Motives and Their Narrow Consequences

The Millian argument depicts motives as prior to the actions they lead to. This is its second error. It incorporates a mistaken view of how motives function when agents act from them. A motive establishes an end or goal for an agent, and she guides her activity accordingly. As she acts she will monitor her activity to be sure that it is succeeding in achieving her end, and she will modify it if it is not. She will look to see that she is actually employing her chosen means appropriately. So, for example, if my motive in driving my car is to attend a certain concert at a certain time, I will modify my driving if I think I am going to be late. This means that it is better to think of a motive as contemporaneous with an action rather than as prior to it. If an agent acts from a certain motive it has not receded into the causally inert past.

The fact that motives guide the performance of actions means that when the same type of action is performed from two different motives it may be performed in somewhat different ways. This fact plays an important role in detective stories and, presumably, in real detective work. Someone who kills in revenge will do so in a way that differs from someone killing out of greed. In the former case, for example, the killer may leave the victim's wallet in place. This means that if some peculiar lover were actually to "kiss his mistress with an eye to the common weal" he would not do this in quite the same way as if he did it from love. Hence, if Smith kisses his mistress from affection, and Jones kisses his mistress "with an eye to the common weal," Smith's mistress might find the kiss to be more satisfying simply as a physical movement. The point applies especially to those actions that Bernard Williams called "human gestures."[18] So a consequentialist cannot suppose that all tokens of an act type are such that they produce the same narrow consequences no matter what motive leads to their performance.[19]

---

18 Bernard Williams, "Morality and the Emotions," in his *Problems of the Self* (Cambridge: Cambridge University Press, 1973), 227. Williams used this idea to criticize Kantian, not consequentialist, moral theorists. However, Michael Stocker, "The Schizophrenia of Modern Ethical Theory," *Journal of Philosophy* 73 (1976): 453–466, argues in a related vein that neither a pure consequentialist nor a pure Kantian would be able to act from the motives that are central to relationships like friendship.

19 This conclusion seems to be endorsed by Brink, *Moral Realism and the Foundations of Ethics*; Parfit, *Reasons and Persons*; and Railton, "Alienation, Consequentialism, and the Demands of Morality." All three are concerned to rebut Stocker, "The Schizophrenia of Modern Ethical Theory,"

There is another reason why motives can make a difference in the narrow consequences of an action. Motives can be of interest to another person, even when they lead to perceptually indistinguishable actions. A number of the points in this paragraph and the following one are made in the excellent discussion of Thomas Scanlon in his *Moral Dimensions*. He speaks of the "meaning" that an action has for an agent and others; this derives from the agent's reasons for acting. If Jones is the recipient of a favor from Smith then Jones might be interested in knowing Smith's motive, that is, her reason, for so acting. Jones might have one sort of reaction to Smith's action if she believes that Smith acted from self-interest, and another sort of reaction if she believes that Smith acted from affection. This important fact about human nature helps to explain why people often try to conceal their motives.

One reason that we care about others' motives is that they are evidence about the further relations that we will have with them, conceived of simply in terms of actions without motives. That is, I may infer from the fact that you acted from a certain motive that you are likely to kick me—or to kiss me—in the future. I may also make further inferences about what motive you will act from. And we care about what use another person will put our interactions to. Scanlon gives the example of Smith wanting to know why Jones invites her "to the big end-of-the-year dance." Smith might want to be reassured that Jones was not merely seeking a chance to associate with the "in crowd" (*MD* 115). These sorts of concern obviously rest in part on a more basic one: to understand an agent's reason for acting on the present occasion. Even if Smith expects never to meet Jones again, she may have a different feeling about the favor that Jones provides her if she believes that Jones acts from one motive rather than another.

---

and Bernard Williams, "Persons, Character and Morality," in *Moral Luck* (Cambridge: Cambridge University Press, 1981), 18. But I have not found a passage in them where they make the point that different tokens of an act type can have different effects because of their motives. See also Thomas Scanlon, *Moral Dimensions: Permissibility, Meaning, Blame* (Cambridge, Mass.: Harvard University Press, 2008), 28–32.

This point has had a particular significance in discussions of what Kantians call "the motive of duty." We saw that Sidgwick raised doubts about whether the recipients of actions motivated by a sense of duty are always gratified to think that this is what led the agent to act (*ME* 223). In our own day Bernard Williams has echoed this thought. In a well-known example, he suggests that a man's wife would be disappointed if she learned that, when he could either rescue a stranger or her, but not both, he reasoned thus: she is my wife and it is morally permissible for me to rescue her. Williams memorably remarks that such a man has "one thought too many."[20] Michael Stocker[21] and Lawrence Blum have endorsed this sort of claim. Blum believes that "in general one prefers to be helped from sympathy [rather] than from duty; for the former response conveys a greater good than does acting from duty."[22] If this is correct then consequentialists can not only take issue with the Kantian claim that the sense of duty is always a praiseworthy motive. They can even assert that sometimes it is wrong-making, as we will see.

In conclusion, motives can affect how an action is done, and people care, for various reasons, why actions are done, that is, what motives lead to their being undertaken. So a consequentialist should not grant that the narrow consequences of a type of action will be the same no matter what motive leads to its performance in a given instance. The Millian argument in effect denies that motives can have these sorts of narrow consequences.

---

20 Williams, "Persons, Character and Morality," 18. Compare Williams, "Morality and the Emotions," 227. Michael Smith has generalized Williams's point in a certain way, claiming that acting from a concern to do what it is right, understood as a *de dicto* commitment, makes such motivation into a kind of fetishism. Michael Smith, *The Moral Problem* (Oxford: Blackwell, 1994), 75–76. For a recent assessment, see Vanessa Carbonell, "*De Dicto* Desires and Morality as Fetish," *Philosophical Studies* 163 (2013): 459–477. See also Julia Markovits, "Acting for the Right Reasons," *Philosophical Review* 119 (2010): 201–242.

21 Stocker, "The Schizophrenia of Modern Ethical Theory," 462. Compare Michael Stocker and Elizabeth Hegeman, *Valuing Emotions* (Cambridge: Cambridge University Press, 1996), 158.

22 Lawrence Blum, *Friendship, Altruism and Morality* (London: Routledge and Kegan Paul, 1980), 168; see all of chap. 7.

4

In this section I draw on my preceding comments and present an example in which an agent's motive is relevant deontically. I intend for this example to be plausible in this sense: it should strike the reader as being a case where a certain motive is part of the reason why a token of an action type is wrong (or where another token of the action type is right in virtue of being performed from another motive). I will argue that consequentialism can explain why motives in this sort of case are relevant deontically. This ability to explain the relevance of motives in such a case is, I believe, a point in favor of the theory. Furthermore, consequentialism can provide such an explanation even if it does not make the Moorean assumption that motives themselves have intrinsic value. That is, it need not assume that motives themselves are pleasures or pains (and thus intrinsically good or bad according to hedonistic versions of the theory), or another psychological state (such as a desire) that is sometimes intrinsically valuable according to pluralistic forms of consequentialism similar to Moore's. So the example is designed to show that motives can be relevant deontically only because they make a difference in the narrow consequences of actions.

We can imagine, then, there are two teenage grandchildren who are expected to visit their grandmother every so often.[23] One of them enjoys playing card games with her. The other does not enjoy such games or any other activity that her grandmother is interested in. She visits her grandmother only because she believes she is obligated to. She finds the visits disagreeable, and although she tries to mask this fact, it is evident to her grandmother. This makes her visits disagreeable to her grandmother as well. We can capture these facts in the following chart, where the numbers represent units of happiness "when all is said and done," that is, taking account of all the effects of the various actions. S is the grandchild who enjoys visiting, T the grandchild who does not, and G the grandmother.

---

23 This example differs from the one in Sverdlik, *Motive and Rightness*, 55–58. In thinking about convincing examples I have benefited from conversations with Richard Galvin and Julia Staffel.

	S's Options		T's Options	
	Visit today	Don't visit	Visit today	Don't visit
S	10	10	T −5	10
G	10	−5	G −5	−5
Total	20	5	−10	5

The numbers represent the following psychological facts. S would enjoy playing cards with her grandmother—a desire to do this will be her motive—and she would enjoy the visit. She will get ten units of happiness from doing so. G will enjoy it to the same extent. The total happiness produced by the visit will be twenty units of happiness. If S does not visit she will enjoy herself doing something else. Her grandmother's unhappiness will amount to five units, so the total amount of happiness produced by this choice would be five. Compare T's options. If she visits today she will do so from a sense of duty—this will be her motive—and be somewhat unhappy, as will her grandmother. The visit will produce ten units of unhappiness in total. If T does not visit she will also enjoy herself doing something else, but her grandmother will be just as unhappy about this as she will be if S does not visit. The total amount of happiness produced by this choice would be five. What these numbers mean is that S will produce more happiness by visiting her grandmother today, and T will produce more happiness by not visiting her grandmother today. Therefore, a utilitarian would say S would act rightly in visiting her grandmother and T would act wrongly in doing so. This difference in the deontic status of the two tokens of the same act is due to the fact that the motives cause the actions to have different narrow consequences.

Some comments are in order about the reasoning just presented. First, certain assumptions are made about the narrow consequences of different motives and the available alternatives. But there is nothing objectionable in making special assumptions, which are in any case not unrealistic, in supporting the claim that motives are relevant deontically. To say that motives are relevant is only to say that they are sometimes relevant. The assumptions can therefore be taken to illustrate a case *when* they are relevant.

Second, I used utilitarian assumptions to structure the example. But it is clear that other forms of consequentialism, employing different assumptions about intrinsic value, can also support the claim that motives are relevant deontically. Indeed, as I have shown, there are forms of consequentialism that assert that some motives are intrinsically valuable, and they also entail that motives are relevant deontically. But these forms of consequentialism are less plausible, in my opinion.[24]

Third, the example can be accepted without holding that motives are often or generally relevant deontically. I have said that consequentialism is unlikely to say that the motive of an action can change the calculation that determines which action has the best consequences. This example is not meant to withdraw this assertion. We can still accept Mill's statement that saving someone from drowning is right, no matter what motive leads a person to do this. It is, again, only with certain kinds of "human gestures" that the consequentialist is likely to see an agent's motives as relevant deontically, and this seems to be correct.

Fourth, saying that S's and T's motives make a difference in whether they act rightly is not to make their moral obligations into objectionable hypothetical imperatives, as Kant might put the point. It might seem to a Kantian as though T is relieved of her obligation simply because she does not want to carry it out. But if there is something objectionable about what we might call a hypothetical moral imperative then this is a difficulty that would tell against any theory that holds that motives are relevant deontically, not just consequentialism. And it does seem that in the realm of personal relations we are in a sphere

24 See Sverdlik, *Motive and Rightness*, chap. 4, for criticism of Hurka's version of pluralistic consequentialism.

where agents' feelings can sometimes make the difference between right and wrong behavior. Furthermore, the consequentialist need not deny that there is *something* that T is obligated to do with regard to her grandmother. For example, T might be obligated to send her grandmother a card expressing her appreciation of her grandmother's affection for her, and, if she is mature, describing why visits are currently problematic. (A sensitive grandmother might take heed and try to find something more enjoyable for the two of them to do.) All of this confirms how intimate relations do need to be shaped by a good understanding of the parties' current motivational tendencies (and a sense of how they might be changed over time). These assertions can be seen as consistent with a consequentialist understanding of what makes any action whatsoever morally right.

If there are cases where motives are relevant deontically, then the distinction between the rightness of an action and the praiseworthiness of its motive probably breaks down. This is because if an action is obligatory because it is done from a certain motive, it is likely that this motive is praiseworthy. Typically in consequentialism an action's deontic status is unaffected by the motive that leads to its performance.

5

The classical consequentialists deny, implicitly or explicitly, that motives are relevant deontically. And they have reason to do this: above all, the fact that in most cases the factors bearing on the moral rightness of an action concern its narrow consequences. But Moore's claim that certain attitudes have intrinsic value leaves room for the possibility of motives being relevant deontically, and it suggests a new way to think about which motives are praiseworthy. More traditional forms of consequentialism will not assert that motives are intrinsically valuable, but they leave room for rare cases in which motives are relevant deontically. I have described such a case. These forms of consequentialism will favor using criteria of moral praiseworthiness that focus on the effects various motives have on human well-being or—more debatably—on the effects on well-being of acts of praising them.

Acknowledgments

I am grateful to the other authors of this volume for helpful discussion and to Iakovos Vasiliou for his encouragement.

Bibliography

PRIMARY SOURCES

Alexander of Aphrodisias. "De anima libri mantissa." In *Supplementum Aristotelicum,* vol. 2, pt. 1 of *Commentaria in Aristotelem Graeca,* edited by I. Bruns, 101–186. Berlin: Reimer, 1887.

Alexander of Aphrodisias. "Ethical Problems." In *Supplementum Aristotelicum.* vol. 2, pt. 1 of *Commentaria in Aristotelem Graeca,* edited by I. Bruns, 117–163. Berlin: Reimer, 1887.

Anselm. "On Free Will." In *Anselm of Canterbury: The Major Works,* edited by Brian Davies and G. R. Evans. Oxford: Oxford University Press, 2008.

Anselm. "On the Fall of the Devil." In *Anselm of Canterbury: The Major Works,* edited by Brian Davies and G. R. Evans. Oxford: Oxford University Press, 2008.

Anselm. "On Truth." In *Anselm of Canterbury: The Major Works,* edited by Brian Davies and G. R. Evans. Oxford: Oxford University Press, 2008.

Aquinas, Thomas. *Disputed Questions on Evil.* Translated by John and Jean Oesterle. Notre Dame, IN: University of Notre Dame Press, 1995.

Aquinas, Thomas. *Summa Theologiae.* In *Introduction to St. Thomas Aquinas,* edited by Anton C. Pegis. New York: Modern Library, 1948.

Aquinas, Thomas. *Summa Theologiae*. In *Thomas Aquinas: Selected Writings*, trans.
    Ralph McInerny. London: Penguin Books, 1998.
Aristotle. *Aristotelis Ethica Eudemia*. Edited by R. R. Walzer and J. M. Mingay.
    Oxford Classical Texts. Oxford: Clarendon Press, 1991.
Aristotle. *Aristotelis Ethica Nicomachea*. Edited by I. Bywater. Oxford Classical
    Texts. Oxford: Clarendon Press, 1894.
Aristotle. *Aristotle: Nicomachean Ethics*. Translation with introduction and
    commentary by Sarah Broadie and Christopher Rowe. Oxford: Oxford
    University Press, 2002.
Aristotle. *Aristotle: Nicomachean Ethics*. Translated and edited by Roger Crisp.
    Cambridge: Cambridge University Press, 2000.
Aristotle. *Nicomachean Ethics*. Translated with introduction, notes, and glossary by
    Terence Irwin. 2nd ed. Indianapolis: Hackett, 1999.
Aristotle. *Metaphysics*. In *Basic Works of Aristotle*. Translated by W. D. Ross. New
    York: Random House, 1941.
Augustine. *On Grace and Free Choice*. In *On the Free Choice of the Will, On Grace
    and Free Choice, and Other Writings*, edited by Peter King, 141–184. Cambridge:
    Cambridge University Press: 2010.
Augustine. *On the Free Choice of the Will*. Translated by Anna Benjamin.
    Indianapolis: Bobbs-Merrill, 1964.
Austin, John. *The Province of Jurisprudence Determined*. Edited by H. L. A. Hart.
    New York: Noonday, 1954.
Bentham, Jeremy. *An Introduction to the Principles of Morals and Legislation*. Edited
    by J. H. Burns and H. L. A. Hart. London: Methuen, 1982.
Butler, Joseph. "A Dissertation upon the Nature of Virtue." In *Five Sermons*, edited
    by Stuart Brown, 81–90. Indianapolis: Library of Liberal Arts, 1956.
Cicero. *De Officiis*. Edited by Michael Winterbottom. Oxford: Oxford University
    Press, 1994.
Cicero. *De Re Publica: Selections*. Edited by James Zetzel. Cambridge: Cambridge
    University Press, 1995.
Cicero. *On Moral Ends*. Edited by J. Annas. Translated by R. Woolf. Cambridge:
    Cambridge University Press, 2001.
Culverwell, Nathaniel. *Elegant and Learned Discourse of the Light of Nature*. Edited
    by Robert A. Greene and Hugh MacCallum. Indianapolis: Liberty Fund, 2002.
Dreiser, Theodore. *Sister Carrie*. Edited by Donald Pizer. New York: Norton, 2006.
Fichte, Johann Gottlieb. *Fichtes Werke*. Edited by I. H. Fichte. Vols. 1–8. Berlin: de
    Gruyter, 1971.
Gaon, Saadia. *The Book of Beliefs and Opinions*. Translated by Samuel Rosenblatt.
    New Haven, CT: Yale University Press, 1976.

Godwin, William. *Enquiry Concerning Political Justice, with Selections from Godwin's Other Writings*. Edited by K. Codell Carter. Oxford: Oxford University Press, 1971.

Hegel, G. W. F. *Elements of the Philosophy of Right*. Translated by H. B. Nisbet. Edited by Allen Wood. Cambridge: Cambridge University Press, 1991.

Hegel, Georg W. F. *Enzyklopädie der philosophischen Wissenschaften in Grundrisse*. Berlin, 1830.

Hegel, G. W. F. *Grundlinien der Philosophie des Rechts*. Vol. 7. Frankfurt: Suhrkamp Verlag, 1970.

Hobbes, Thomas. *Leviathan, with Selected Variants from the Latin Edition of 1668*. Edited by E. Curley. Indianapolis: Hackett, 1994.

Hume, David. *An Enquiry Concerning the Principles of Morals*. Edited by Tom L. Beauchamp. Oxford: Clarendon Press, 1998.

Hume, David. *Essays Moral, Political, and Literary*. Edited by Eugene F. Miller. Indianapolis: Liberty Classics, 1985.

Hume, David. "Hume's Letter to Francis Hutcheson, Jan. 10, 1743." In *The Letters of David Hume*, vol. 1, edited by J. Y. T. Greig, 46. Oxford: Clarendon Press, 1932.

Hume, David. *A Treatise on Human Nature*. Edited by David Fate Norton and Mary J. Norton. 2 vols. Oxford: Clarendon Press, 2007.

Ibn Pakuda, Bahya. *The Book of Direction to the Duties of the Heart*. Translated by Menahem Mansoor. Oxford: Littman Library of Jewish Civilizations, 2004.

Kant, Immanuel. *Kants gesammelte Schriften*. Hrsg. v. der Preußischen Akademie der Wissenschaften. Berlin: de Gruyter, 1910–.

Locke, John. *An Essay Concerning Human Understanding*. Edited by P. H. Nidditch. Based on the 4th ed. Oxford: Oxford University Press, 1975.

Locke, John. *Essays on the Law of Nature*. Edited by W. Von Leyden. Oxford: Oxford University Press, 1954.

Maimonides, Moses. "Eight Chapters." Translated by Raymond L. Weiss and Charles Butterworth. In *Ethical Writings of Maimonides*, edited by Raymond L. Weiss and Charles Butterworth, 59–104. New York: Dover, 1983.

Maimonides, Moses. "Laws Concerning Character Traits." Translated by Raymond L. Weiss. In *Ethical Writings of Maimonides*, edited by Raymond L. Weiss and Charles Butterworth, 27–58. New York: Dover, 1983.

Mill, John Stuart. *Utilitarianism*. Edited by George Sher. Indianapolis: Hackett, 1979.

Moore, George E. *Ethics*. Oxford: Oxford University Press, 1965.

Moore, George E. *Principia Ethica*. Cambridge: Cambridge University Press, 1903.

Plato. *Plato's "Republic."* Translated by G. M. A. Grube. Revised by C. D. C. Reeve. Indianapolis: Hackett Press, 1992.

Plato. *Plato: "Symposium."* Translated by Alexander Nehamas and Paul Woodruff. Indianapolis: Hackett Press, 1989.

Plato. *Plato: The Republic.* Translated by Paul Shorey. 2 vols. Cambridge, MA: Harvard University Press, 1930.

Reid, Thomas. *Essays on the Active Powers of Man* (1788). Edited by Knud Haakonssen and James Harris. Edinburgh: Edinburgh University Press, 2010.

Schiller, Friedrich. *On the Aesthetic Education of Man in a Series of Letters* (1794). Translated by E. Wilkinson and L. Willoughby. Oxford: Oxford University Press, 1967.

Schiller, Friedrich. *Xenien* (1797). In Goethe, *Werke I*, edited by Erich Trunz. Hamburg: Christian Wegner Verlag, 1949.

Sidgwick, Henry. *The Methods of Ethics.* 7th ed. Indianapolis: Hackett, 1981.

Spinoza, Baruch. *The Collected Works of Spinoza.* Vol. 1. Translated by Edwin Curley. Princeton, NJ: Princeton University Press, 1984.

Spinoza, Baruch. *Spinoza Opera.* Vol. 5. Edited by Carl Gebhardt. Heidelberg: Carl Winters Universitaetsbuchandlung, 1925.

Stobaeus, John. *Anthology.* Vol. 2. Edited by C. Wachsmuth. Berlin: Weidmann, 1884.

Stoicorum Veterum Fragmenta. Edited by H. Von Arnim. Vol. 3. Stuttgart: Teubner, 1903.

SECONDARY SOURCES

Ackrill, John. 1980. "Eudaimonia in Aristotle's Ethics." In *Essays on Aristotle's Ethics*, edited by A. O. Rorty, 15–33. Berkeley: University of California Press. Reprinted from *Proceedings of the British Academy* 60 (1974): 339–359.

Adams, Robert M. "Motive Utilitarianism." *Journal of Philosophy* 73 (1976): 467–481.

Adkins, Arthur W. H. *Merit and Responsibility.* Oxford: Oxford University Press, 1960.

Allison, Henry. *Kant's Theory of Freedom.* Cambridge: Cambridge University Press, 1990.

Annas, Julia. *An Introduction to Plato's "Republic."* Oxford: Oxford University Press, 1981.

Annas, Julia. "The Hellenistic Version of Aristotle's Ethics." *Monist* 73 (1990): 80–96.

Annas, Julia. *The Morality of Happiness.* Oxford: Oxford University Press, 1993.

Árdal, Páll. "Some Implications of the Virtue of Reasonableness in Hume's *Treatise.*" In *Hume: A Re-Evaluation*, edited by Donald W. Livingston and James T. King, 91–106. New York: Fordham University Press, 1976.

Arendt, Hannah. *The Human Condition*. Chicago: Chicago University Press, 1958.

Audi, Robert. "Moral Judgment and Reasons for Action." In *Ethics and Practical Reason*, edited by Garrett Cullity and Berys Gaut, 125–160. Oxford: Oxford University Press, 1997.

Baier, Annette C. *Justice: The Cautious Jealous Virtue*. Cambridge, MA: Harvard University Press, 2010.

Baier, Annette C. "Master Passions." In *Explaining Emotions*, edited by Amelie O. Rorty, 403–423. Berkeley: University of California Press, 1980.

Baier, Annette C. *A Progress of Sentiments: Reflections on Hume's Treatise*. Cambridge, MA: Harvard University Press, 1991.

Barney, Rachel, Tad Brennan, and Charles Brittain, eds. *Plato and the Divided Self*. Cambridge: Cambridge University Press, 2012.

Bencivenga, Ermanno. "Kant's Sadism." *Philosophy and Literature* 20:1 (1996): 39–46.

Bennett, Jonathan. *A Study of Spinoza's "Ethics."* Indianapolis: Hackett, 1984.

Besser-Jones, Lorraine. "Hume on Pride-in-Virtue: A Reliable Motive?" *Hume Studies* 36 (2010): 171–192.

Björnsson, Gunnar, Caj Strandberg, Ragnar Francén Olinder, John Eriksson, and Fredrik Björklund, eds. *Motivational Internalism*. Oxford: Oxford University Press, 2015.

Blackburn, Simon. *Ruling Passions: A Theory of Practical Reasoning*. Oxford: Clarendon Press, 1998.

Blum, Lawrence. *Friendship, Altruism and Morality*. London: Routledge and Kegan Paul, 1980.

Blundell, Mary W. *Helping Friends and Harming Enemies: A Study in Sophocles and Greek Ethics*. Cambridge: Cambridge University Press, 1989.

Bobonich, Christopher. *Plato's Utopia Recast*. Oxford: Oxford University Press, 2002.

Brickhouse, Thomas, and Nicholas Smith. *Socratic Moral Psychology*. Cambridge: Cambridge University Press, 2010.

Brink, David. "Moral Motivation." *Ethics* 108:1 (October 1997): 4–32.

Brink, David. *Moral Realism and the Foundations of Ethics*. Cambridge: Cambridge University Press, 1989.

Broadie, Alexander. "The Scotist Thomas Reid." *American Catholic Philosophical Quarterly* 74:3 (2000): 385–407.

Broadie, Sarah. *Ethics with Aristotle*. New York: Oxford University Press, 1991.

Brown, Eric. "Minding the Gap in Plato's *Republic*." *Philosophical Studies* 117 (2004): 275–302.

Brunschwig, Jacques. "The Cradle Argument in Epicureanism and Stoicism." In *The Norms of Nature*, edited by M. Schofield and G. Striker, 113–144. Cambridge: Cambridge University Press, 1986.

Burnyeat, Myles F. "Aristotle on Learning to be Good." In *Essays on Aristotle's Ethics*, edited by A. O. Rorty. Berkeley: University of California Press, 1980.

Burrell, David. *Freedom and Creation in Three Traditions.* Notre Dame, IN: University of Notre Dame Press, 1993.

Butler, Judith. *Giving an Account of Oneself.* New York: Fordham University Press, 2005.

Carbonell, Vanessa. "*De Dicto*: Desires and Morality as Fetish." *Philosophical Studies* 163 (2013): 459–477.

Carter, Tim. "Re-reading *Poppea*: Some Thoughts on Music and Meaning in Monteverdi's Last Opera." *Journal of the Royal Music Association* 122:2 (1997): 194.

Cavarero, Adriana. *Relating Narratives: Story-telling and Selfhood.* New York: Routledge, 2000.

Chappell, Vere. *The Cambridge Companion to Locke.* Cambridge: Cambridge University Press, 1994.

Charles, David. "Aristotle, Ontology, and Moral Reasoning." *Oxford Studies in Ancient Philosophy* 4 (1986): 119–144.

Cohon, Rachel. *Hume's Morality: Feeling and Fabrication.* New York: Oxford University Press, 2008.

Cooper, John. "The Psychology of Justice in Plato." *American Philosophical Quarterly* 14 (1977): 151–157. Reprinted in Cooper, *Reason and Emotion* (Princeton, NJ: Princeton University Press, 1999), 138–149.

Cooper, John. *Reason and Emotion.* Princeton, NJ: Princeton University Press, 1999.

Cooper, John. *Reason and Human Good in Aristotle.* Cambridge, MA: Harvard University Press, 1975.

Cooper, John. "Reason, Moral Virtue, and Moral Value." In *Rationality in Greek Thought,* edited by M. Frede and G. Striker. Oxford: Oxford University Press, 1986, 81–114.

Cooper, John. "Two Theories of Justice." *Proceedings and Addresses of the American Philosophical Association* 74:2 (2000): 5–27. Reprinted in Cooper, *Knowledge, Nature, and the Good.* Princeton, NJ: Princeton University Press, 2004, 247–269.

Crisp, Roger. *Reasons and the Good.* Oxford: Oxford University Press, 2006.

Cullity, Garrett, and Berys Gaut, eds. *Ethics and Practical Reason.* Oxford: Oxford University Press, 1997.

Cummisky, David. *Kantian Consequentialism.* Oxford: Oxford University Press, 1996.

Cuneo, Terence. "A Puzzle Regarding Reid's Theory of Motives." *British Journal for the History of Philosophy* 19:5 (2011): 963–981.

Curley, Edwin. *Behind the Geometric Method.* Princeton, NJ: Princeton University Press, 1988.

Curley, Edwin. "Spinoza's Moral Philosophy." In *Spinoza: A Collection of Critical Essays,* edited by Marjorie Grene, 354–376. Notre Dame, IN: University of Notre Dame Press, 1973.

Curzer, Howard. *Aristotle and the Virtues.* Oxford: Oxford University Press, 2012.

Dahl, Norman O. *Practical Reason, Aristotle, and Weakness of the Will.* Minneapolis: University of Minnesota Press, 1984.

Dancy, Jonathan. "Mill's Puzzling Footnote." *Utilitas* 12 (2000): 219–222.

Darwall, Stephen. *The British Moralists and the Internal "Ought": 1640–1740.* Cambridge: Cambridge University Press, 1995.

Darwall, Stephen. "Hume: Norms and the Obligation to be Just." In *The British Moralists and the Internal "Ought": 1640–1740,* 284–318. Cambridge: Cambridge University Press, 1995.

Della Rocca, Michael. "Egoism and the Imitation of the Affects in Spinoza." In *Spinoza on Reason and the Free Man,* edited by Yirmiyahu Yovel and Gideon Segal, 123–148. New York: Little Room Press, 2004.

Dirlmeier, F. "Die Oikeiosis-Lehre Theophrasts." *Philologus Supplementband* 30 (1937).

Driscoll, Edward A. "The Influence of Gassendi on Locke's Hedonism." *International Philosophical Quarterly* 12 (1972): 87–110.

Driver, Julia. *Uneasy Virtue.* Cambridge: Cambridge University Press, 2001.

Eagleton, Terry. *Trouble with Strangers: A Study of Ethics.* Malden, MA: Wiley-Blackwell, 2009.

Echeñique, Javier. *Aristotle's Ethics and Moral Responsibility.* Cambridge: Cambridge University Press, 2012.

Falcon, A. *Aristotelianism in the First Century bce: Xenarchus of Seleucia.* Cambridge: Cambridge University Press, 2012.

Fenlon, Iain, and Peter Miller. *The Song of the Soul: Understanding "Poppea."* London: Royal Music Association, 1992.

Fonnesu, Luca. *Antropologia e idealismo. La destinazione dell' uomo nell'etica di Fichte.* Roma-Bari: Laterza, 1993.

Foot, Philippa. *Natural Goodness.* Oxford: Oxford University Press, 2003.

Foot, Philippa. *Virtues and Vices and Other Essays in Moral Philosophy.* Oxford: Oxford University Press, 2003.

Fortenbaugh, William W. "Arius, Theophrastus and the *Eudemian Ethics*." In *On Stoic and Peripatetic Ethics*, edited by Fortenbaugh, 203–223. New Brunswick, NJ: Transaction Books, 1983.

Fortenbaugh, William W., ed. *On Stoic and Peripatetic Ethics: The Work of Arius Didymus*. New Brunswick, NJ: Transaction Books, 1983.

Frankfurt, Harry. "Freedom of the Will and the Concept of a Person." *Journal of Philosophy* 68:1 (1971): 5–20.

Garrett, Don. "The First Motive to Justice: Hume's Circle Argument Squared." *Hume Studies* 33 (2007): 257–277.

Garrett, Don. "Spinoza's Ethical Theory." In *The Cambridge Companion to Spinoza*, edited by Don Garrett, 267–314. Cambridge: Cambridge University Press, 1996.

Gauthier, R. A., and J. Y. Jolif. *L'Éthique à Nicomaque: Introduction, Traduction et Commentaire*. 3 vols. Louvain: Publications Universitaires de Louvain, 1958–59.

Göransson, T. *Albinus, Alcinous, Arius Didymus*. Studia Graeca et Latina Gothoburgensia 61. Göteborg, Sweden: Acta Universitatis Gothoburgensis, 1995.

Gottlieb, P. 2009. *The Virtue of Aristotle's Ethics*. Cambridge: Cambridge University Press.

Gottschalk, H. B. "Aristotelian Philosophy in the Roman Empire from the Time of Cicero to the End of the Second Century AD." In *Aufstieg und Niedergang der Römischen Welt* II.36.2, edited by H. Temporini and W. Haase, 1079–1174. Berlin: de Gruyter, 1987.

Grant, A. 1885. *The "Ethics" of Aristotle Illustrated with Essays and Notes*. 4th ed. 2 vols. London: Longmans, Green. Reprint, New York: Arno Press, 1973.

Greenwood, L. 1909. *Aristotle: Nicomachean Ethics Book VI*. Cambridge: Cambridge University Press. Reprint, New York: Arno Press, 1973.

Griswold, Charles. *Adam Smith and the Virtues of Enlightenment*. Cambridge: Cambridge University Press, 1999.

Guyer, Paul. "Kant on the Theory and Practice of Autonomy." In Guyer, *Kant's System of Nature and Freedom: Selected Essays*, 115–145. Oxford: Oxford University Press, 2005.

Guyer, Paul. "Kant's Morality of Law and Morality of Freedom." In Guyer, *Kant on Freedom, Law, and Happiness*, 129–171. Cambridge: Cambridge University Press, 2000.

Hardie, W. 1980. *Aristotle's Ethical Theory*. 2nd ed. Oxford: Clarendon Press.

Hare, R. M. *Moral Thinking*. Oxford: Oxford University Press, 1981.

Harris, James A. "Hume on the Moral Obligation to Justice." *Hume Studies* 36 (2010): 25–50.

Heller, Wendy. "Chastity, Heroism, and Allure: Women in the Opera of Seventeenth-Century Venice." PhD diss., Brandeis University, 1995.

Herman, Barbara. "Leaving Deontology Behind." In Herman, *The Practice of Moral Judgment*, 208–240. Cambridge, MA: Harvard University Press, 1993.

Herman, Barbara. "On the Value of Acting from the Motive of Duty." In Herman, *The Practice of Moral Judgment*, 1–22. Cambridge, MA: Harvard University Press, 1993.

Hurka, Thomas. *Virtue, Vice, and Value*. Oxford: Oxford University Press, 2001.

Hursthouse, Rosalind. "Reply to Bernard Williams." In *Aristotle on Moral Realism*, edited by Robert Heinaman, 14–33. San Francisco: Westview Press, 1995.

Inwood, Brad. *Ethics after Aristotle*. Cambridge, MA: Harvard University Press, 2014.

Inwood, Brad. *Ethics and Human Action in Early Stoicism*. Oxford: Oxford University Press, 1985.

Inwood, Brad. "Moral Causes: The Role of Physical Explanation in Ancient Ethics." In *Thinking about Causes: From Greek Philosophy to Modern Physics,* edited by P. Machamer and G. Wolters, 14–36. Pittsburgh: University of Pittsburgh Press, 2007.

Inwood, Brad. "Moral Judgment in Seneca." In Inwood, *Reading Seneca: Stoic Philosophy at Rome*. Oxford: Oxford University Press 2005.

Inwood, Brad. Review of Göransson, *Albinus, Alcinous, Arius Didymus. Bryn Mawr Classical Review* 7 (1996): 25–30.

Inwood, Brad. *Seneca: Selected Philosophical Letters*. Oxford: Oxford University Press, 2007.

Inwood, Brad. "The Voice of Nature." In *Cicero's "De Finibus": Philosophical Approaches,* edited by Julia Annas and Gábor Betegh, 147–166. Cambridge: Cambridge University Press, 2016.

Irwin, Terence. "Aristotle's Conception of Morality." *Proceedings of the Boston Area Colloquium in Ancient Philosophy,* vol. 1, 115–143. Leiden: Brill, 1985.

Irwin, Terence. *Aristotle's First Principles*. Oxford: Oxford University Press, 1988.

Irwin, Terence. "The Platonic Corpus." In *The Oxford Handbook of Plato*, edited by G. Fine, 63–87. Oxford: Oxford University Press, 2008.

Irwin, Terence. *Plato's Ethics*. Oxford: Oxford University Press, 1995.

Irwin, Terence. *Plato's Moral Theory*. Oxford: Oxford University Press, 1977.

Irwin, Terence. "Scotus and the Possibility of Moral Motivation." In *Morality and Self-Interest*, edited by Paul Bloomfield, 159–176. New York: Oxford University Press, 2008.

Irwin, Terence. "The Sense and Reference of *Kalon* in Aristotle." *Classical Philology* 105 (2010): 381–396.

Jacobs, Jonathan. "Aristotle and Maimonides on Virtue and Natural Law." *Hebraic Political Studies* 2:1 (Spring 2007): 46–77.

Jacobs, Jonathan. *Law, Reason, and Morality in Medieval Jewish Philosophy*. Oxford: Oxford University Press, 2010.

Kamtekar, Rachana. "What's the Good of Agreeing? Homonoia in Platonic Politics." *Oxford Studies in Ancient Philosophy* 26 (2004): 131–170.

Kamian, Roger. *Music, An Appreciation*. 6th brief ed. New York: McGraw-Hill, 2008.

Kenny, Anthony. *The Aristotelian Ethics*. Oxford: Oxford University Press, 1978.

Kenny, Anthony. *Aristotle's Theory of the Will*. London: Duckworth. 1979.

Kerman, Joseph. *Opera as Drama*. Berkeley: University of California Press, 1988.

Kisner, Matthew J. *Spinoza on Human Freedom: Reason, Autonomy and the Good Life*. Cambridge: Cambridge University Press, 2011.

Korsgaard, Christine. *Creating the Kingdom of Ends*. Cambridge: Cambridge University Press, 1996.

Korsgaard, Christine. "Creating the Kingdom of Ends: Reciprocity and Responsibility in Personal Relations." In Korsgaard, *Creating the Kingdom of Ends*, 188–223. Cambridge: Cambridge University Press, 1996.

Korsgaard, Christine. "From Duty and for the Sake of the Noble." In *Aristotle, Kant and the Stoics*, edited by Stephen Engstrom and Jennifer Whiting, 203–236. Cambridge: Cambridge University Press, 1996.

Korsgaard, Christine. "Skepticism about Practical Reason." *Journal of Philosophy* 83 (1986): 5–25.

Korsgaard, Christine. *The Sources of Normativity*. Cambridge: Cambridge University Press, 1996.

Kraut, Richard. *Aristotle on the Human Good*. Princeton, NJ: Princeton University Press, 1989.

Kraut, Richard. "The Defense of Justice in the *Republic*." In *Cambridge Companion to Plato*, edited by Richard Kraut, 311–337. Cambridge: Cambridge University Press, 1992.

Kraut, Richard. "Return to the Cave: *Republic* 519–521." In *Plato*, vol. 2, *Ethics, Politics, Religion, and the Soul*, edited by Gail Fine, 235–254. Oxford: Oxford University Press, 1999.

Lawrence, Gavin. "Acquiring Character: Becoming Grown-Up." In *Moral Psychology and Human Action in Aristotle*, edited by M. Pakaluk and G. Pearson. Oxford: Oxford University Press, 2011.

Lear, Gabriel Richardson. "Aristotle on Moral Virtue and the Fine." In *The Blackwell Guide to Aristotle's Nicomachean Ethics*, edited by R. Kraut, 116–136. Oxford: Blackwell, 2006.

Lear, Gabriel Richardson. *Happy Lives and the Highest Good*. Princeton, NJ: Princeton University Press, 2004.

LeBuffe, Michael. *From Bondage to Freedom: Spinoza on Human Excellence*.
    Oxford: Oxford University Press, 2010.
Lévi-Strauss, Claude. *Structural Anthropology*. Translated by Claire Jacobson and
    Brooke Grundfest Schoepf. New York: Basic Books, 1963.
Long, Anthony A. "Morals and Values in Homer." *Journal of Hellenic Studies*
    90 (1970): 121–139.
Lorenz, Hendrik. *The Brute Within: Appetitive Desire in Plato and Aristotle*.
    Oxford: Oxford University Press, 2006.
Lorenz, Hendrik. "Natural Goals of Action in Aristotle." *Journal of the American
    Philosophical Association* 1.4 (2015): 583–600.
Lorenz, Hendrik. "Virtue of Character in Aristotle's *Nicomachean Ethics*." *Oxford
    Studies in Ancient Philosophy* 37 (Winter 2009): 177–212.
Mackie, John L. *Ethics: Inventing Right and Wrong*. New York: Penguin, 1977.
Mackie, John L. *Hume's Moral Theory*. London: Routledge and Kegan Paul, 1980.
Magri, Tito. "Natural Obligation and Normative Motivation in Hume's *Treatise*."
    Hume Studies 22 (1996): 231–253.
Markovits, Julia. "Acting for the Right Reasons." *Philosophical Review* 119 (2010):
    201–242.
Marshall, John. *John Locke: Resistance, Religion, and Responsibility*. Cambridge:
    Cambridge University Press, 1994.
McClary, Susan. *Feminine Endings: Music, Gender, and Sexuality*. Minneapolis:
    University of Minnesota Press, 1991.
McDowell, John. "The Role of Eudaimonia in Aristotle's Ethics." In McDowell,
    Mind, Value, and Reality, 3–22. Cambridge, MA: Harvard University Press, 1998.
McDowell, John. "Some Issues in Aristotle's Moral Psychology." In McDowell, *Mind,
    Value, and Reality*, 22–49. Cambridge, MA: Harvard University Press, 1998.
Meyer, Susan Sauvé. *Ancient Ethics*. London: Routledge, 2008.
Meyer, Susan Sauvé. *Aristotle on Moral Responsibility*. Oxford: Blackwell, 1993.
    Reprint, Oxford: Oxford University Press, 2011.
Meyer, Susan Sauvé. "Living for the Sake of an Ultimate End." In *Aristotle's
    Nicomachean Ethics: A Critical Guide*, edited by Jon Miller, 47–65. Cambridge:
    Cambridge University Press, 2011.
Meyer, Susan Sauvé, and Adrienne M. Martin. "Emotion and the Emotions." In
    The Oxford Handbook of the History of Ethics, edited by Roger Crisp, 638–671.
    Oxford: Oxford University Press, 2013.
Michael, Fred, and Emily Michael. "Gassendi's Modified Epicureanism and British
    Moral Philosophy." *History of European Ideas* 21:6 (1995): 743–761.
Miller, Jon. "Spinoza's Axiology." *Oxford Studies in Early Modern Philosophy*
    2 (2005): 149–172.

Mitsis, Phillip. "Locke's Offices." In *Hellenistic and Early Modern Philosophy,* edited by J. Miller and B. Inwood, 45–61. Cambridge: Cambridge University Press, 2003.

Moiso, Francesco. "*Wille* e *Willkür* in Fichte." *Revue Internationale de Philosophie* 191 (1995): 5–38.

Moran, Kate. *Community and Progress in Kant's Moral Philosophy*. Washington, DC: Catholic University Press, 2012.

Moraux, P. *Der Aristotelismus bei den Griechen*. Vol. 1. Berlin: de Gruyter, 1973.

Moss, Jessica. *Aristotle on the Apparent Good: Perception, Phantasia, Thought, and Desire*. Oxford: Oxford University Press, 2012.

Nagel, Thomas. *The Possibility of Altruism*. Oxford: Oxford University Press, 1970.

Natali, Carlo. *The Wisdom of Aristotle*, translated by Gerald Parks. Albany, NY: State University of New York Press, 2001.

Neiman, Susan. *The Unity of Reason: Rereading Kant*. Oxford: Oxford University Press, 1994.

Norton, David Fate. *David Hume: Common-Sense Moralist, Sceptical Metaphysician*. Princeton, NJ: Princeton University Press, 1982.

Nussbaum, Martha. *The Fragility of Goodness*. Cambridge: Cambridge University Press, 1986.

Nuzzo, Angelica. "Contradiction in the Ethical World: Hegel's Challenge for Times of Crisis." In *Freiheit*, Akten der Stuttgarter Hegel Kongress 2011, edited by G. Hindrich and A. Honneth, 627–648. Stuttgart: Klostermann, 2011.

Nuzzo, Angelica. *Ideal Embodiment: Kant's Theory of Sensibility*. Bloomington: Indiana University Press, 2008.

Nuzzo, Angelica. *Rappresentatione e concetto nella logica della Filosofia del diritto di Hegel*. Naples: Guida, 1990.

Oakley, Francis. "Locke, Natural Law, and God; Note" (1966). Natural Law Forum. Paper 119. http://scholarship.law.nd.edu/nd_naturallaw_forum/119.

Parfit, Derek. *Reasons and Persons*. Oxford: Oxford University Press, 1984.

Paton, H. J. *The Categorical Imperative: A Study in Kant's Moral Philosophy*. London: Hutchinson, 1947.

Pembroke, S. "Oikeiōsis." In *Problems in Stoicism,* edited by A. A. Long, 114–149. London: Athlone Press, 1971.

Peperzak, Adriaan. *Hegels praktische Philosophie*. Stuttgart: Frommann, 1991.

Peperzak, Adriaan. *Modern Freedom: Hegel's Legal, Moral, and Political Philosophy*. Dordrecht: Kluwer, 2001.

Piper, Adrian. *Out of Order, Out of Sight*. Cambridge, MA: MIT Press, 1996.

Pippin, Robert. *Hegel's Practical Philosophy: Rational Agency as Ethical Life*. Cambridge: Cambridge University Press, 2008.

Porter, James. *The Origins of Aesthetic Thought in Ancient Greece: Matter, Sensation, and Experience.* Cambridge: Cambridge University Press, 2010.

Price, Anthony W. *Virtue and Reason in Plato and Aristotle.* Oxford: Clarendon Press, 2011.

Quante, Michael. *Hegel's Concept of Action.* Cambridge: Cambridge University Press, 2004.

Radcliffe, Elizabeth. "Moral Sentimentalism and the Reasonableness of Being Good." *Revue Internationale de Philosophie* 1 (2013): 9–27.

Railton, Peter. "Alienation, Consequentialism, and the Demands of Morality." In Railton, *Facts, Values, and Norms*, 151–186. Cambridge: Cambridge University Press, 2003.

Reeve, C. D. C. *Aristotle on Practical Wisdom: Nicomachean Ethics Book 6.* Cambridge, MA: Harvard University Press, 2013.

Reeve, C. D. C. *Philosopher-Kings: The Argument of Plato's Republic.* Princeton, NJ: Princeton University Press, 1988.

Ridge, Michael. "Mill's Intentions and Motives." *Utilitas* 14 (2002): 54–70.

Rosand, Ellen. "Seneca and the Interpretation of *L'incoronazione di Poppea.*" *Journal of the American Musicological Society* 38 (1985): 69.

Rosati, Connie S. "Moral Motivation." In *Stanford Encyclopedia of Philosophy* (Spring 2014 ed.), edited by Edward Zalta. http://plato.stanford.edu/entries/moral-motivation/.

Rowe, Christopher. *Plato: "Symposium."* Warminster, England: Aris and Phillips, 1998.

Rutherford, Donald. "In Pursuit of Happiness: Hobbes's New Science of Ethics." *Philosophical Topics* 31 (2003): 360–393.

Sachs, David. "A Fallacy in Plato's *Republic.*" *Philosophical Review* 72 (1963): 141–158.

Santas, Gerasimos, ed. *The Blackwell Guide to Plato's "Republic."* Oxford: Blackwell, 2006.

Sarasohn, Lisa T. *Gassendi's Ethics: Freedom in a Mechanistic Universe.* Ithaca, NY: Cornell University Press, 1996.

Scanlon, Thomas. *Moral Dimensions: Permissibility, Meaning, Blame.* Cambridge, MA: Harvard University Press, 2008.

Schenker, Heinrich. *Der Tonwille: Pamphlets in Witness of the Immutable Laws of Music, Volume I: Issues 1–5 (1921–1923).* Edited by William Drabkin. New York: Oxford University Press, 2004.

Schneewind, Jerome B. *The Invention of Autonomy: A History of Modern Moral Philosophy.* Cambridge: Cambridge University Press, 1998.

Schneewind, Jerome B. "Locke's Moral Philosophy." In *The Cambridge Companion to Locke,* edited by V. Chappell, 199–225. Cambridge: Cambridge University Press, 1994.

Schneewind, Jerome B. *Sidgwick's Ethics and Victorian Moral Philosophy*. Oxford: Oxford University Press, 1977.

Schouls, Peter A. *Reasoned Freedom: John Locke and the Enlightenment*. Ithaca, NY: Cornell University Press, 1992.

Segvic, Heda. "Deliberation and Choice in Aristotle." In Segvic, *From Protagoras to Aristotle*, 144–171. Princeton, NJ: Princeton University Press, 2009. Reprinted in *Moral Psychology and Human Action in Aristotle*, edited by M. Pakaluk and G. Pearson, 159–185. Oxford: Oxford University Press, 2011.

Setiya, Kieran. "Hume on Practical Reason." *Philosophical Perspectives* 18 (2004): 365–389.

Shaffer-Landau, Russ. *Moral Realism: A Defense*. Oxford: Oxford University Press, 2003.

Sharples, Robert. *Peripatetic Philosophy 200 BC to 200 AD*. Cambridge: Cambridge University Press, 2010.

Sheffield, Frisbee. *Plato's "Symposium": The Ethics of Desire*. Oxford: Oxford University Press, 2006.

Sheridan, Patricia. *Locke: A Guide for the Perplexed*. London: Continuum, 2010.

Sheridan, Patricia. "Pirates, Kings and Reasons to Act: Moral Motivation and the Role of Sanctions in Locke's Moral Theory." *Canadian Journal of Philosophy* 37:1 (2007): 35–48.

Sherman, Nancy. 1989. *The Fabric of Character: Aristotle's Theory of Virtue*. Oxford: Clarendon Press.

Siep, Ludwig. "Was heisst: 'Aufhebung der Moralität in Sittlichkeit' in Hegels Rechtsphilosophie?" *Hegel Studien* 12 (1982): 75–96.

Singh, Raghuveer. "John Locke and the Theory of Natural Law." *Political Studies* 9 (1961): 105–118.

Slote, Michael. *Morals from Motives*. Oxford: Oxford University Press, 2001.

Smith, Michael. *The Moral Problem*. Malden, MA: Blackwell, 1994.

Stocker, Michael. "The Schizophrenia of Modern Ethical Theory." *Journal of Philosophy* 73 (1976): 453–466.

Stocker, Michael, and Elizabeth Hegeman. *Valuing Emotions*. Cambridge: Cambridge University Press, 1996.

Svavarsdottir, Sigrun. "Moral Cognitivism and Motivation." *Philosophical Review* 108 (1999): 161–219.

Sverdlik, Steven. *Motive and Rightness*. Oxford: Oxford University Press, 2011.

Taylor, Christopher. *Aristotle: Nicomachean Ethics Books 2–4*. Translation with commentary. Oxford: Clarendon Press, 2006.

Taylor, Jacqueline. "Hume on the Standard of Virtue." *Journal of Ethics* 6 (2002): 43–62.

Taylor, Jacqueline. "Hume's Later Moral Philosophy." In *The Cambridge Companion to Hume,* 2nd ed., edited by David Norton and Jacqueline Taylor, 311–340. Cambridge: Cambridge University Press, 2009.

Taylor, Jacqueline. "Moral Sentiments and the Sources of Moral Identity." In *Morality and the Emotions,* edited by Carla Bagnoli, 257–274. Oxford: Oxford University Press, 2011.

Trapp, Michael. *Philosophy in the Roman Empire: Ethics, Politics, and Society.* Aldershot, England: Ashgate, 2007.

Tsouni, G. "Antiochus and Peripatetic Ethics." PhD diss., Cambridge University, 2010.

Uleman, Jennifer. *An Introduction to Kant's Moral Philosophy*. Cambridge: Cambridge University Press, 2010.

Vasiliou, Iakovos. *Aiming at Virtue in Plato*. Cambridge: Cambridge University Press, 2008.

Vasiliou, Iakovos. "Aristotle, Agents, and Actions." In *Aristotle's "Nicomachean Ethics": A Critical Guide,* edited by Jon Miller, 170–190. Cambridge: Cambridge University Press, 2011.

Vasiliou, Iakovos. "From the *Phaedo* to the *Republic*: Plato's Tripartite Soul and the Possibility of Non-philosophical Virtue." In *Plato and the Divided Self,* edited by Rachel Barney, Tad Brennan, and Charles Brittain, 9–32. Cambridge: Cambridge University Press, 2012.

Vasiliou, Iakovos. "Plato, Forms, and Moral Motivation." *Oxford Studies in Ancient Philosophy* 49 (2015): 37–70.

Vasiliou, Iakovos. "Platonic Virtue: An Alternative Approach." *Philosophy Compass* 9:9 (2014): 605–614.

Vasiliou, Iakovos. "Virtue and Argument in Aristotle's Ethics." In *Moral Psychology,* Poznan Studies in the Philosophy of the Sciences and Humanities, vol. 94, edited by Sergio Tenenbaum, 35–76. Amsterdam: Rodopi, 2007.

Vivenza, Gloria. *Adam Smith and the Classics*. Oxford: Oxford University Press, 2001.

Vogt, Katja. "Seneca." In *The Stanford Encyclopedia of Philosophy* (Summer 2013 ed.), edited by Edward N. Zalta, http://plato.stanford.edu/archives/sum2013/entries/seneca/.

Watson, Gary. "Free Agency." *Journal of Philosophy* 72:8 (1975): 205–220.

Weller, Cass. "Scratched Fingers, Ruined Lives, and Acknowledged Lesser Goods." *Hume Studies* 30 (2004): 51–85.

Whiting, Jennifer. "*Eudaimonia*, External Results, and Choosing Virtuous Actions for Themselves." *Philosophy and Phenomenological Research* 65:2 (2002): 270–290.

Whiting, Jennifer. "The Lockeanism of Aristotle." *Antiquorum Philosophia*
  2 (2008): 101–136.

Whiting, Jennifer. "Psychic Contingency in the *Republic*." In *Plato and the Divided
  Self*, edited by Rachel Barney, Tad Brennan, and Charles Brittain, 174–208.
  Cambridge: Cambridge University Press, 2012.

Wielenberg, Erik. "Pleasure as a Sign of Moral Virtue in the *Nicomachean Ethics*."
  Journal of Value Inquiry 34 (2000): 439–448.

Wiggins, David. 1980. "Deliberation and Practical Reason." In *Essays on Aristotle's
  Ethics,* edited by A. O. Rorty, 221–240. Berkeley: University of California Press.
  Revised from its original publication in *Proceedings of the Aristotelian Society*
  76 (1975–76): 29–51.

Williams, Bernard. "Acting as the Virtuous Person Acts." In *Aristotle on Moral
  Realism*, edited by Robert Heinaman, 13–23. San Francisco: Westview Press,
  1995.

Williams, Bernard. *Ethics and the Limits of Philosophy*. Cambridge, MA: Harvard
  University Press, 1985.

Williams, Bernard. 1981. "Internal and External Reasons." In Williams, *Moral Luck*,
  101–113. Cambridge: Cambridge University Press, 1981.

Williams, Bernard. "Morality and the Emotions." In Williams, *Problems of the Self*,
  207–229. Cambridge: Cambridge University Press, 1973.

Williams, Bernard. "Persons, Character and Morality." In Williams, *Moral Luck*,
  1–19. Cambridge: Cambridge University Press, 1981.

Williams, Bernard. *Shame and Necessity*. Berkeley: University of California Press,
  1993.

Wolf, Susan. *Freedom within Reason*. Oxford: Oxford University Press, 1990.

Wood, Allen. *Hegel's Ethical Thought*. Cambridge: Cambridge University Press,
  1990.

Woolf, Virginia. *A Room of One's Own* (1929). New York: Harcourt Brace
  Jovanovich, 1981.

Woolf, Virginia. *To the Lighthouse* (1927). New York: Harcourt Brace Jovanovich,
  1981.

Worman, Nancy. *The Cast of Character: Style in Greek Literature*. Austin: University
  of Texas Press, 2002.

Yaffe, Gideon. *Liberty Worth the Name: Locke on Free Agency*. Princeton, NJ:
  Princeton University Press, 2000.

Yolton, John. "Locke on the Laws of Nature." *Philosophical Review* 67:4
  (1958): 490.

Index

Achilles, 40–43
actions,
  altruistic, 40, 137
  as done for their own sake vs. for the sake
    of something further, 8–10, 46–53
  free, 169–172
  praiseworthy,
  right, 133, 137–138
  as source of morality, 9
  virtuous, 9–10, 17–20, 34–37, 44–64,
    76–80, 103, 133, 140
  vicious, 20, 35, 60
aesthetic perception, 88–91
Agamemnon, 41–42
agency. *See* agents
agents (*see also* will, free will),
  egoistic, *see* egoism
  moral, 9, 258
  rational, 71–73, 137–138, 140, 144–145,
    163, 172–175
  vicious, 52, 59, 61–62, 89, 104, 111, 179

  virtuous, 9–10, 17–20, 44–64, 103,
    104–105, 137–138, 141–142, 145,
    179, 267, 269
Alexander of Aphrodisias, 65, 80–82
Alfarabi, 103
Anselm, 11, 100–102, 113–115, 118
Aquinas, 11, 102–103, 106n.25, 115–119,
    158n.8, 165
Arendt, H., 222n.19
Aristo, 158n.8
Aristotle, 4, 8–11, 19n.9, 31, 33n.32, 37, 44–64,
    65–69, 74–76, 80–81, 95–98, 102–105,
    107, 112, 119, 138n.14, 161, 176–177, 203
Arius Didymus, 66
Aspasius, 65, 74
ataraxia (tranquility), 165, 167
Atticus, 195
Audi, R., 7
Augustine, 11, 99–100, 103, 115
Augustus, 66
Austin, J., 265–266